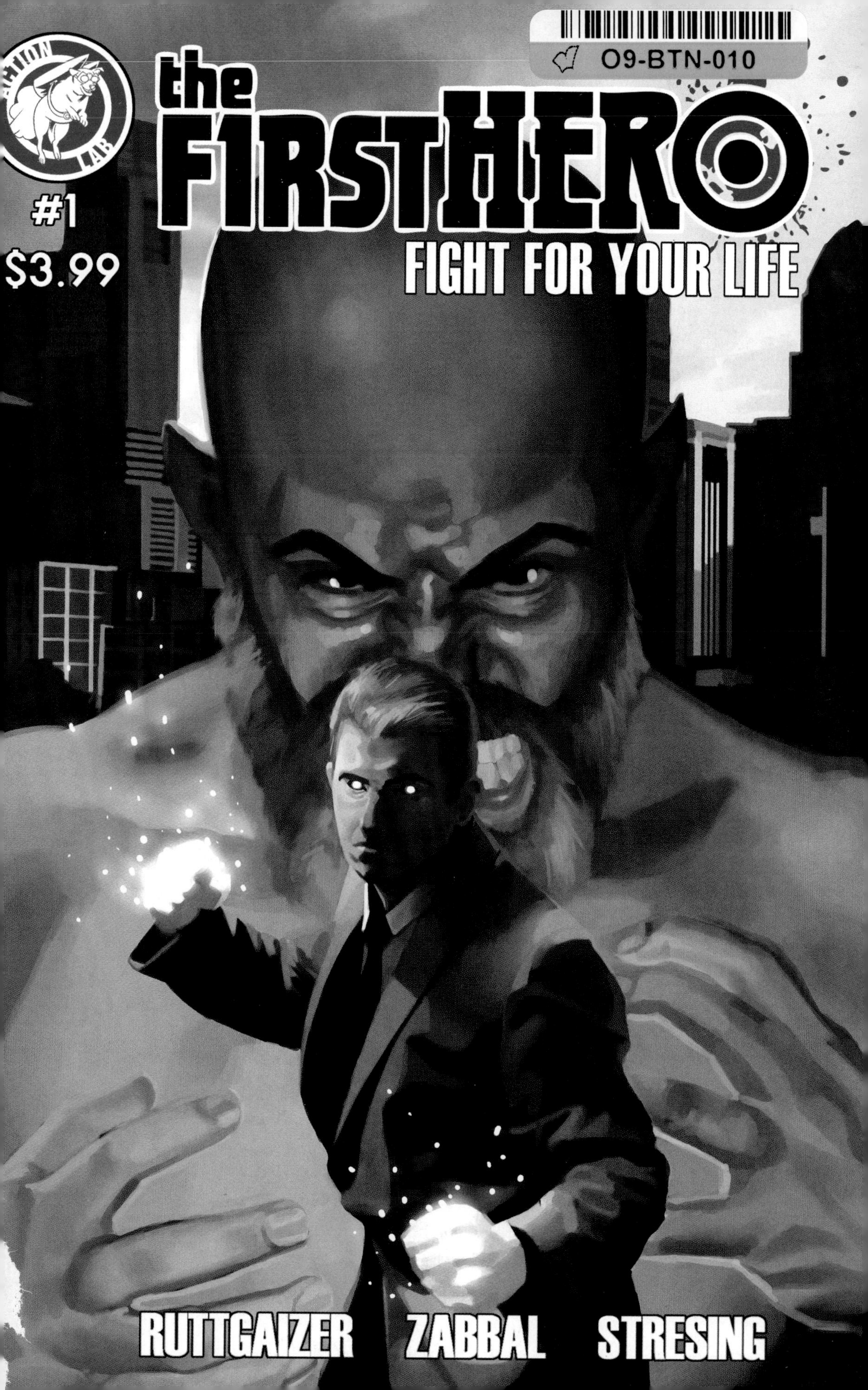
ACTION LAB
the FIRST HERO
#1
$3.99
FIGHT FOR YOUR LIFE
RUTTGAIZER ZABBAL STRESING
O9-BTN-010

FROM JAY FAERBER AND JAMAL IGL

VENTURE

PRESS
Baxter,
Reginald

AVAILABLE IN FINER STORES EVERYWHER

Down-on-his-luck reporter Reggie Baxter has stumbled onto one of the greatest secrets of all time...superpowered high school history teacher Joe Campbell! But who is Joe Campbell and more importantly, how rich will Reggie become by blackmailing him?

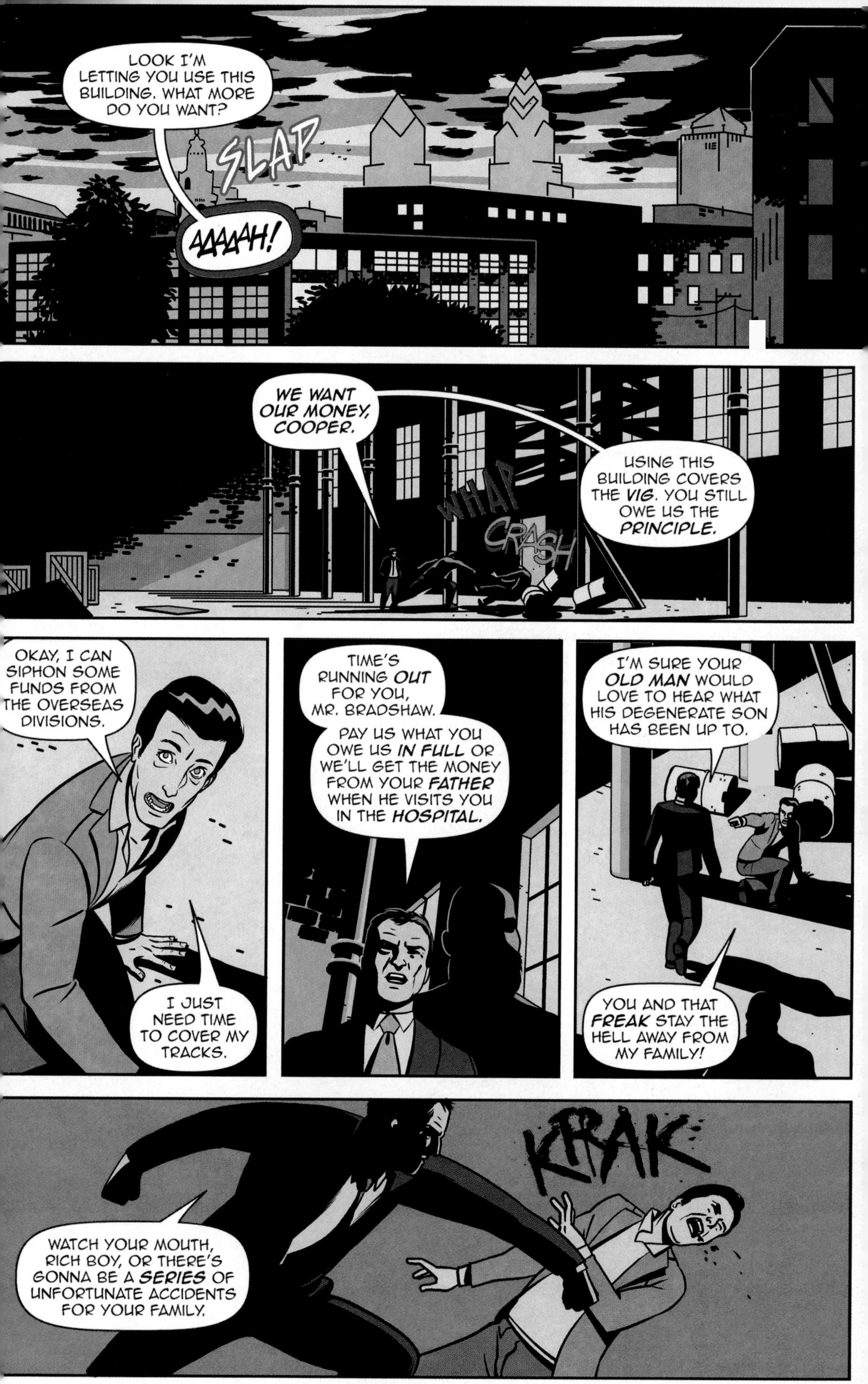
LOOK I'M LETTING YOU USE THIS BUILDING. WHAT MORE DO YOU WANT?
SLAP
AAAAAH!
WE WANT OUR MONEY, COOPER.
USING THIS BUILDING COVERS THE VIG. YOU STILL OWE US THE PRINCIPLE.
WHAP
CRASH
OKAY, I CAN SIPHON SOME FUNDS FROM THE OVERSEAS DIVISIONS.
I JUST NEED TIME TO COVER MY TRACKS.
TIME'S RUNNING OUT FOR YOU, MR. BRADSHAW.
PAY US WHAT YOU OWE US IN FULL OR WE'LL GET THE MONEY FROM YOUR FATHER WHEN HE VISITS YOU IN THE HOSPITAL.
I'M SURE YOUR OLD MAN WOULD LOVE TO HEAR WHAT HIS DEGENERATE SON HAS BEEN UP TO.
YOU AND THAT FREAK STAY THE HELL AWAY FROM MY FAMILY!
KRAK
WATCH YOUR MOUTH, RICH BOY, OR THERE'S GONNA BE A SERIES OF UNFORTUNATE ACCIDENTS FOR YOUR FAMILY.

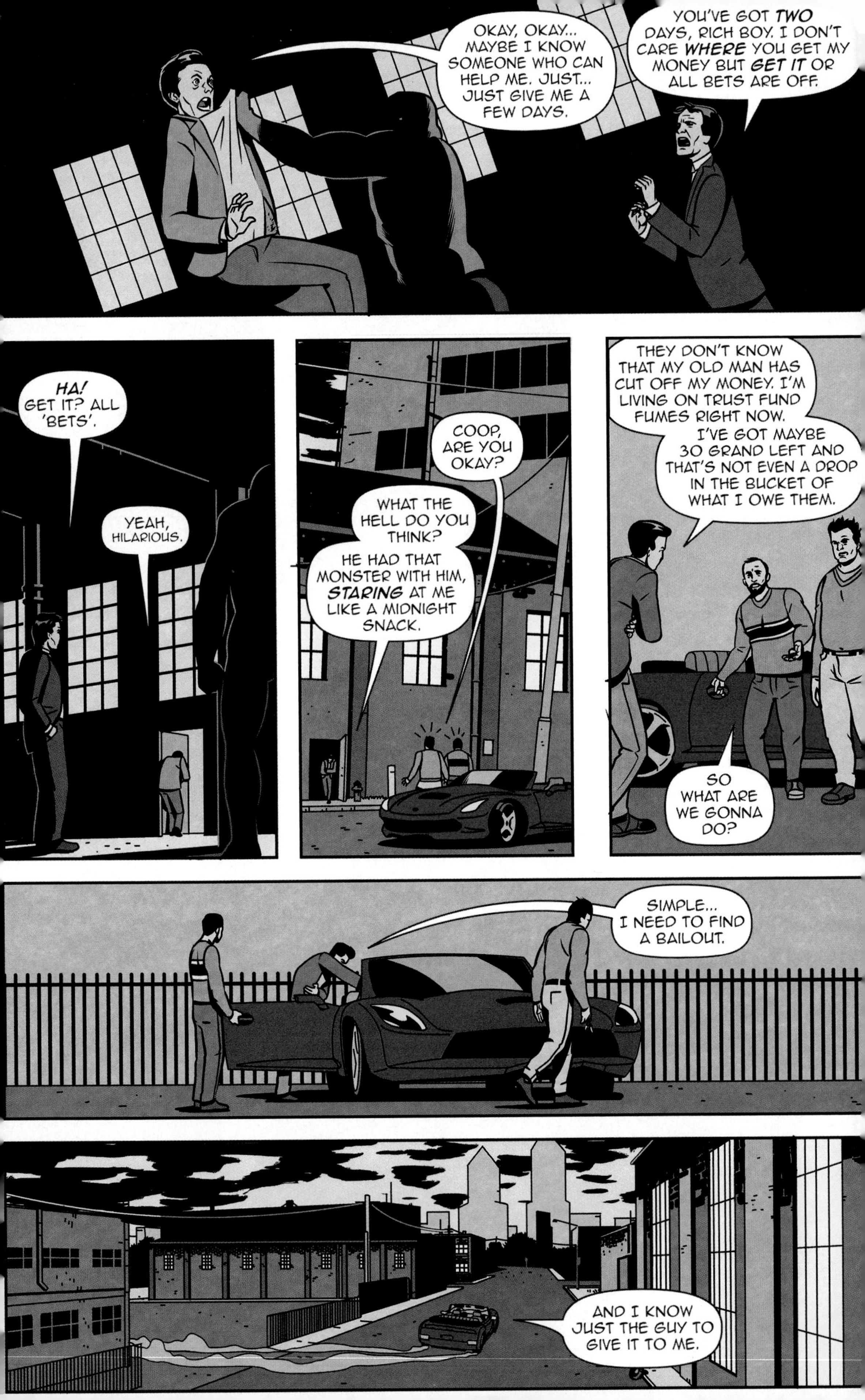
OKAY, OKAY... MAYBE I KNOW SOMEONE WHO CAN HELP ME. JUST... JUST GIVE ME A FEW DAYS.
YOU'VE GOT TWO DAYS, RICH BOY. I DON'T CARE WHERE YOU GET MY MONEY BUT GET IT OR ALL BETS ARE OFF.
HA! GET IT? ALL 'BETS'.
YEAH, HILARIOUS.
COOP, ARE YOU OKAY?
WHAT THE HELL DO YOU THINK?
HE HAD THAT MONSTER WITH HIM, STARING AT ME LIKE A MIDNIGHT SNACK.
THEY DON'T KNOW THAT MY OLD MAN HAS CUT OFF MY MONEY. I'M LIVING ON TRUST FUND FUMES RIGHT NOW.
I'VE GOT MAYBE 30 GRAND LEFT AND THAT'S NOT EVEN A DROP IN THE BUCKET OF WHAT I OWE THEM.
SO WHAT ARE WE GONNA DO?
SIMPLE... I NEED TO FIND A BAILOUT.
AND I KNOW JUST THE GUY TO GIVE IT TO ME.

ACTION LAB ENTERTAINMENT PROUDLY PRESENTS

the FIRST HERO

VOLUME 2: FIGHT FOR YOUR LIFE

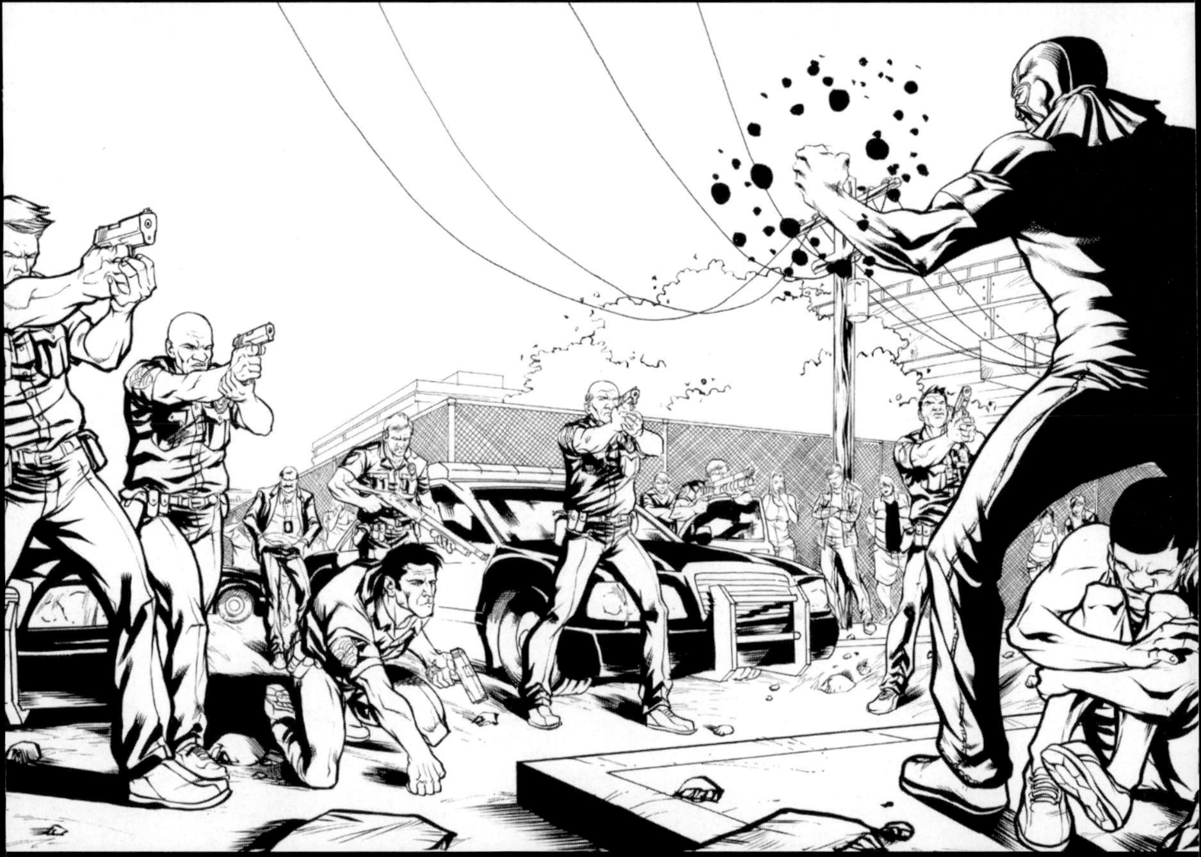

CHAPTER FIVE: THE FOUR HORSEMEN RIDE AGAIN

for SIXTEEN HECTARES AND A MOOSE, INK.

Created/Written by ANTHONY RUTTGAIZER
Cover/Interior Art by DANNY ZABBAL
Letters/Colors by FRED C. STRESING
Variant Cover by JERRY GAYLORD
frontispiece art by PHILLIP SEVY

For More Info, visit SixteenHectares.com

for ACTION LAB ENTERTAINMENT

BRYAN SEATON Publisher
KEVIN FREEMAN President
SHAWN GABBORIN Editor-in-Chief
DAVE DWONCH Creative Driector
JIM DIETZ Social Media Director
JAMAL IGLE Director of Marketing
VITO DELSANTE Director of Marketing
COLLEEN BOYD Associate Editor
CHAD CICCONI Kumite Champion

Read More Now at ActionLabComics.com

The entire world knows the stark reality: everyone who develops superpowers goes criminally or clinically insane. These so-called "extrahumans" have been stripped of all their rights and are hunted down by the government because of the threat they pose to society... until Jake Roth. When Jake manifests superpowers --but somehow keeps his sanity-- he must decide whether to put himself at risk by using his powers to save people, or to hide his new abilities while innocent people he could have helped are hurt around him every day.

Previously in The First Hero...

As a United States Marine nearing the end of active duty in Afghanistan, Jake manifests extrahuman powers while under fire. Scared and confused by his sudden transformation, Jake is able to use his new abilities --an energy pulse that gives him immense strength and makes him seemingly invulnerable-- to defeat several enemy combatants and escape capture.

With his mind in tact and his new powers still a secret, Jake returns home to Philadelphia and tries to settle into his normal life. But when the police attempt a violent takedown on an extrahuman teenager, Jake feels compelled to step in and help the boy. The situation gets out of control when both the U.S. Extrahuman Task Force and a rogue gang of extrahuman thugs arrive and turn South Philly into a full-blown battlefield.

The young extrahuman Jake is trying to save suffers a catastrophic loss of control of his powers and dies in the resulting massive explosion. Jake escapes again but ends up making powerful enemies on both sides of the growing human/extrahuman conflict. Saddened by the young man's death, Jake vows to use his power to prevent what he sees as the impending all-out war coming to the streets of Philadelphia.

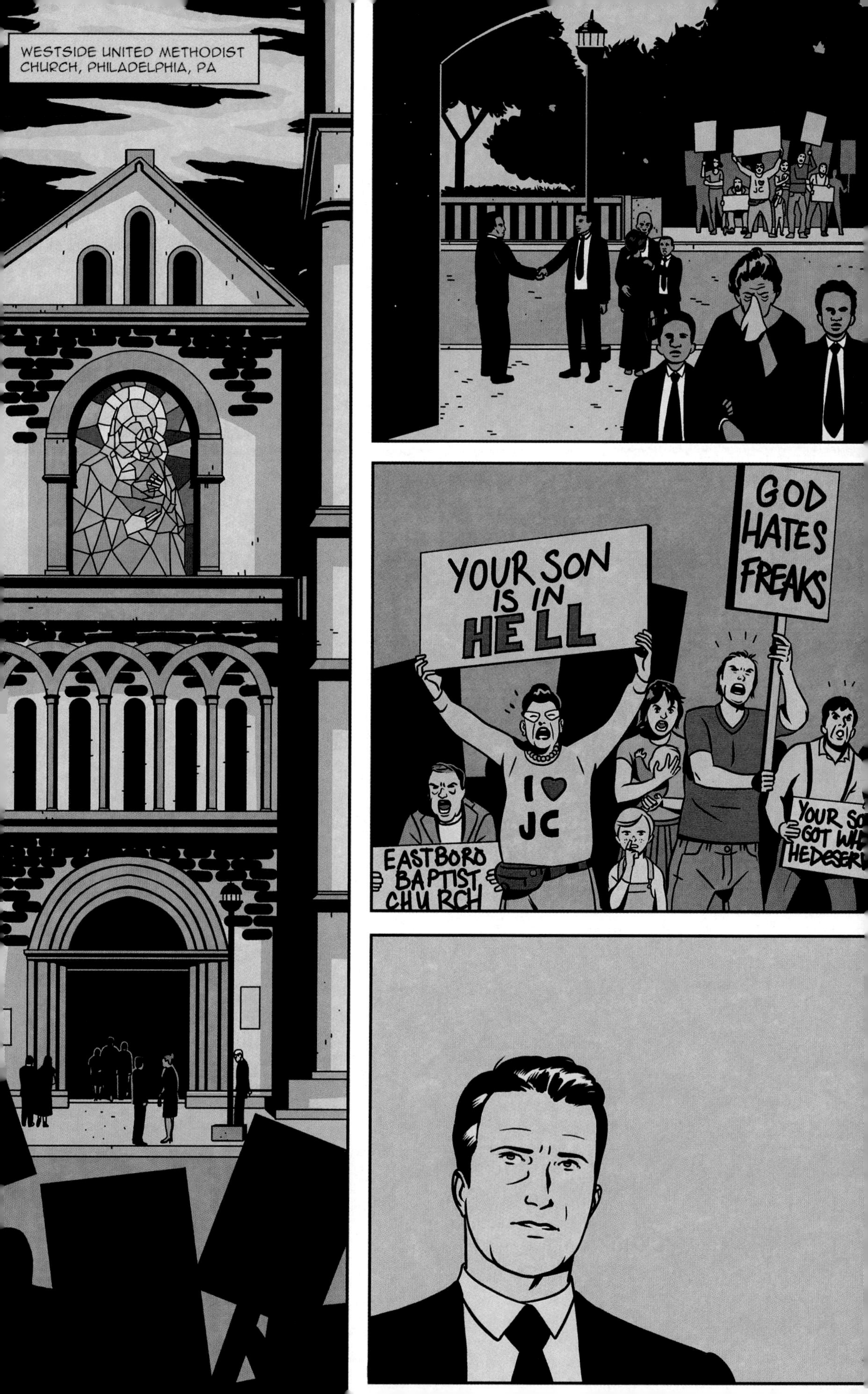
WESTSIDE UNITED METHODIST CHURCH, PHILADELPHIA, PA
YOUR SON IS IN HELL
GOD HATES FREAKS
I ♥ JC
EASTBORO BAPTIST CHURCH

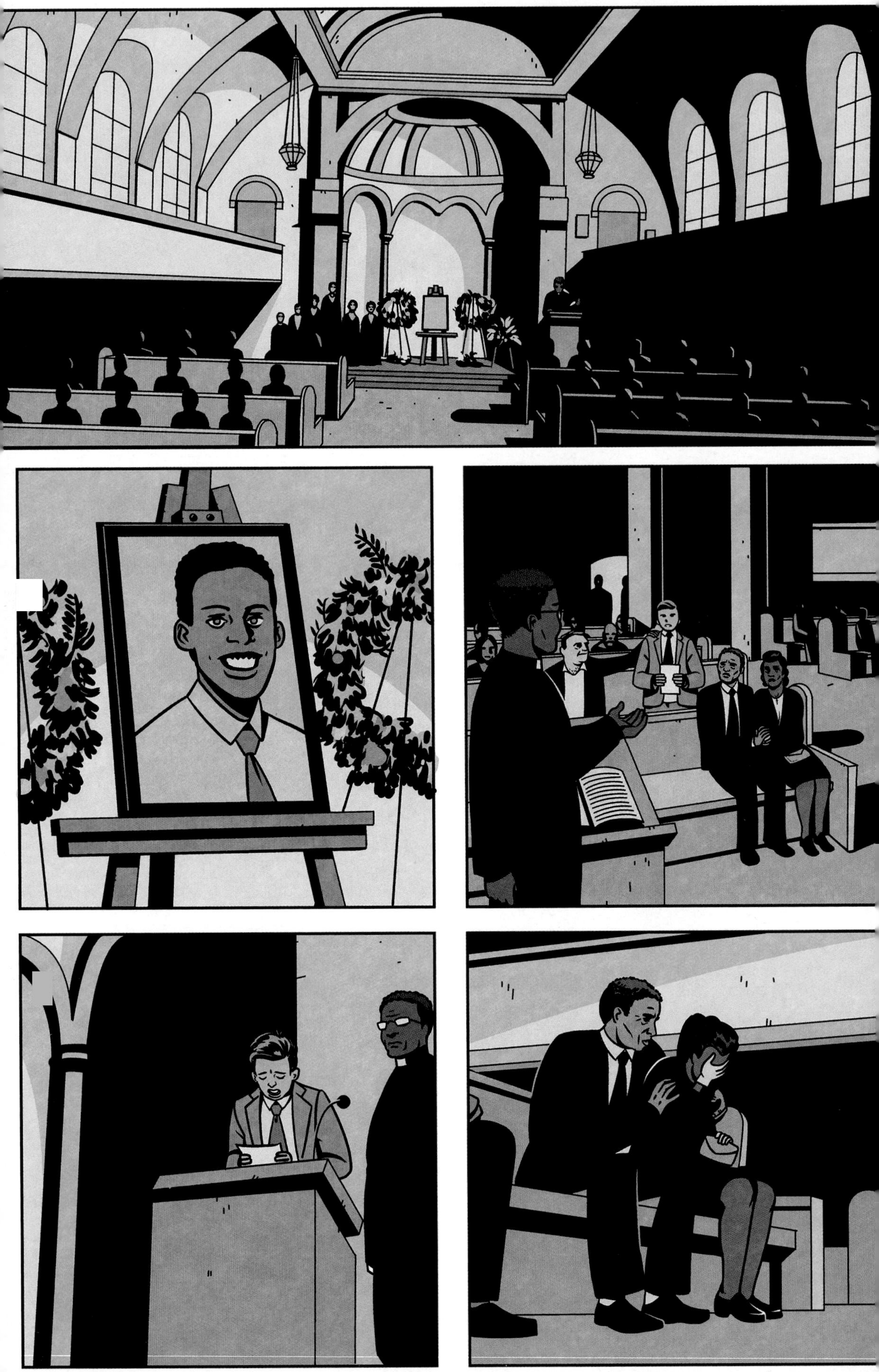

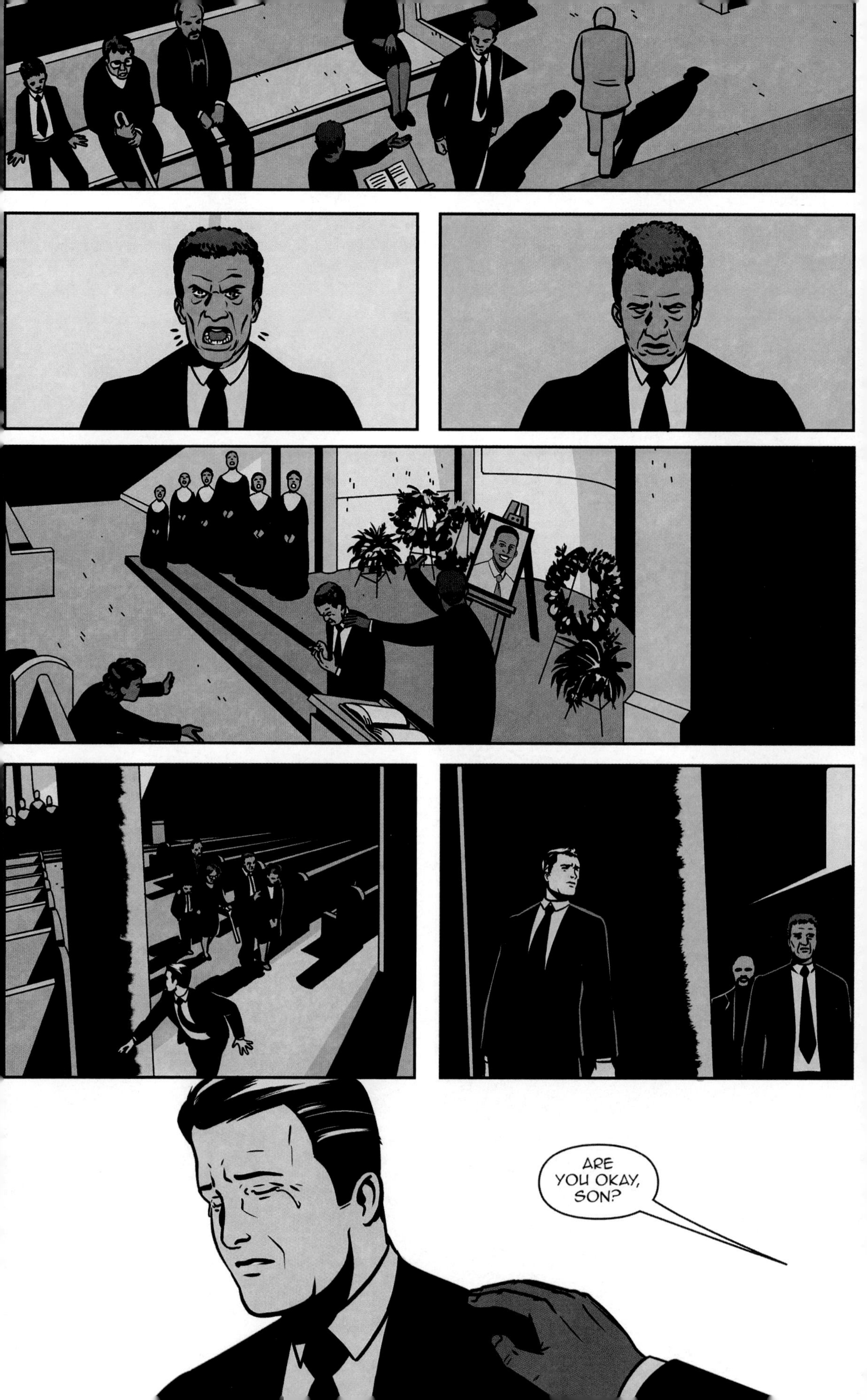
ARE YOU OKAY, SON?

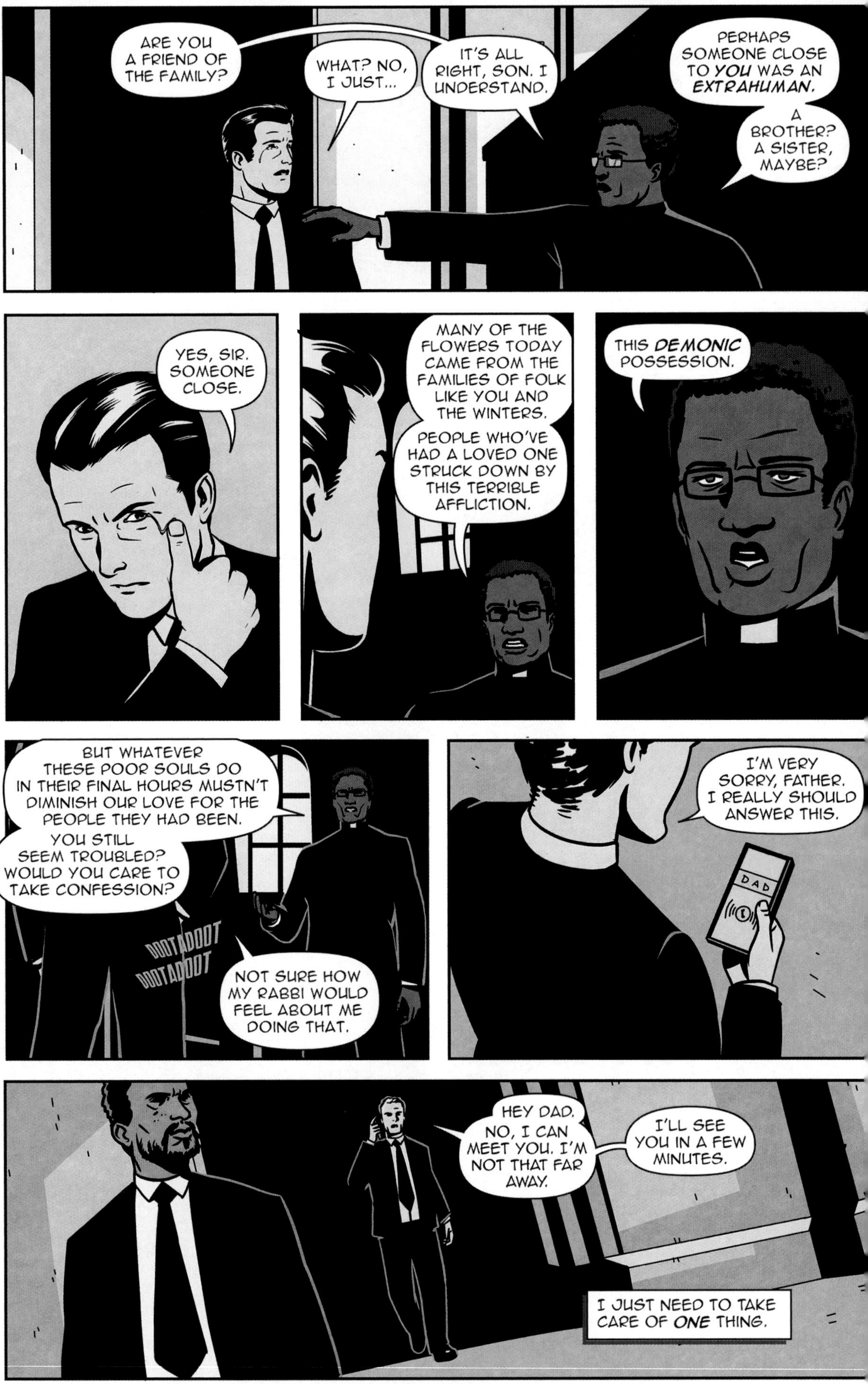

ARE YOU A FRIEND OF THE FAMILY?
WHAT? NO, I JUST...
IT'S ALL RIGHT, SON. I UNDERSTAND.
PERHAPS SOMEONE CLOSE TO *YOU* WAS AN *EXTRAHUMAN.*
A BROTHER? A SISTER, MAYBE?
YES, SIR. SOMEONE CLOSE.
MANY OF THE FLOWERS TODAY CAME FROM THE FAMILIES OF FOLK LIKE YOU AND THE WINTERS.
PEOPLE WHO'VE HAD A LOVED ONE STRUCK DOWN BY THIS TERRIBLE AFFLICTION.
THIS *DEMONIC* POSSESSION.
BUT WHATEVER THESE POOR SOULS DO IN THEIR FINAL HOURS MUSTN'T DIMINISH OUR LOVE FOR THE PEOPLE THEY HAD BEEN.
YOU STILL SEEM TROUBLED? WOULD YOU CARE TO TAKE CONFESSION?
DOOTADOOT DOOTADOOT
NOT SURE HOW MY RABBI WOULD FEEL ABOUT ME DOING THAT.
I'M VERY SORRY, FATHER. I REALLY SHOULD ANSWER THIS.
DAD
HEY DAD. NO, I CAN MEET YOU. I'M NOT THAT FAR AWAY.
I'LL SEE YOU IN A FEW MINUTES.
I JUST NEED TO TAKE CARE OF *ONE* THING.

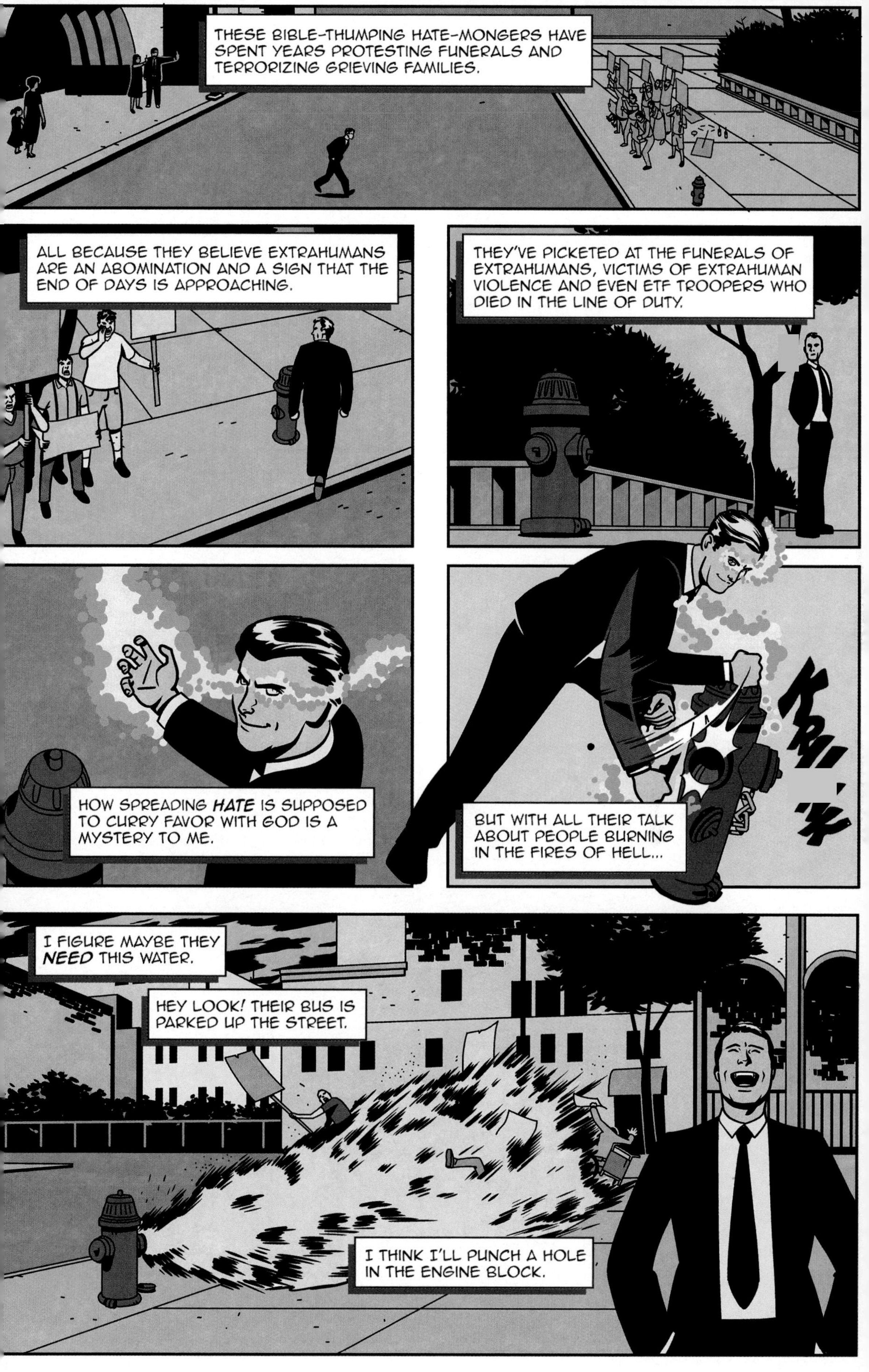
THESE BIBLE-THUMPING HATE-MONGERS HAVE SPENT YEARS PROTESTING FUNERALS AND TERRORIZING GRIEVING FAMILIES.
ALL BECAUSE THEY BELIEVE EXTRAHUMANS ARE AN ABOMINATION AND A SIGN THAT THE END OF DAYS IS APPROACHING.
THEY'VE PICKETED AT THE FUNERALS OF EXTRAHUMANS, VICTIMS OF EXTRAHUMAN VIOLENCE AND EVEN ETF TROOPERS WHO DIED IN THE LINE OF DUTY.
HOW SPREADING ***HATE*** IS SUPPOSED TO CURRY FAVOR WITH GOD IS A MYSTERY TO ME.
BUT WITH ALL THEIR TALK ABOUT PEOPLE BURNING IN THE FIRES OF HELL...
I FIGURE MAYBE THEY ***NEED*** THIS WATER.
HEY LOOK! THEIR BUS IS PARKED UP THE STREET.
I THINK I'LL PUNCH A HOLE IN THE ENGINE BLOCK.

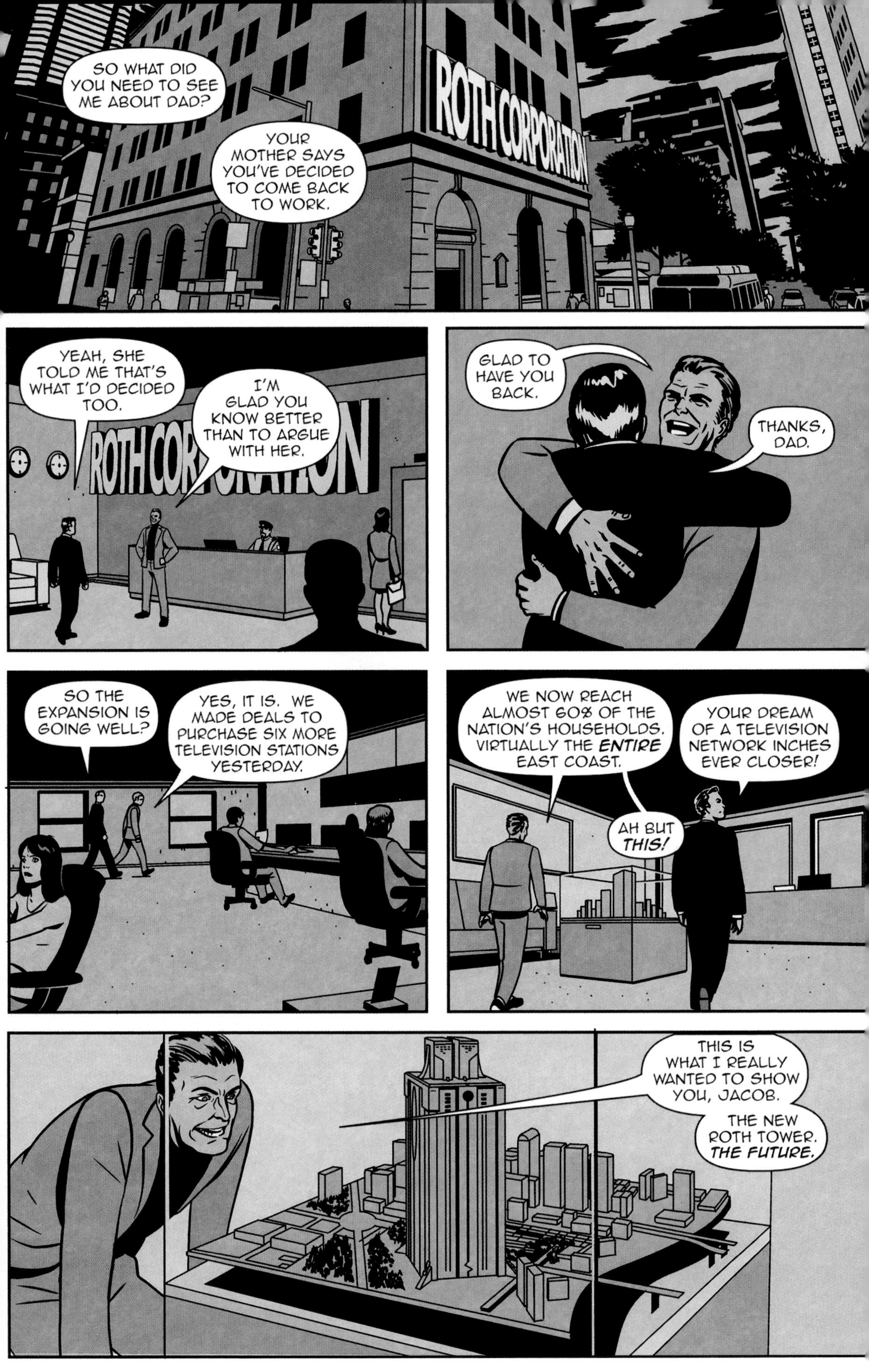
ROTH CORPORATION
SO WHAT DID YOU NEED TO SEE ME ABOUT DAD?
YOUR MOTHER SAYS YOU'VE DECIDED TO COME BACK TO WORK.
YEAH, SHE TOLD ME THAT'S WHAT I'D DECIDED TOO.
I'M GLAD YOU KNOW BETTER THAN TO ARGUE WITH HER.
GLAD TO HAVE YOU BACK.
THANKS, DAD.
SO THE EXPANSION IS GOING WELL?
YES, IT IS. WE MADE DEALS TO PURCHASE SIX MORE TELEVISION STATIONS YESTERDAY.
WE NOW REACH ALMOST 60% OF THE NATION'S HOUSEHOLDS. VIRTUALLY THE *ENTIRE* EAST COAST.
YOUR DREAM OF A TELEVISION NETWORK INCHES EVER CLOSER!
AH BUT *THIS!*
THIS IS WHAT I REALLY WANTED TO SHOW YOU, JACOB.
THE NEW ROTH TOWER. *THE FUTURE.*

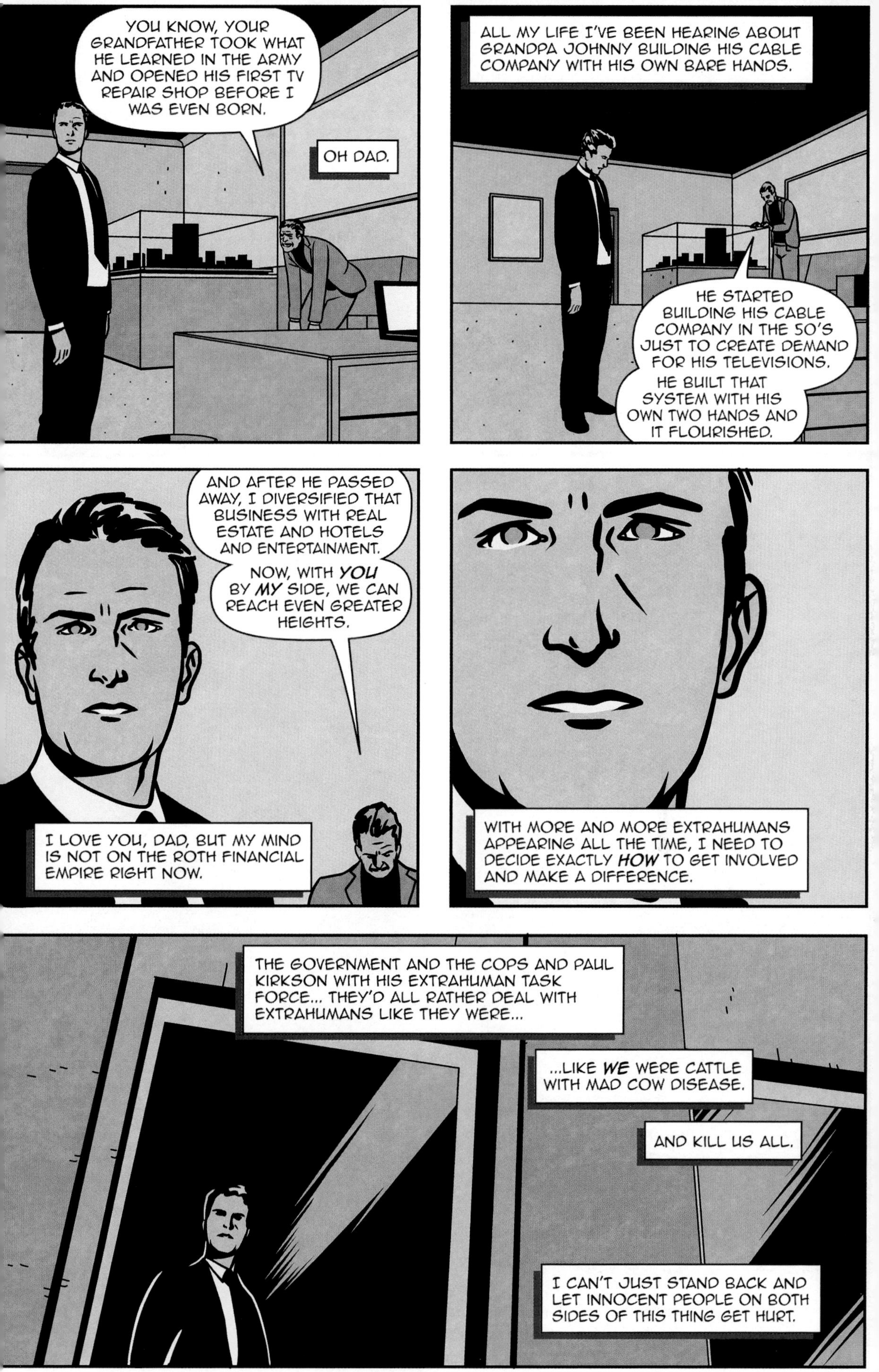
YOU KNOW, YOUR GRANDFATHER TOOK WHAT HE LEARNED IN THE ARMY AND OPENED HIS FIRST TV REPAIR SHOP BEFORE I WAS EVEN BORN.
OH DAD.
ALL MY LIFE I'VE BEEN HEARING ABOUT GRANDPA JOHNNY BUILDING HIS CABLE COMPANY WITH HIS OWN BARE HANDS.
HE STARTED BUILDING HIS CABLE COMPANY IN THE 50'S JUST TO CREATE DEMAND FOR HIS TELEVISIONS.
HE BUILT THAT SYSTEM WITH HIS OWN TWO HANDS AND IT FLOURISHED.
AND AFTER HE PASSED AWAY, I DIVERSIFIED THAT BUSINESS WITH REAL ESTATE AND HOTELS AND ENTERTAINMENT.
NOW, WITH *YOU* BY *MY* SIDE, WE CAN REACH EVEN GREATER HEIGHTS.
I LOVE YOU, DAD, BUT MY MIND IS NOT ON THE ROTH FINANCIAL EMPIRE RIGHT NOW.
WITH MORE AND MORE EXTRAHUMANS APPEARING ALL THE TIME, I NEED TO DECIDE EXACTLY *HOW* TO GET INVOLVED AND MAKE A DIFFERENCE.
THE GOVERNMENT AND THE COPS AND PAUL KIRKSON WITH HIS EXTRAHUMAN TASK FORCE... THEY'D ALL RATHER DEAL WITH EXTRAHUMANS LIKE THEY WERE...
...LIKE *WE* WERE CATTLE WITH MAD COW DISEASE.
AND KILL US ALL.
I CAN'T JUST STAND BACK AND LET INNOCENT PEOPLE ON BOTH SIDES OF THIS THING GET HURT.

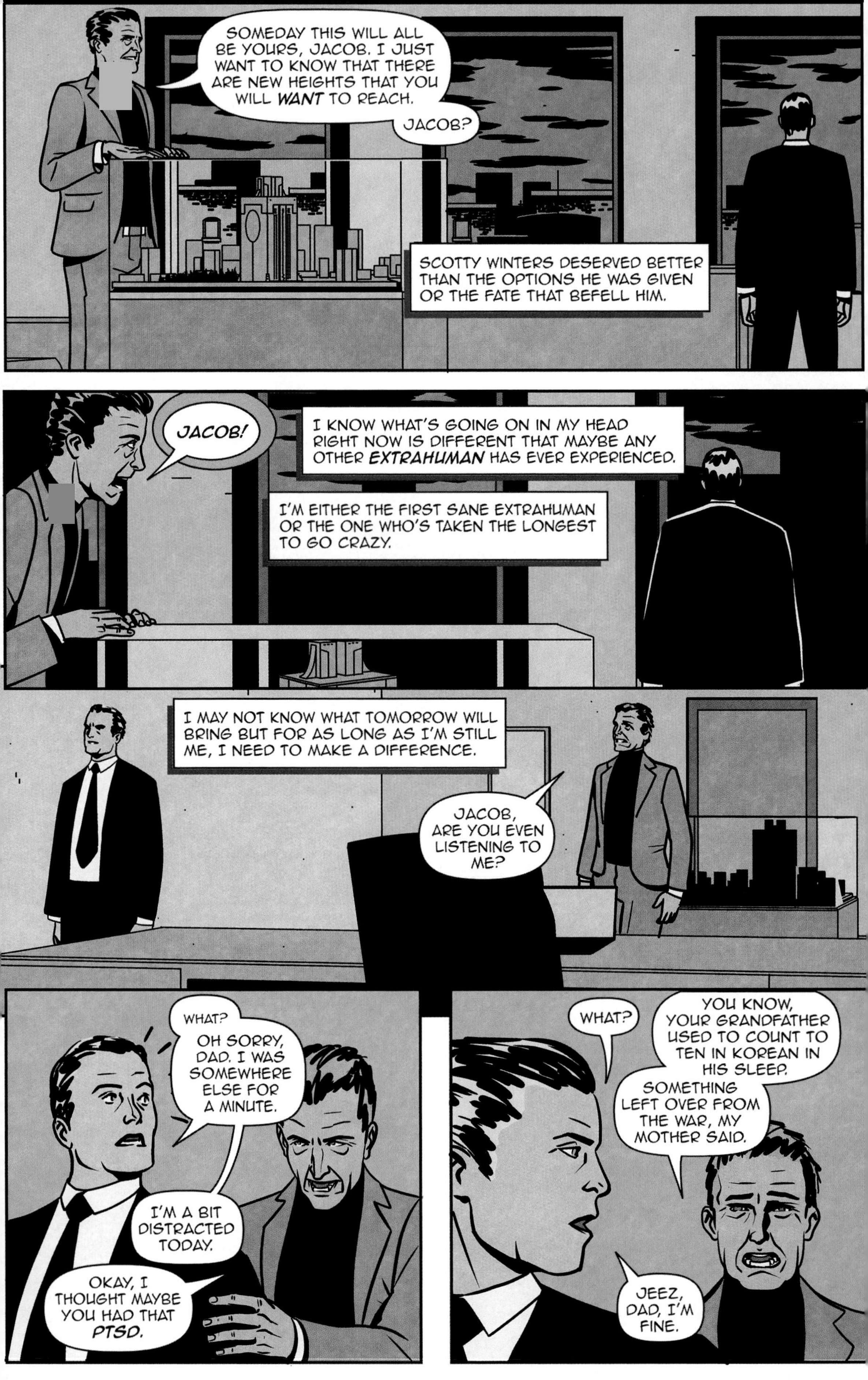
SOMEDAY THIS WILL ALL BE YOURS, JACOB. I JUST WANT TO KNOW THAT THERE ARE NEW HEIGHTS THAT YOU WILL *WANT* TO REACH.
JACOB?
SCOTTY WINTERS DESERVED BETTER THAN THE OPTIONS HE WAS GIVEN OR THE FATE THAT BEFELL HIM.
JACOB!
I KNOW WHAT'S GOING ON IN MY HEAD RIGHT NOW IS DIFFERENT THAT MAYBE ANY OTHER ***EXTRAHUMAN*** HAS EVER EXPERIENCED.
I'M EITHER THE FIRST SANE EXTRAHUMAN OR THE ONE WHO'S TAKEN THE LONGEST TO GO CRAZY.
I MAY NOT KNOW WHAT TOMORROW WILL BRING BUT FOR AS LONG AS I'M STILL ME, I NEED TO MAKE A DIFFERENCE.
JACOB, ARE YOU EVEN LISTENING TO ME?
WHAT?
OH SORRY, DAD. I WAS SOMEWHERE ELSE FOR A MINUTE.
I'M A BIT DISTRACTED TODAY.
OKAY, I THOUGHT MAYBE YOU HAD THAT *PTSD*.
WHAT?
YOU KNOW, YOUR GRANDFATHER USED TO COUNT TO TEN IN KOREAN IN HIS SLEEP.
SOMETHING LEFT OVER FROM THE WAR, MY MOTHER SAID.
JEEZ, DAD, I'M FINE.

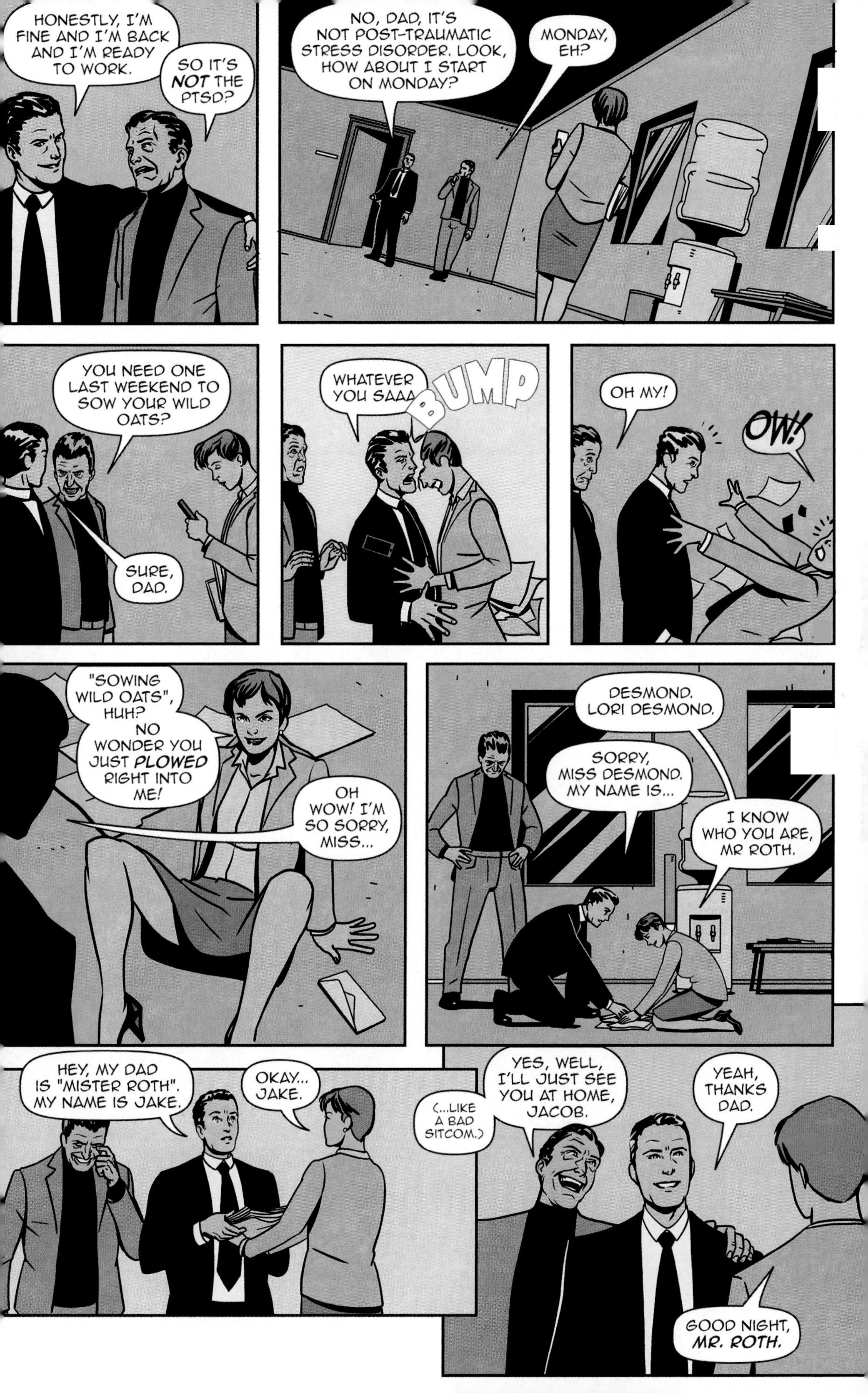
HONESTLY, I'M FINE AND I'M BACK AND I'M READY TO WORK.
SO IT'S NOT THE PTSD?
NO, DAD, IT'S NOT POST-TRAUMATIC STRESS DISORDER. LOOK, HOW ABOUT I START ON MONDAY?
MONDAY, EH?
YOU NEED ONE LAST WEEKEND TO SOW YOUR WILD OATS?
SURE, DAD.
WHATEVER YOU SAAA
BUMP
OH MY!
OW!
"SOWING WILD OATS", HUH?
NO WONDER YOU JUST PLOWED RIGHT INTO ME!
OH WOW! I'M SO SORRY, MISS...
DESMOND. LORI DESMOND.
SORRY, MISS DESMOND. MY NAME IS...
I KNOW WHO YOU ARE, MR ROTH.
HEY, MY DAD IS "MISTER ROTH". MY NAME IS JAKE.
OKAY... JAKE.
(...LIKE A BAD SITCOM.)
YES, WELL, I'LL JUST SEE YOU AT HOME, JACOB.
YEAH, THANKS DAD.
GOOD NIGHT, MR. ROTH.

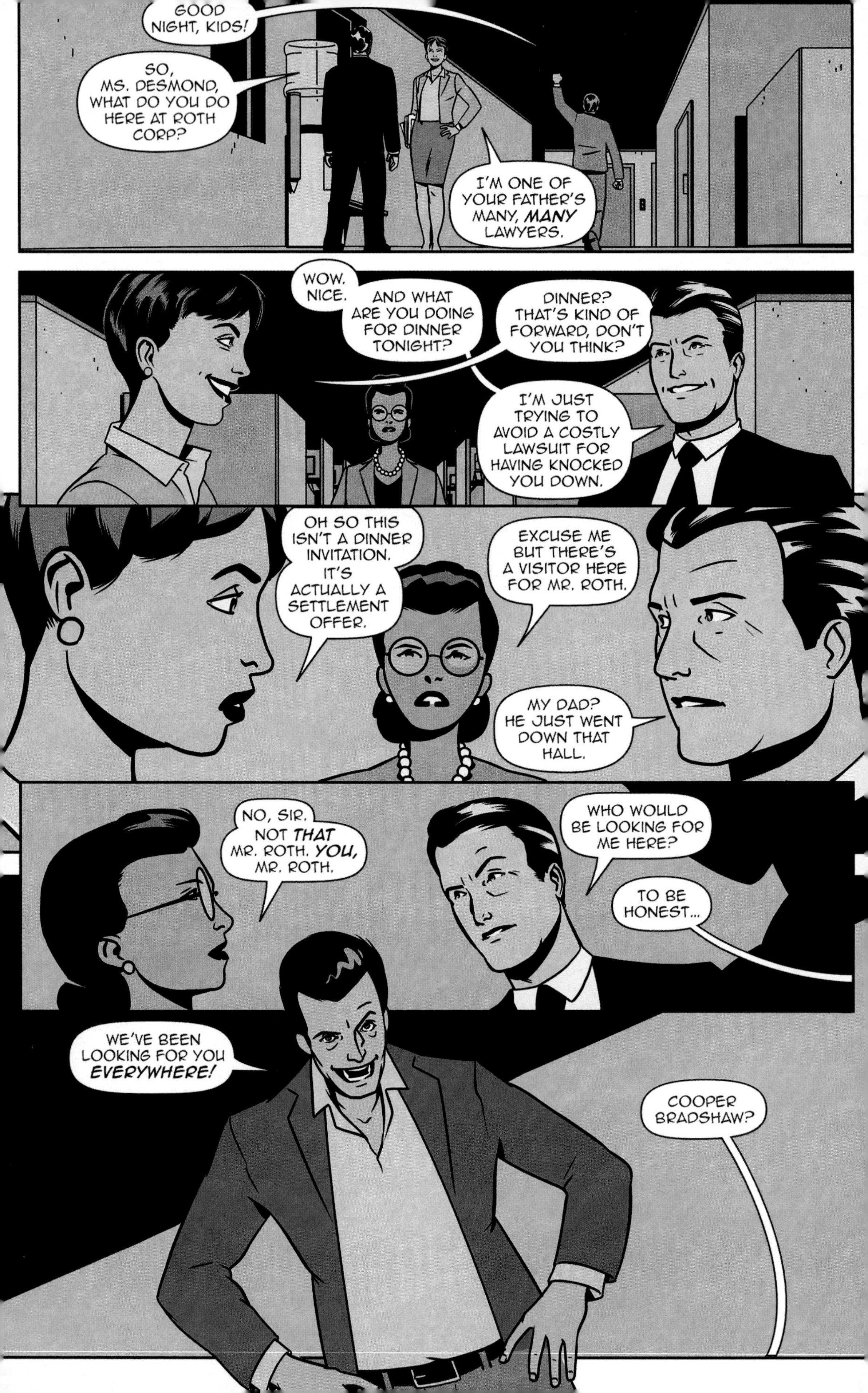
GOOD NIGHT, KIDS!
SO, MS. DESMOND, WHAT DO YOU DO HERE AT ROTH CORP?
I'M ONE OF YOUR FATHER'S MANY, MANY LAWYERS.
WOW. NICE.
AND WHAT ARE YOU DOING FOR DINNER TONIGHT?
DINNER? THAT'S KIND OF FORWARD, DON'T YOU THINK?
I'M JUST TRYING TO AVOID A COSTLY LAWSUIT FOR HAVING KNOCKED YOU DOWN.
OH SO THIS ISN'T A DINNER INVITATION. IT'S ACTUALLY A SETTLEMENT OFFER.
EXCUSE ME BUT THERE'S A VISITOR HERE FOR MR. ROTH.
MY DAD? HE JUST WENT DOWN THAT HALL.
NO, SIR. NOT THAT MR. ROTH. YOU, MR. ROTH.
WHO WOULD BE LOOKING FOR ME HERE?
TO BE HONEST...
WE'VE BEEN LOOKING FOR YOU EVERYWHERE!
COOPER BRADSHAW?

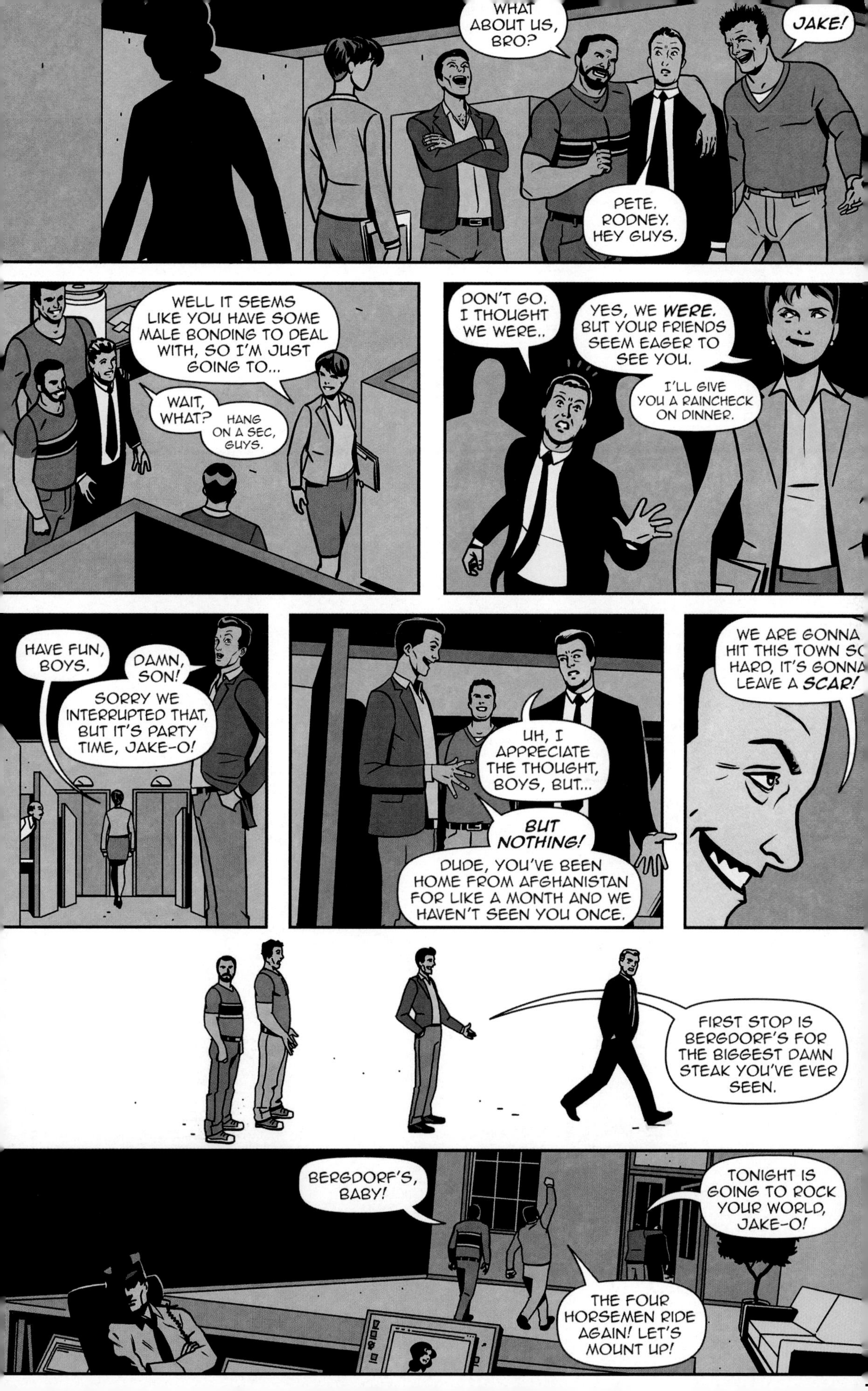
WHAT ABOUT US, BRO?
JAKE!
PETE. RODNEY. HEY GUYS.
WELL IT SEEMS LIKE YOU HAVE SOME MALE BONDING TO DEAL WITH, SO I'M JUST GOING TO...
WAIT, WHAT?
HANG ON A SEC, GUYS.
DON'T GO. I THOUGHT WE WERE..
YES, WE WERE. BUT YOUR FRIENDS SEEM EAGER TO SEE YOU.
I'LL GIVE YOU A RAINCHECK ON DINNER.
HAVE FUN, BOYS.
DAMN, SON!
SORRY WE INTERRUPTED THAT, BUT IT'S PARTY TIME, JAKE-O!
UH, I APPRECIATE THE THOUGHT, BOYS, BUT...
BUT NOTHING!
DUDE, YOU'VE BEEN HOME FROM AFGHANISTAN FOR LIKE A MONTH AND WE HAVEN'T SEEN YOU ONCE.
WE ARE GONNA HIT THIS TOWN SO HARD, IT'S GONNA LEAVE A SCAR!
FIRST STOP IS BERGDORF'S FOR THE BIGGEST DAMN STEAK YOU'VE EVER SEEN.
BERGDORF'S, BABY!
TONIGHT IS GOING TO ROCK YOUR WORLD, JAKE-O!
THE FOUR HORSEMEN RIDE AGAIN! LET'S MOUNT UP!

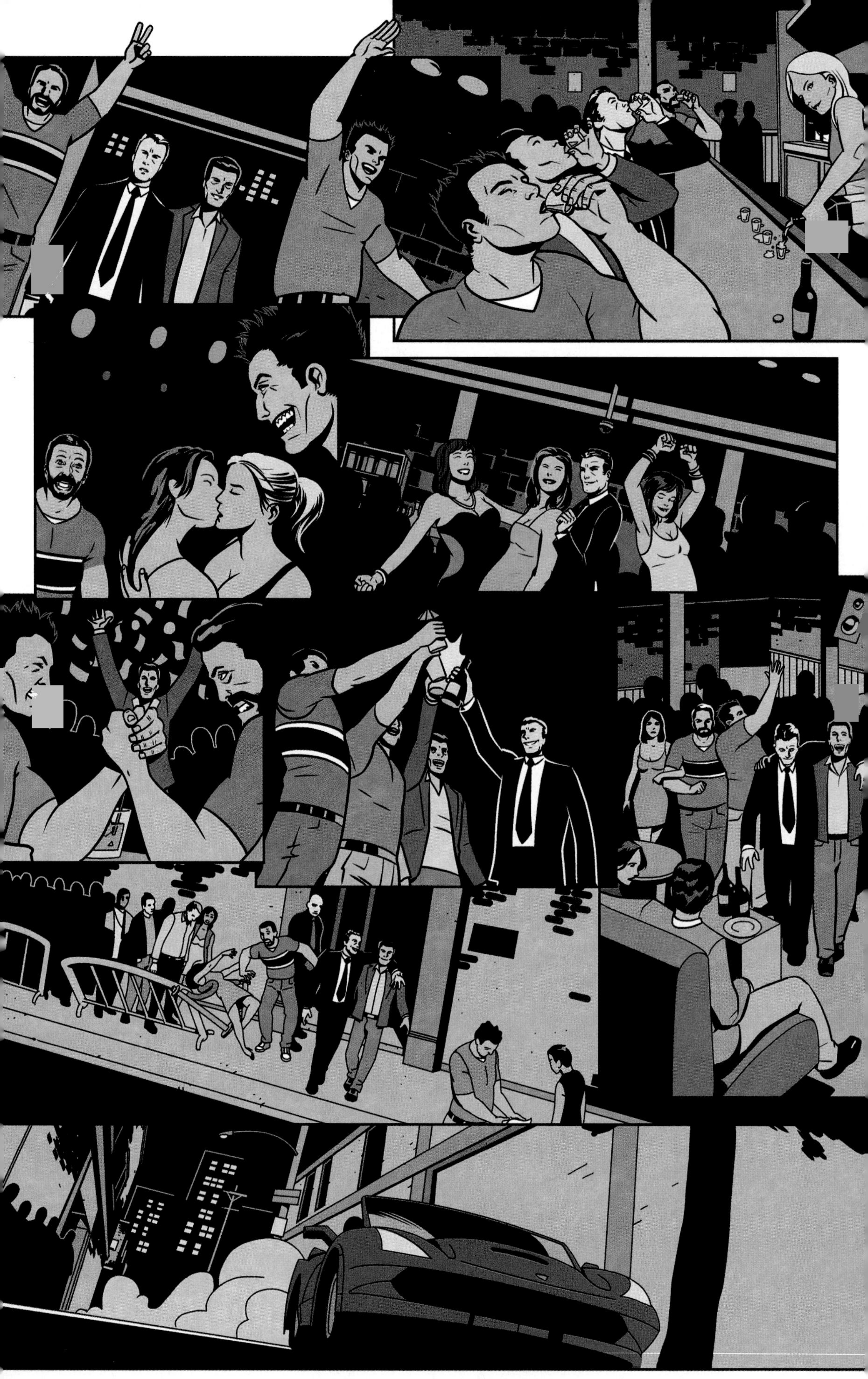

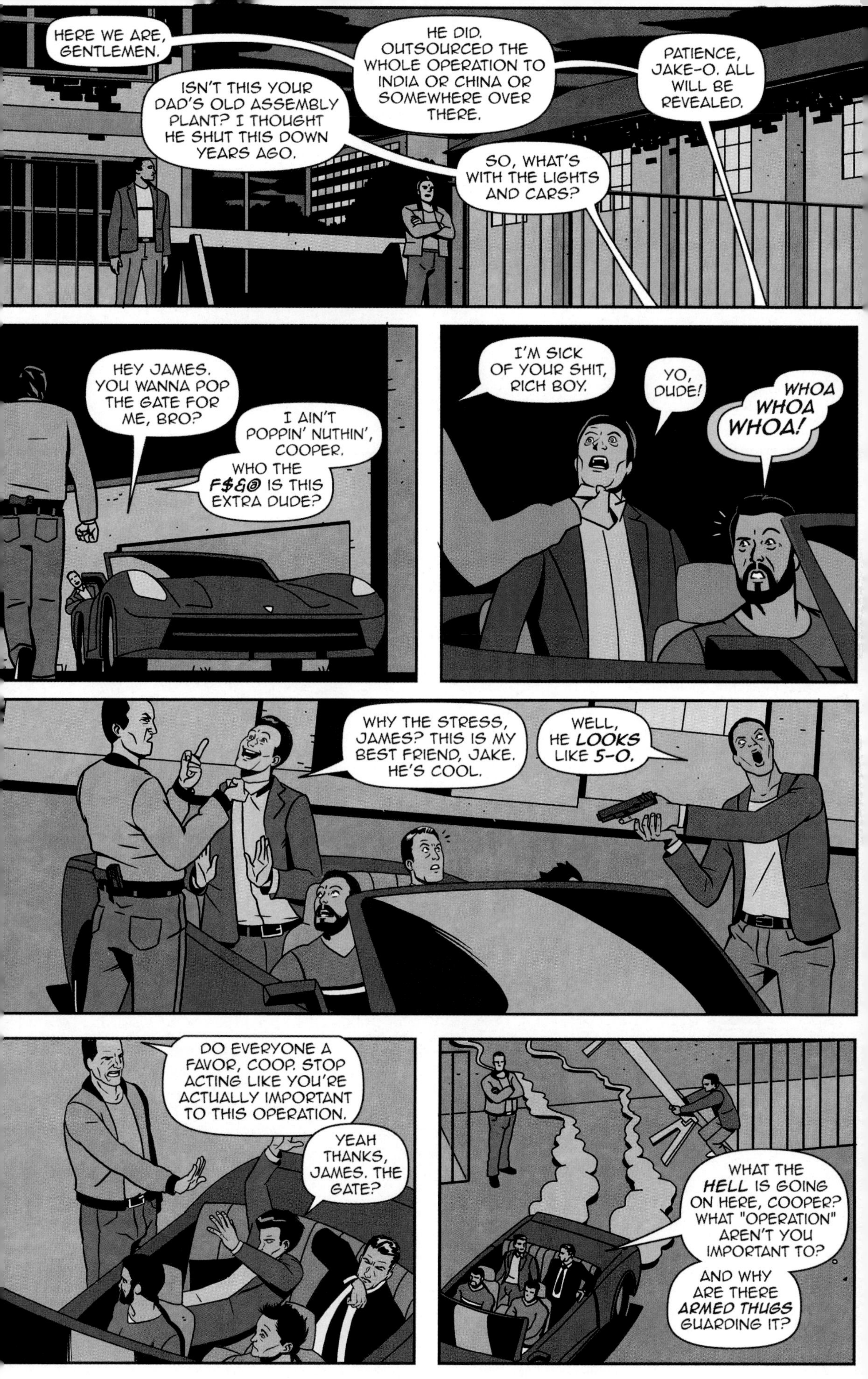
HERE WE ARE, GENTLEMEN.
ISN'T THIS YOUR DAD'S OLD ASSEMBLY PLANT? I THOUGHT HE SHUT THIS DOWN YEARS AGO.
HE DID. OUTSOURCED THE WHOLE OPERATION TO INDIA OR CHINA OR SOMEWHERE OVER THERE.
SO, WHAT'S WITH THE LIGHTS AND CARS?
PATIENCE, JAKE-O. ALL WILL BE REVEALED.
HEY JAMES. YOU WANNA POP THE GATE FOR ME, BRO?
I AIN'T POPPIN' NUTHIN', COOPER.
WHO THE F$&@ IS THIS EXTRA DUDE?
I'M SICK OF YOUR SHIT, RICH BOY.
YO, DUDE!
WHOA WHOA WHOA!
WHY THE STRESS, JAMES? THIS IS MY BEST FRIEND, JAKE. HE'S COOL.
WELL, HE LOOKS LIKE 5-O.
DO EVERYONE A FAVOR, COOP. STOP ACTING LIKE YOU'RE ACTUALLY IMPORTANT TO THIS OPERATION.
YEAH THANKS, JAMES. THE GATE?
WHAT THE HELL IS GOING ON HERE, COOPER? WHAT "OPERATION" AREN'T YOU IMPORTANT TO?
AND WHY ARE THERE ARMED THUGS GUARDING IT?

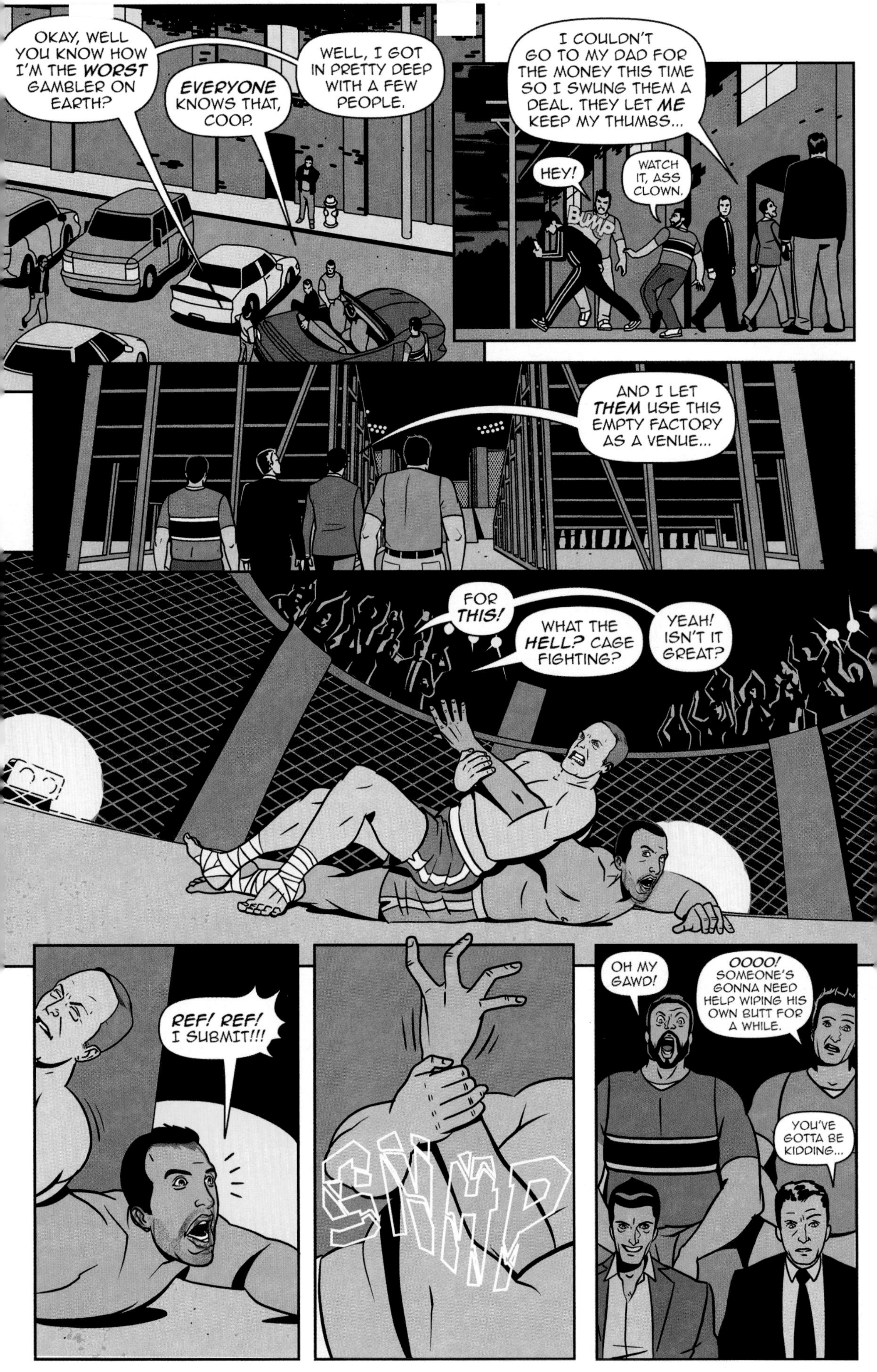
OKAY, WELL YOU KNOW HOW I'M THE *WORST* GAMBLER ON EARTH?
EVERYONE KNOWS THAT, COOP.
WELL, I GOT IN PRETTY DEEP WITH A FEW PEOPLE.
I COULDN'T GO TO MY DAD FOR THE MONEY THIS TIME SO I SWUNG THEM A DEAL. THEY LET *ME* KEEP MY THUMBS...
HEY!
BUMP
WATCH IT, ASS CLOWN.
AND I LET *THEM* USE THIS EMPTY FACTORY AS A VENUE...
FOR *THIS!*
WHAT THE *HELL?* CAGE FIGHTING?
YEAH! ISN'T IT GREAT?
REF! REF! I SUBMIT!!!
SNAP
OH MY GAWD!
OOOO! SOMEONE'S GONNA NEED HELP WIPING HIS OWN BUTT FOR A WHILE.
YOU'VE GOTTA BE KIDDING...

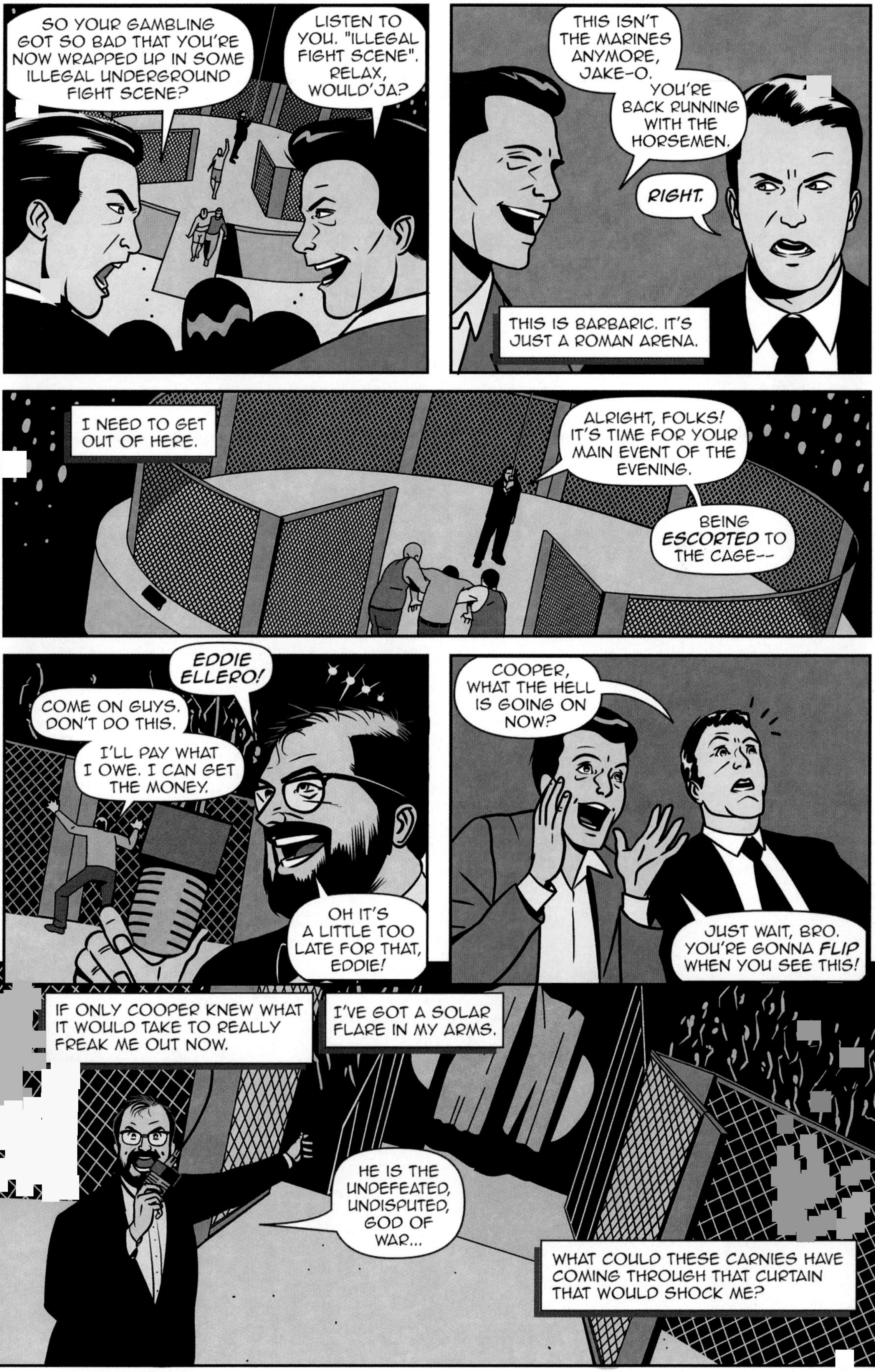
SO YOUR GAMBLING GOT SO BAD THAT YOU'RE NOW WRAPPED UP IN SOME ILLEGAL UNDERGROUND FIGHT SCENE?
LISTEN TO YOU. "ILLEGAL FIGHT SCENE". RELAX, WOULD'JA?
THIS ISN'T THE MARINES ANYMORE, JAKE-O.
YOU'RE BACK RUNNING WITH THE HORSEMEN.
RIGHT.
THIS IS BARBARIC. IT'S JUST A ROMAN ARENA.
I NEED TO GET OUT OF HERE.
ALRIGHT, FOLKS! IT'S TIME FOR YOUR MAIN EVENT OF THE EVENING.
BEING ESCORTED TO THE CAGE--
EDDIE ELLERO!
COME ON GUYS. DON'T DO THIS.
I'LL PAY WHAT I OWE. I CAN GET THE MONEY.
OH IT'S A LITTLE TOO LATE FOR THAT, EDDIE!
COOPER, WHAT THE HELL IS GOING ON NOW?
JUST WAIT, BRO. YOU'RE GONNA FLIP WHEN YOU SEE THIS!
IF ONLY COOPER KNEW WHAT IT WOULD TAKE TO REALLY FREAK ME OUT NOW.
I'VE GOT A SOLAR FLARE IN MY ARMS.
HE IS THE UNDEFEATED, UNDISPUTED, GOD OF WAR...
WHAT COULD THESE CARNIES HAVE COMING THROUGH THAT CURTAIN THAT WOULD SHOCK ME?

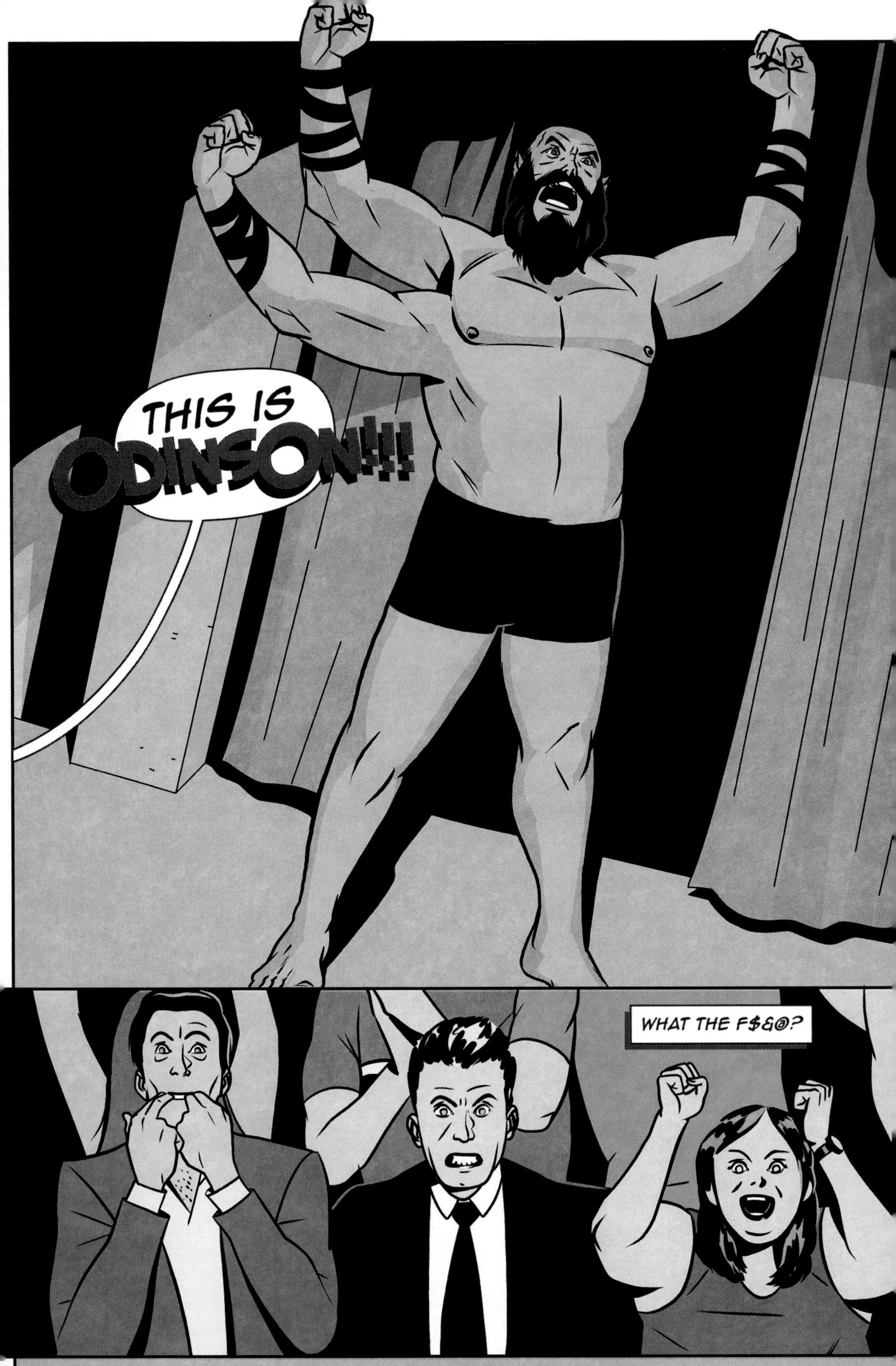
THIS IS ODINSON!!!
WHAT THE F$&@?

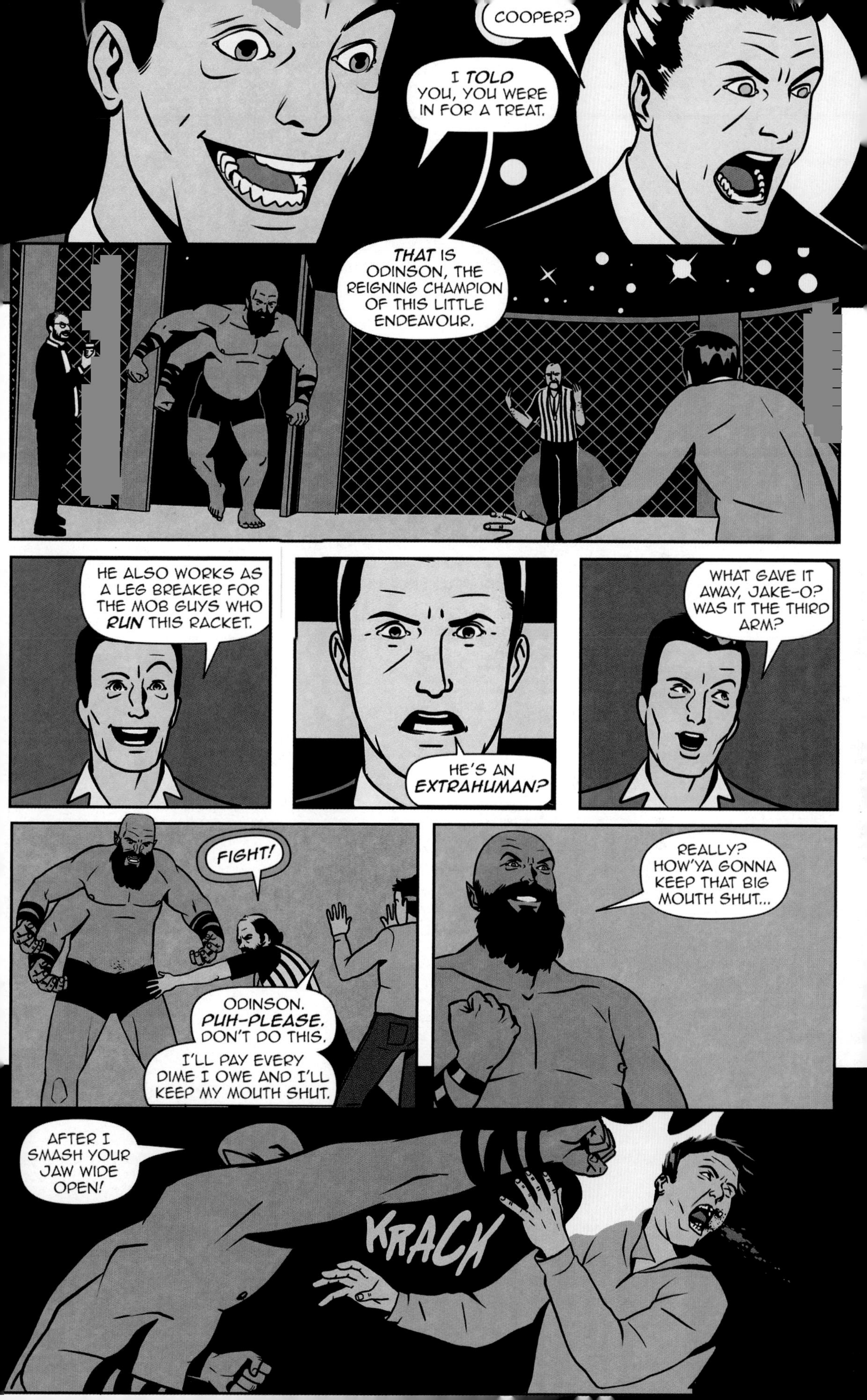
COOPER?
I TOLD YOU, YOU WERE IN FOR A TREAT.
THAT IS ODINSON, THE REIGNING CHAMPION OF THIS LITTLE ENDEAVOUR.
HE ALSO WORKS AS A LEG BREAKER FOR THE MOB GUYS WHO RUN THIS RACKET.
HE'S AN EXTRAHUMAN?
WHAT GAVE IT AWAY, JAKE-O? WAS IT THE THIRD ARM?
FIGHT!
ODINSON. PUH-PLEASE. DON'T DO THIS.
I'LL PAY EVERY DIME I OWE AND I'LL KEEP MY MOUTH SHUT.
REALLY? HOW'YA GONNA KEEP THAT BIG MOUTH SHUT...
AFTER I SMASH YOUR JAW WIDE OPEN!
KRACK

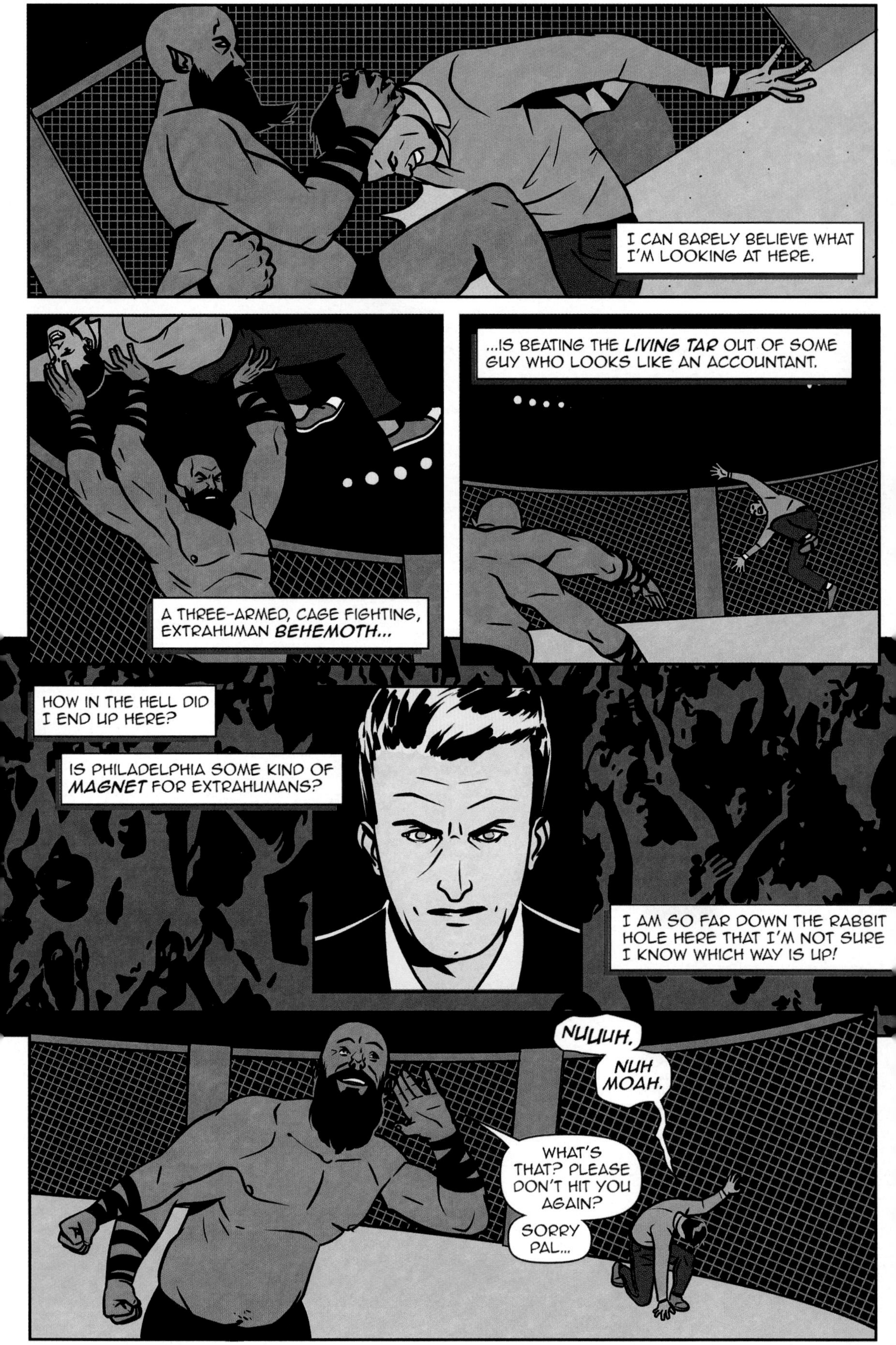
I CAN BARELY BELIEVE WHAT I'M LOOKING AT HERE.
A THREE-ARMED, CAGE FIGHTING, EXTRAHUMAN *BEHEMOTH...*
...IS BEATING THE *LIVING TAR* OUT OF SOME GUY WHO LOOKS LIKE AN ACCOUNTANT.
HOW IN THE HELL DID I END UP HERE?
IS PHILADELPHIA SOME KIND OF *MAGNET* FOR EXTRAHUMANS?
I AM SO FAR DOWN THE RABBIT HOLE HERE THAT I'M NOT SURE I KNOW WHICH WAY IS UP!
NUUUH.
NUH MOAH.
WHAT'S THAT? PLEASE DON'T HIT YOU AGAIN?
SORRY PAL...

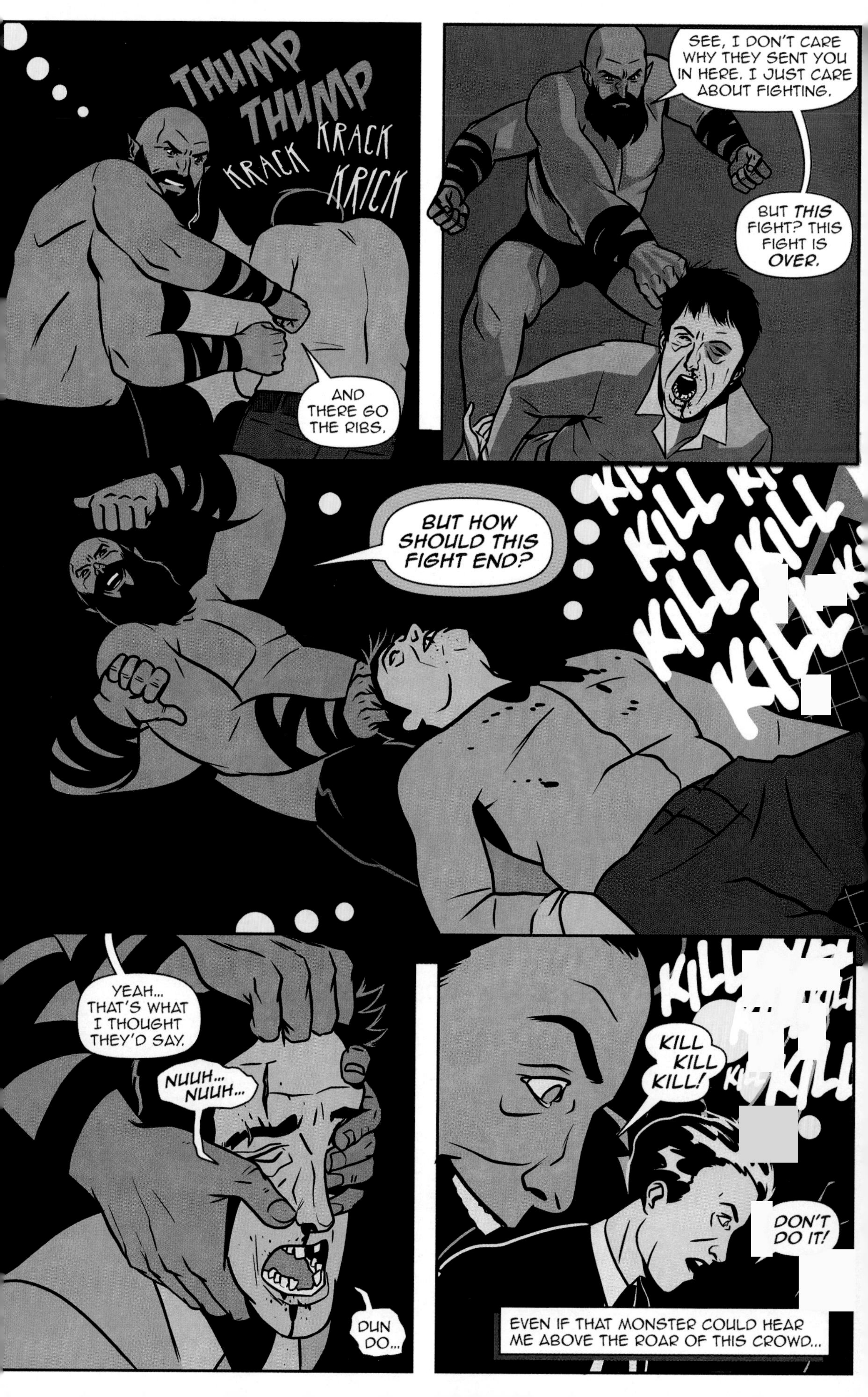
THUMP
THUMP
KRACK
KRACK
KRICK
AND THERE GO THE RIBS.
SEE, I DON'T CARE WHY THEY SENT YOU IN HERE. I JUST CARE ABOUT FIGHTING.
BUT *THIS* FIGHT? THIS FIGHT IS *OVER.*
BUT HOW SHOULD THIS FIGHT END?
KILL KILL
KILL KILL
YEAH... THAT'S WHAT I THOUGHT THEY'D SAY.
NUUH... NUUH...
DUN DO...
KILL
KILL KILL KILL!
DON'T DO IT!
EVEN IF THAT MONSTER COULD HEAR ME ABOVE THE ROAR OF THIS CROWD...

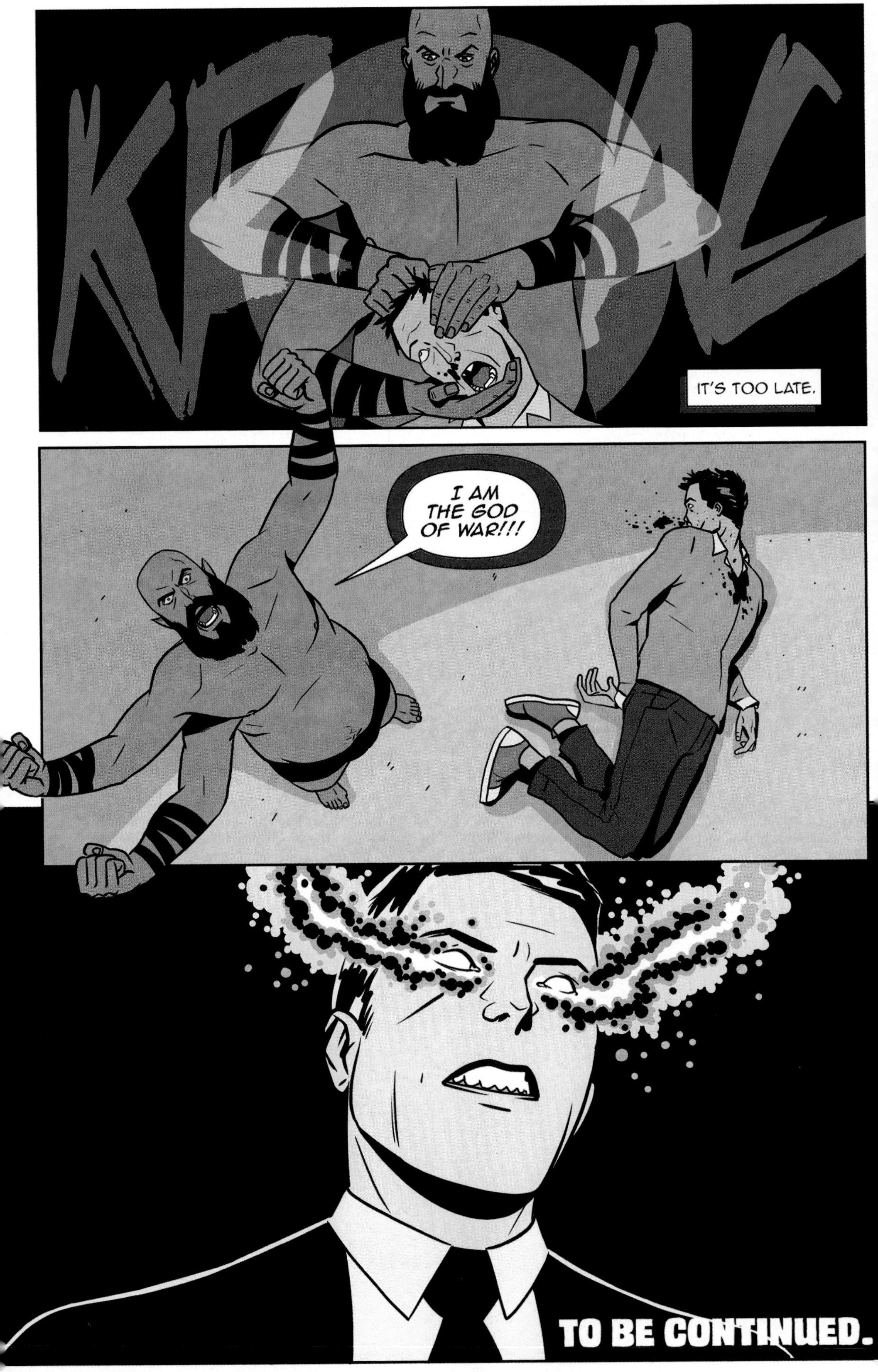
IT'S TOO LATE.
I AM THE GOD OF WAR!!!
TO BE CONTINUED.

EXTRA WORDS

Website: thef1rsthero.com / Twitter: 16Hectares / Instagram: SixteenHectares / Facebook: thef1rsthero
Questions, comments, need some life advice? Contact us directly at sixteenhectares@gmail.com

…elcome back.

…welcome aboard, if you're new. Either way, welcome to the fifth issue of THE FIRST HERO. I am your humble host, Anthony …ttgaizer. As I sit here, tapping away at the virtual keyboard on my iPad Mini in the waning days of May, a lot has changed since …e last time I had to write an editorial page for this book. And a lot is changing again as I am midstream in my writing process for …l.3. But let's not get ahead of ourselves. Let's talk about what happened between Volumes 1 and 2.

…e biggest change, obviously, was Phillip Sevy leaving the series and Danny Zabbal picking up the reins. I am so damn proud of what …il and I did with the first mini-series. Finding Phil made me look like a genius. His art is undeniably fantastic and he turned my …ripts into something beautiful. I will never not love that guy and it's a source of pride for me that I had anything at all to do with …e beginning of what is going to be a tremendous career for Mr. Sevy.

…ter finishing the art for Vol.1, Phil started work on a large-scale project of his own. When the timing of that couldn't jibe with my …ans to get Vol.2 going, he had to bow out. Phil's project, by the way, is called "Second Best" and it will hit stands in 2016. Follow him …Twitter (@phillipsevy) to find out more about the book and get the heads up on when it will be released.

…l's departure left a huge hole in the heart of my batting lineup. I had scripts ready to go and Fred was ready to colour and letter …em (and I should mention what a superstar Fred C Stresing is and how indispensable he has become to my creative efforts) but who …s going to draw the damn books?

…etty quickly in the process of finding a new artist, I got a message from a longtime friend: Danny Zabbal. I've known Danny for …obably 20 years now, when his older brother worked at the Silver Snail, the comic shop in Toronto where I spent my time in a very …orm from Cheers" manner. In the intervening years, Danny had gone on to build a pretty healthy career as a design artist in the …eo game industry. But he still had dreams of becoming a comic book artist and when he saw that I was looking for someone for …l.2, he got in touch with me pretty quickly. And as you've already seen with this issue, I look like a genius once again by virtue of …ving another incredible new artist turning my words into drawings.

…ne to thank some people for helping make THE FIRST HERO: FIGHT FOR YOUR LIFE happen. First and foremost, my creative team, …nny Zabbal and Fred C Stresing. Danny is a tremendous artist who will someday soon be drawing a big time book for a large …mpany. Working with him has been a dream. As I write this, Dan has completed work on the series for almost a month (with the …ception of some nitpicky edits we're making and the covers to issues 3 and 4) so I'm a little sad to not wake up each morning to emails …l of new pages. And Fred? Fred adapted his colouring style to fit Danny's art with such skill and ease. More than anyone working …this series, Fred Stresing deserves an Eisner Award. He's that damn good.

…like to thank the usual suspects at Action Lab: Dave Dwonch, Bryan Seaton, Chad Cicconi, Shawn Gabborin, Kevin Freeman, Jamal …e, Vito Delsante and crew. They've been patient, supportive and wise as we sheppard this series into print and I look forward to …rking with them on many more volumes of THE FIRST HERO… and maybe a few other projects, he said coyly.

…also like to thank a handful of people who have been massively supportive to me on a personal and creative level: Raymond Rowe …r allowing me to base our three-armed killing machine Odinson on him), Phillip Sevy, Tim McCarthy, Kris Erickson, Jason Clark and …An Elegant Weapon podcast, Julian Micevski, Chuck Suffel, Steve Buckley and the GTA Comic Con staff, Tiziano De Santis and the …ff of Fan Expo Canada, Jerry Gaylord (this issue's variant cover artist), George Zotti and the staff of the Silver Snail Comic Shop …Toronto and Matt Polinsky.

…ally, I would like to acknowledge and say a very heartfelt thank you to the family, friends and fans who pledged money to the …ckstarter campaign that helped make this book possible.

…chael Kingston	Haneiro Perez	Sandy Lu	Paul Mansfield	Paul Pintner	Duncan M'gregor	
…ly Hunt	Mario Jamal	Dave Handley	Embreate	Kevin Brown	Martin Anderson-Clutz	
…n Chisholm	Kelly	Derek Simpson	Justin Renard	Dev Mohabir	Ryan Clark	
…rre Zabbal	Paul Lazenby	Marcus Dodd	Krissy Myers	Suzanne & Kevin	Melwyn "Bud" Walwyn	
…din Turgay	Jason Clark	Graig Kent	Brian Isidro	Ryan Davey	Daniel D Hastings	
…e Portoghese	David Clark	Ty Hudson	Chad Cicconi	Youri Zabbal	Joel Jackson	
…ke Jacobs	Marco Carating	Charles Palmer	Kevin Freeman	Andrew Lima	Christopher Batori	
…drew Lorenz	Conall	Ryan Nedeff	Richard N.	Andrew Church	Barbara Sarpong	
…n Fleischer	Luis Silva	Matthew Terry	SC	Nick Kingsland	Jean-Francois Lurette	
…ctor C	Kat Kan	Ed Garrett	Greg Oliver	Dany	Cedric Neil Milton	
…am Farr	Jamal Igle	Phillip Gauthier	Katie Halliday	Geoff Connor	Murtis McKellar	
…l MacGregor	Melanie Somers	Marc Hauss	Roger Pettet	Valerie Renee	Dandy Lion Creations	
…n Claude Z	James P. Senft	Rebekah Church	Michael Kudrac	Bruce Peck	Michael MacGowan Smith	
…aig Henshaw	David Rynax	Michael Bedard	Jim Gardner	Brian Morton	Colin Douglas Brackenridge	

Thank you,
Anthony Ruttgaizer
Toronto, 26 May 2015

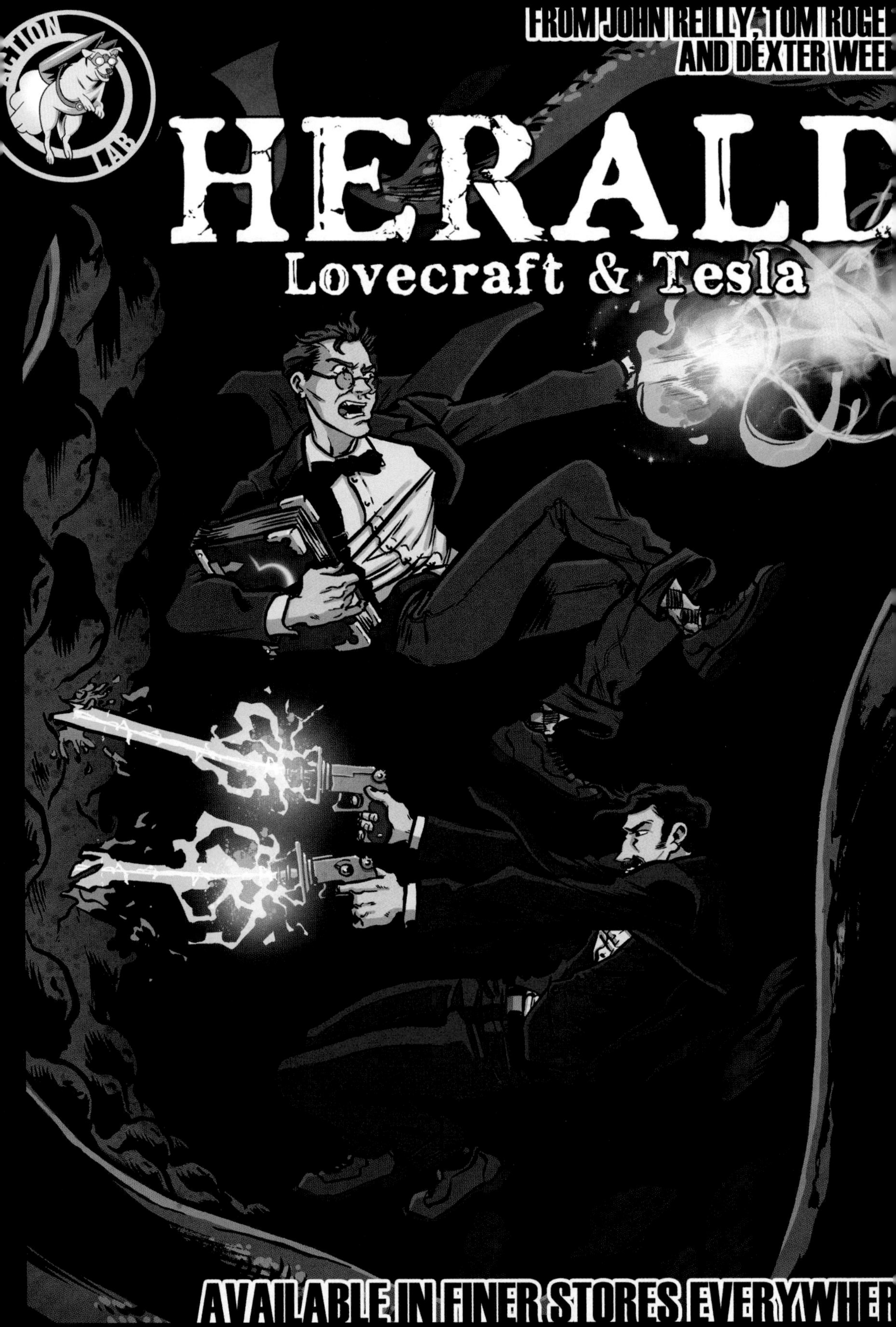
FROM JOHN REILLY, TOM ROGE
AND DEXTER WEE
HERALD
Lovecraft & Tesla
AVAILABLE IN FINER STORES EVERYWHER

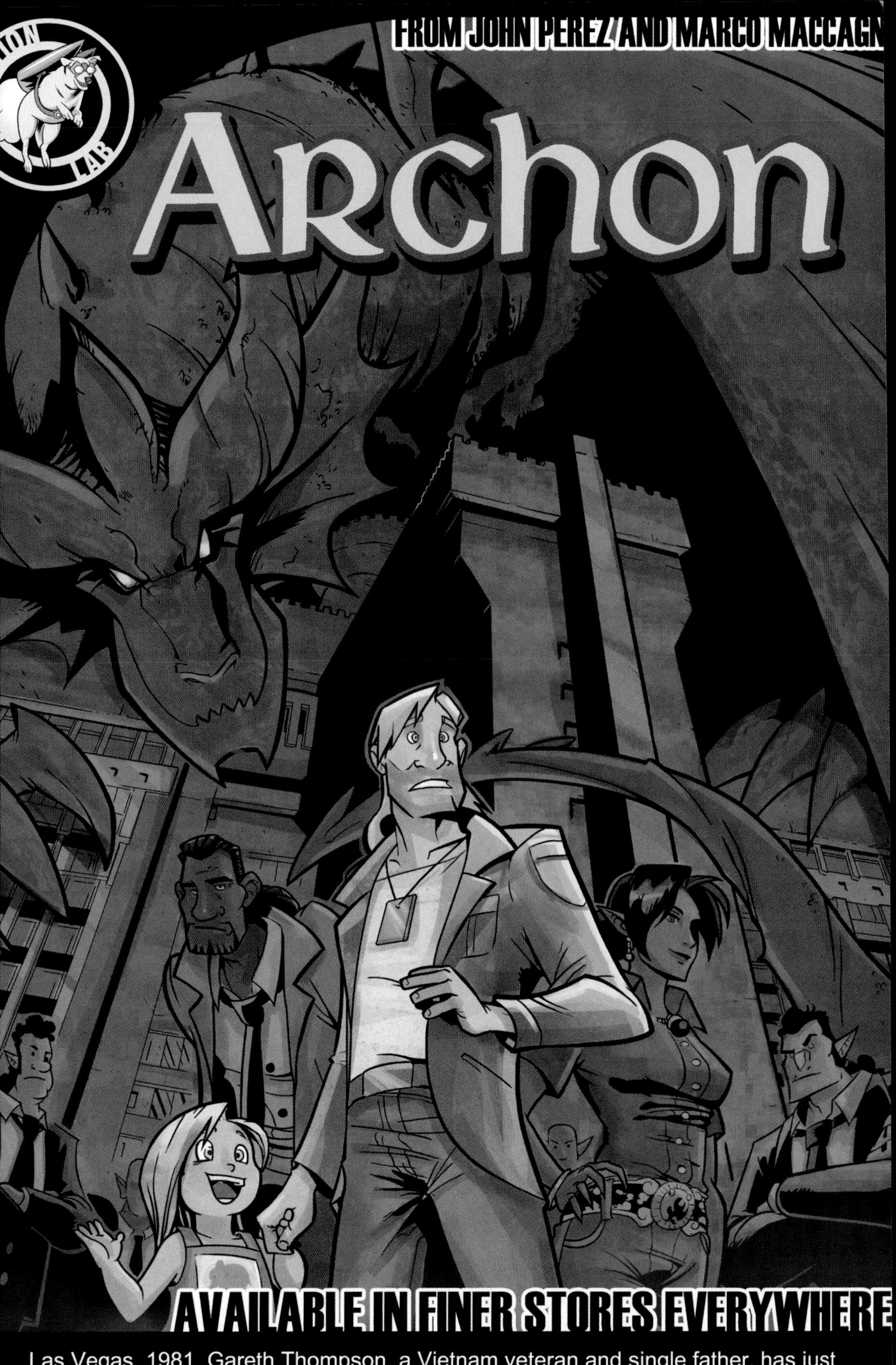

FROM JOHN PEREZ AND MARCO MACCAGN[I]

Archon

AVAILABLE IN FINER STORES EVERYWHERE

Las Vegas, 1981. Gareth Thompson, a Vietnam veteran and single father, has just accepted a security job at the new fantasy-themed "Archon Hotel and Casino." However, he'll soon discover all the Orcs, Elves and Dragons at the Resort are not people in costumes, but actual creatures of myth and legend.

ACTION LAB

READ MORE NOW

F1rst Hero - Action Lab
www.actionlabcomics.com
00511
7 00465 77238 1

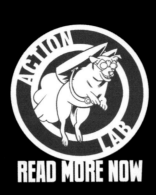

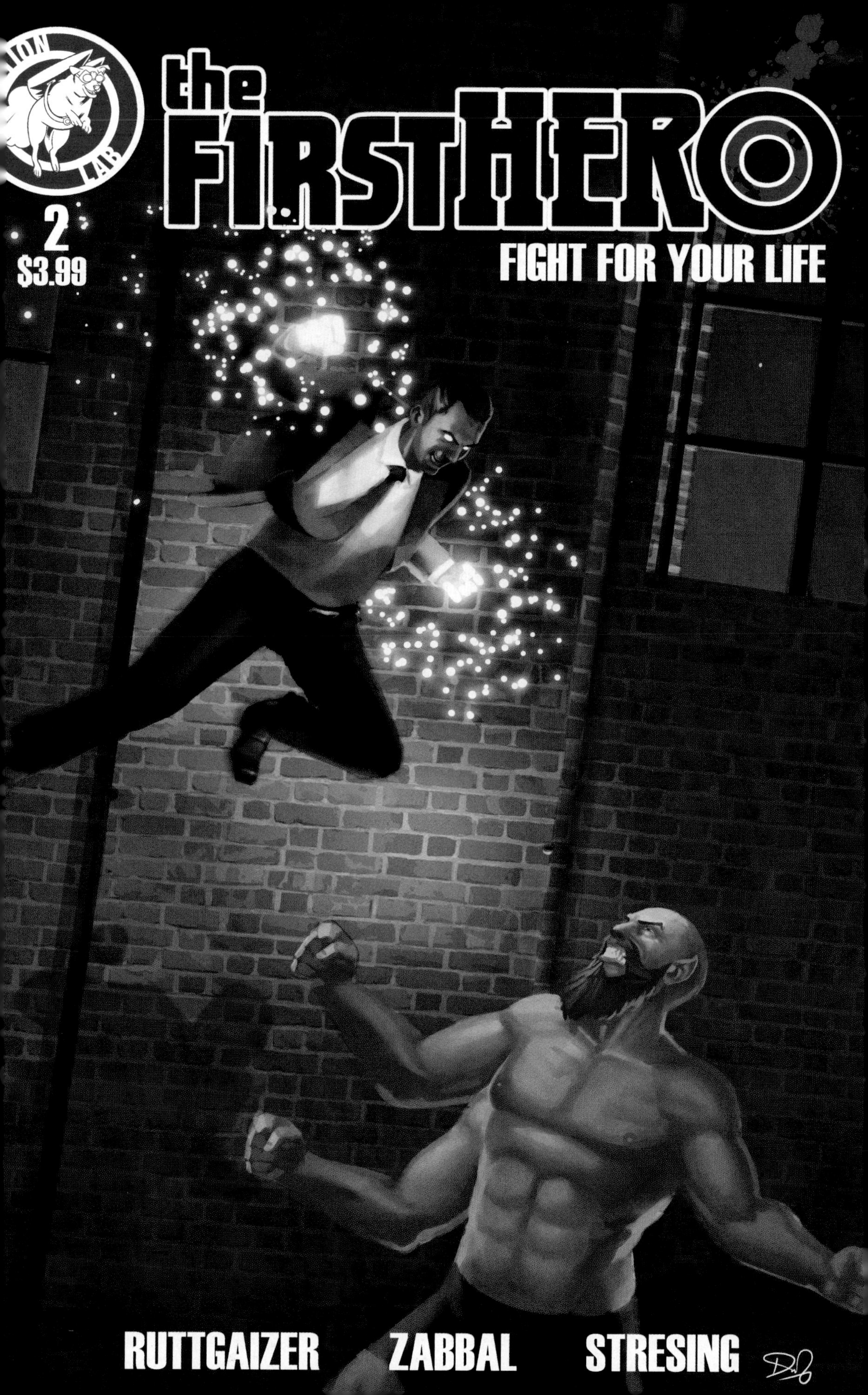
ACTION LAB
the FIRST HERO
2
$3.99
FIGHT FOR YOUR LIFE
RUTTGAIZER
ZABBAL
STRESING

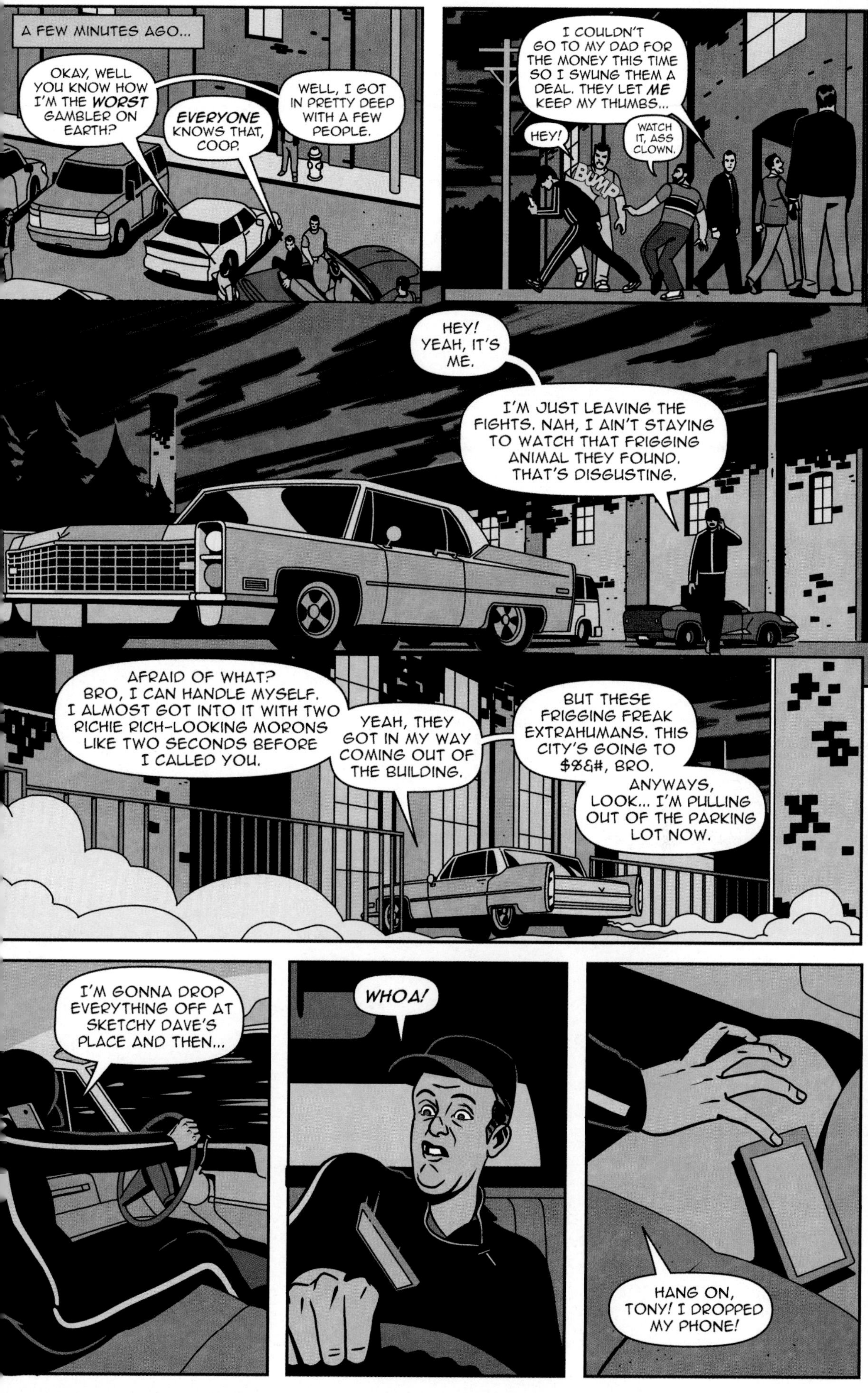
A FEW MINUTES AGO...
OKAY, WELL YOU KNOW HOW I'M THE WORST GAMBLER ON EARTH?
EVERYONE KNOWS THAT, COOP.
WELL, I GOT IN PRETTY DEEP WITH A FEW PEOPLE.
I COULDN'T GO TO MY DAD FOR THE MONEY THIS TIME SO I SWUNG THEM A DEAL. THEY LET ME KEEP MY THUMBS...
HEY!
BUMP
WATCH IT, ASS CLOWN.
HEY! YEAH, IT'S ME.
I'M JUST LEAVING THE FIGHTS. NAH, I AIN'T STAYING TO WATCH THAT FRIGGING ANIMAL THEY FOUND. THAT'S DISGUSTING.
AFRAID OF WHAT? BRO, I CAN HANDLE MYSELF. I ALMOST GOT INTO IT WITH TWO RICHIE RICH-LOOKING MORONS LIKE TWO SECONDS BEFORE I CALLED YOU.
YEAH, THEY GOT IN MY WAY COMING OUT OF THE BUILDING.
BUT THESE FRIGGING FREAK EXTRAHUMANS. THIS CITY'S GOING TO $%&#, BRO.
ANYWAYS, LOOK... I'M PULLING OUT OF THE PARKING LOT NOW.
I'M GONNA DROP EVERYTHING OFF AT SKETCHY DAVE'S PLACE AND THEN...
WHOA!
HANG ON, TONY! I DROPPED MY PHONE!

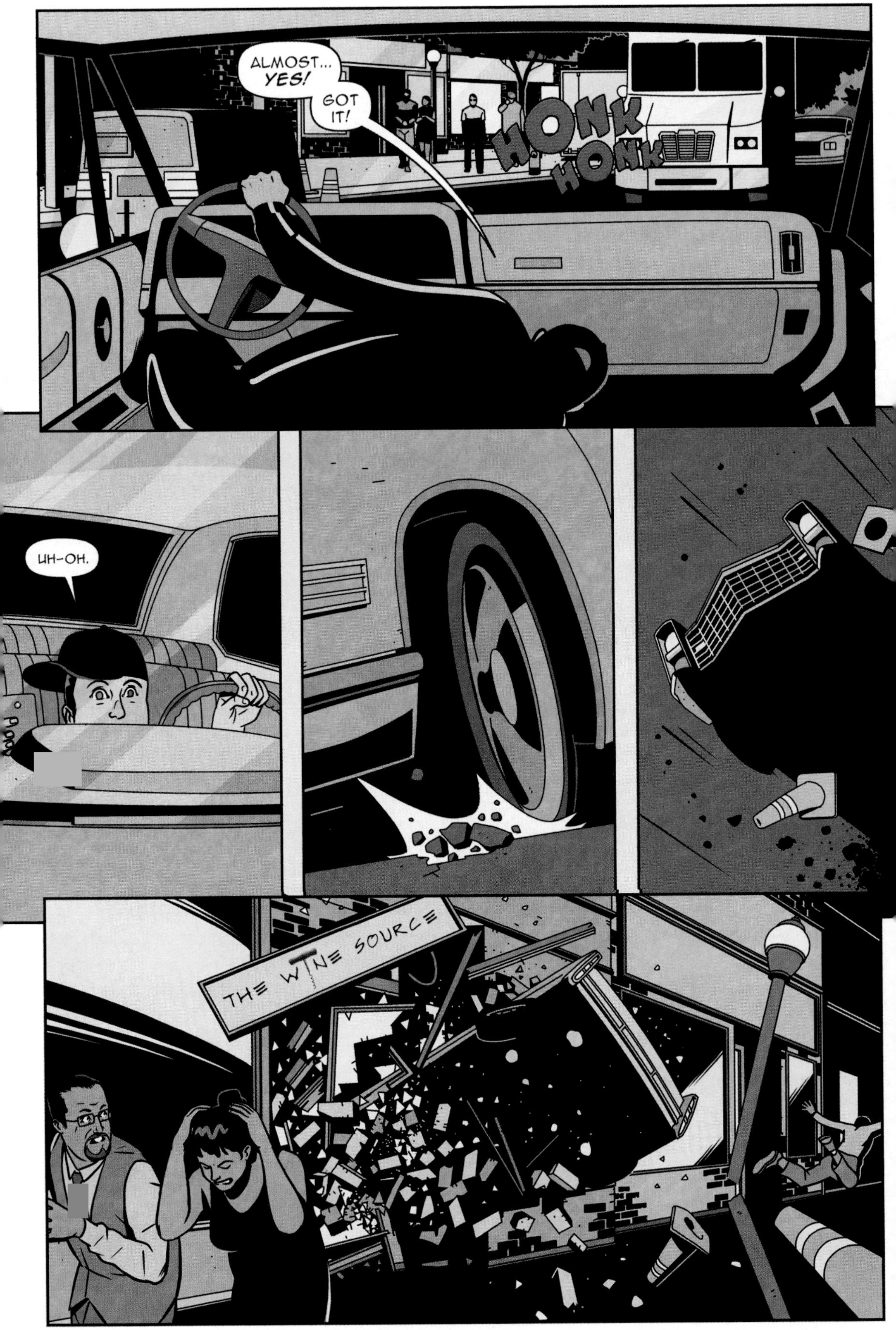
ALMOST... YES!
GOT IT!
HONK
HONK
UH-OH.
THE WINE SOURCE

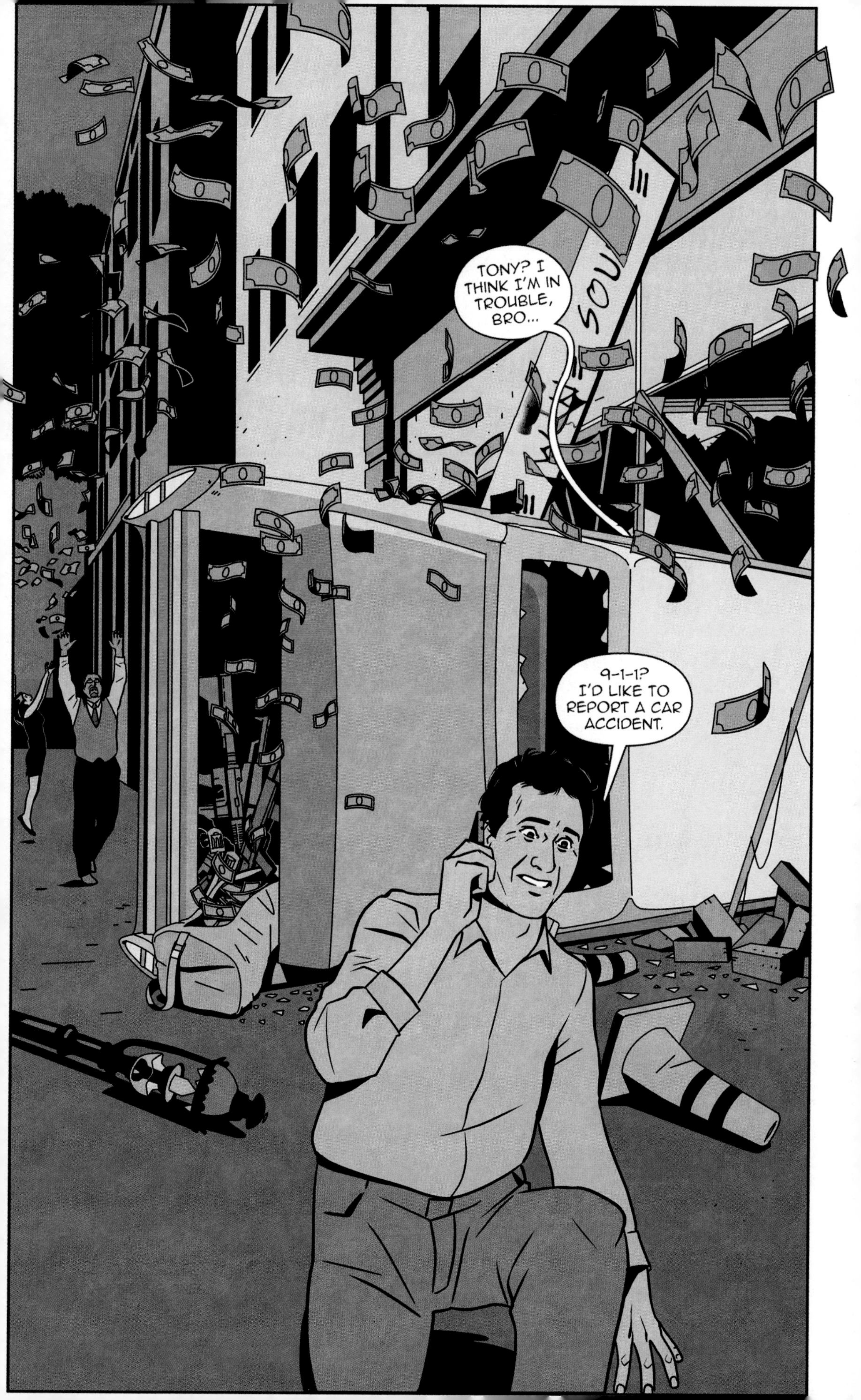
TONY? I THINK I'M IN TROUBLE, BRO...
9-1-1? I'D LIKE TO REPORT A CAR ACCIDENT.
SOU

ACTION LAB ENTERTAINMENT PROUDLY PRESENTS

the FIRST HERO

VOLUME 2: FIGHT FOR YOUR LIFE

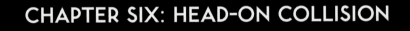

CHAPTER SIX: HEAD-ON COLLISION

for SIXTEEN HECTARES AND A MOOSE, INK.

Created/Written by ANTHONY RUTTGAIZER
Cover/Interior Art by DANNY ZABBAL
Letters/Colors by FRED C. STRESING
Variant Cover by ANTHONY RUTTGAIZER

For More Info. visit SixteenHectares.com

for ACTION LAB ENTERTAINMENT

BRYAN SEATON Publisher
KEVIN FREEMAN President
SHAWN GABBORIN Editor-in-Chief
DAVE DWONCH Creative Driector
JIM DIETZ Social Media Director
JAMAL IGLE Director of Marketing
VITO DELSANTE Director of Marketing
COLLEEN BOYD Associate Editor
CHAD CICCONI Three-Armed Psychopath

Read Now at ActionLabComics.com

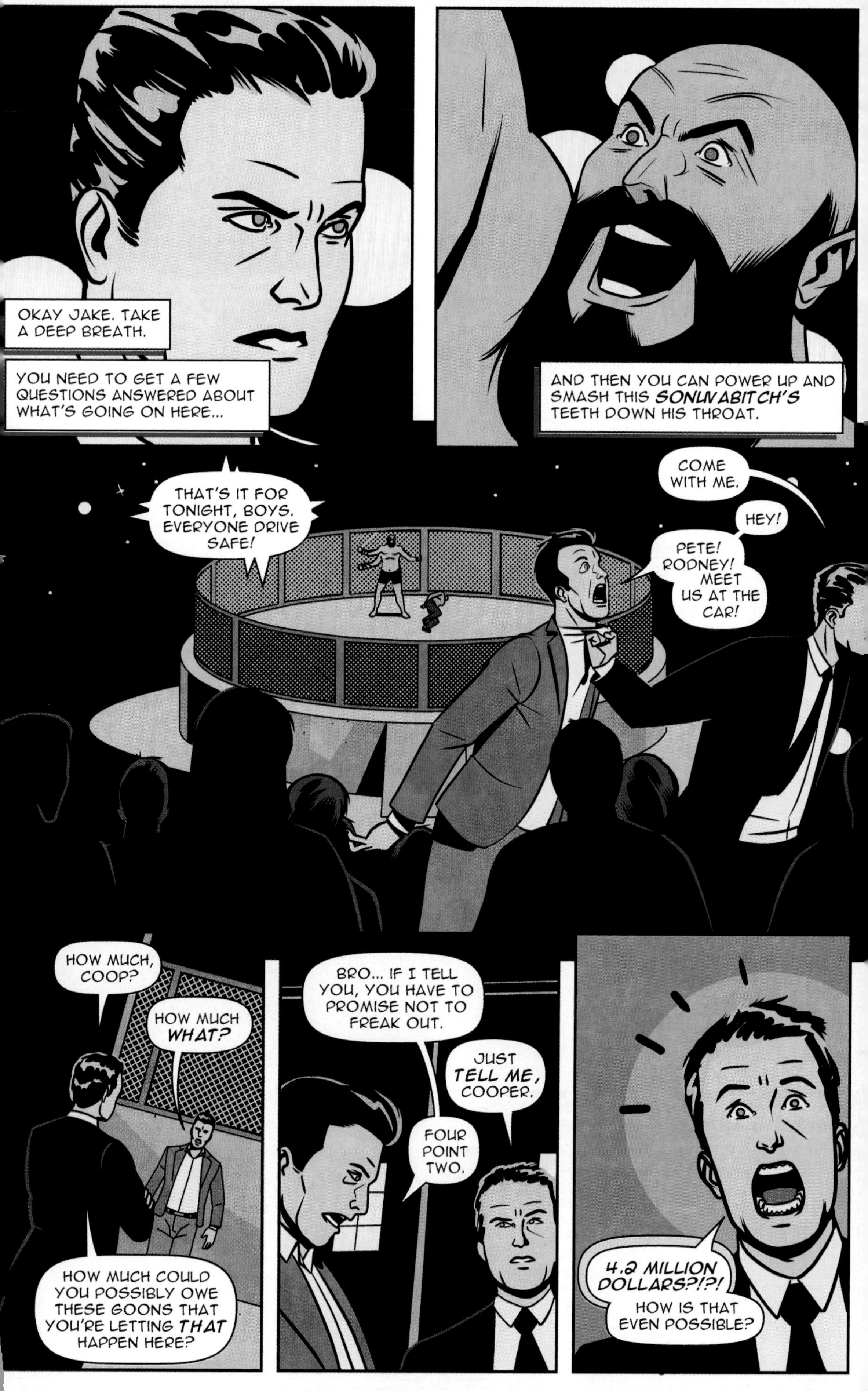
OKAY JAKE. TAKE A DEEP BREATH.
YOU NEED TO GET A FEW QUESTIONS ANSWERED ABOUT WHAT'S GOING ON HERE...
AND THEN YOU CAN POWER UP AND SMASH THIS *SONUVABITCH'S* TEETH DOWN HIS THROAT.
THAT'S IT FOR TONIGHT, BOYS. EVERYONE DRIVE SAFE!
COME WITH ME.
HEY!
PETE! RODNEY! MEET US AT THE CAR!
HOW MUCH, COOP?
HOW MUCH *WHAT?*
HOW MUCH COULD YOU POSSIBLY OWE THESE GOONS THAT YOU'RE LETTING *THAT* HAPPEN HERE?
BRO... IF I TELL YOU, YOU HAVE TO PROMISE NOT TO FREAK OUT.
JUST *TELL ME,* COOPER.
FOUR POINT TWO.
4.2 MILLION DOLLARS?!?!
HOW IS THAT EVEN POSSIBLE?

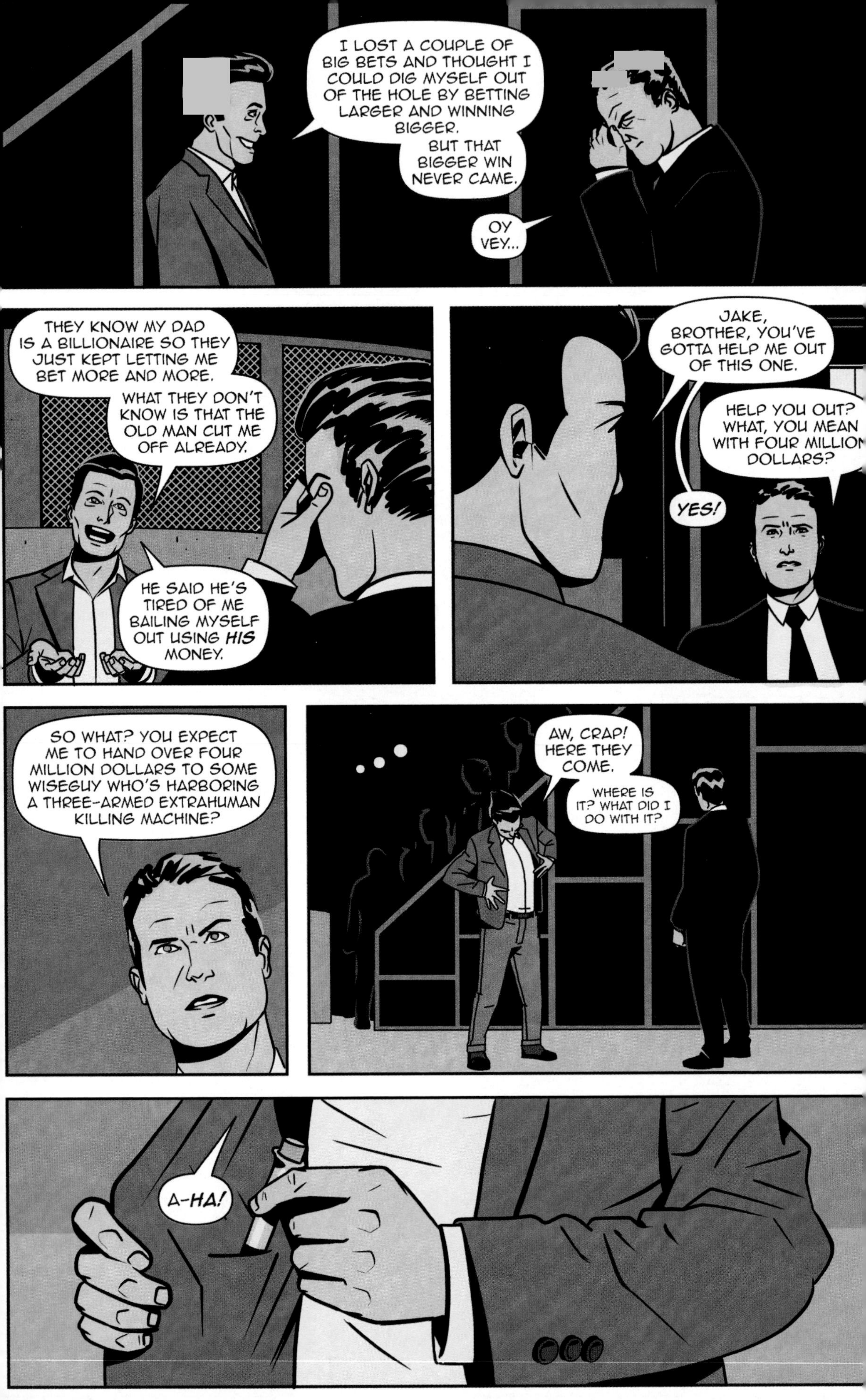
I LOST A COUPLE OF BIG BETS AND THOUGHT I COULD DIG MYSELF OUT OF THE HOLE BY BETTING LARGER AND WINNING BIGGER.
BUT THAT BIGGER WIN NEVER CAME.
OY VEY...
THEY KNOW MY DAD IS A BILLIONAIRE SO THEY JUST KEPT LETTING ME BET MORE AND MORE.
WHAT THEY DON'T KNOW IS THAT THE OLD MAN CUT ME OFF ALREADY.
HE SAID HE'S TIRED OF ME BAILING MYSELF OUT USING *HIS* MONEY.
JAKE, BROTHER, YOU'VE GOTTA HELP ME OUT OF THIS ONE.
HELP YOU OUT? WHAT, YOU MEAN WITH FOUR MILLION DOLLARS?
YES!
SO WHAT? YOU EXPECT ME TO HAND OVER FOUR MILLION DOLLARS TO SOME WISEGUY WHO'S HARBORING A THREE-ARMED EXTRAHUMAN KILLING MACHINE?
AW, CRAP! HERE THEY COME.
WHERE IS IT? WHAT DID I DO WITH IT?
A-*HA!*

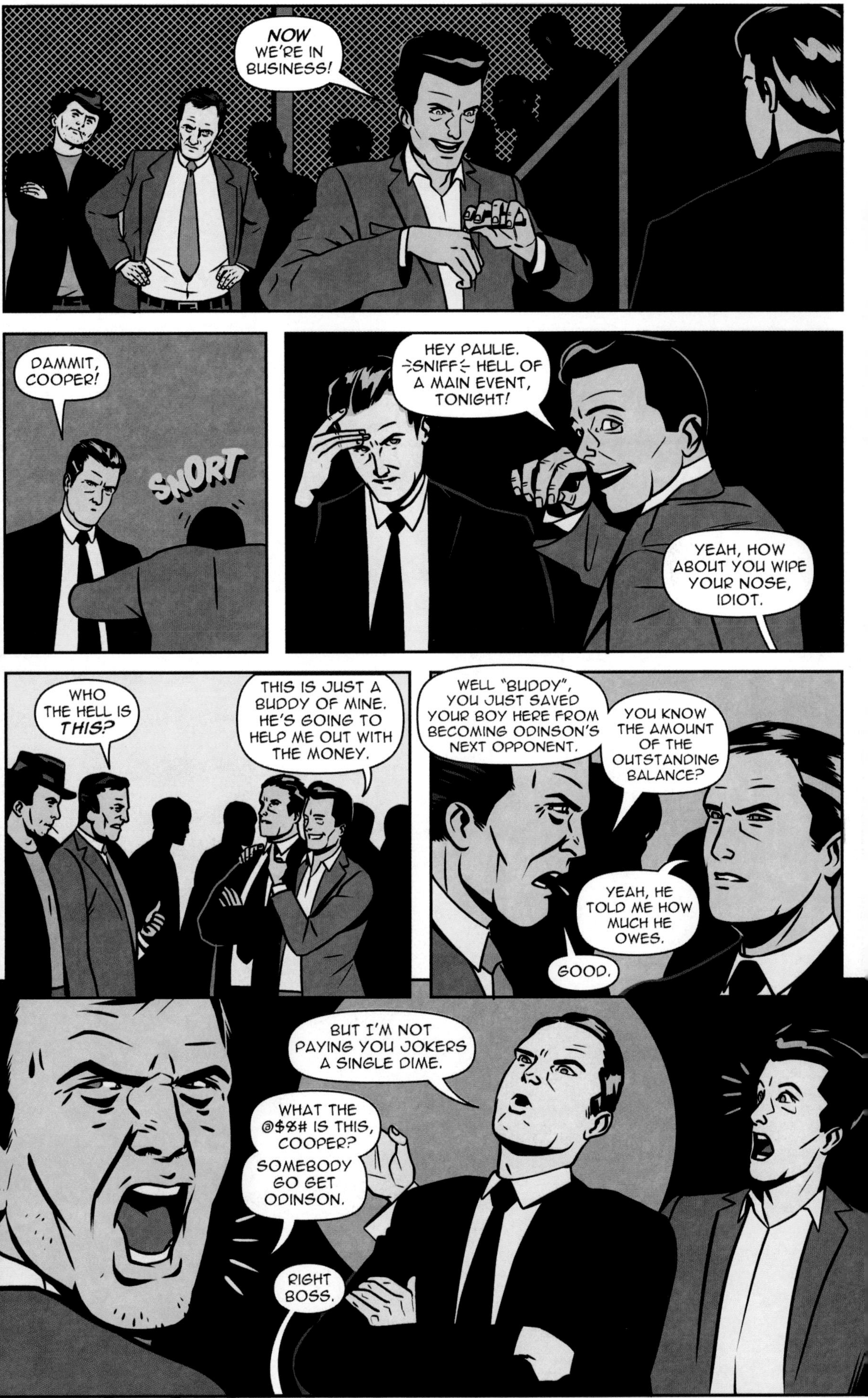
NOW WE'RE IN BUSINESS!
DAMMIT, COOPER!
SNORT
HEY PAULIE. -SNIFF- HELL OF A MAIN EVENT, TONIGHT!
YEAH, HOW ABOUT YOU WIPE YOUR NOSE, IDIOT.
WHO THE HELL IS THIS?
THIS IS JUST A BUDDY OF MINE. HE'S GOING TO HELP ME OUT WITH THE MONEY.
WELL "BUDDY", YOU JUST SAVED YOUR BOY HERE FROM BECOMING ODINSON'S NEXT OPPONENT.
YOU KNOW THE AMOUNT OF THE OUTSTANDING BALANCE?
YEAH, HE TOLD ME HOW MUCH HE OWES.
GOOD.
BUT I'M NOT PAYING YOU JOKERS A SINGLE DIME.
WHAT THE @$%# IS THIS, COOPER?
SOMEBODY GO GET ODINSON.
RIGHT BOSS.

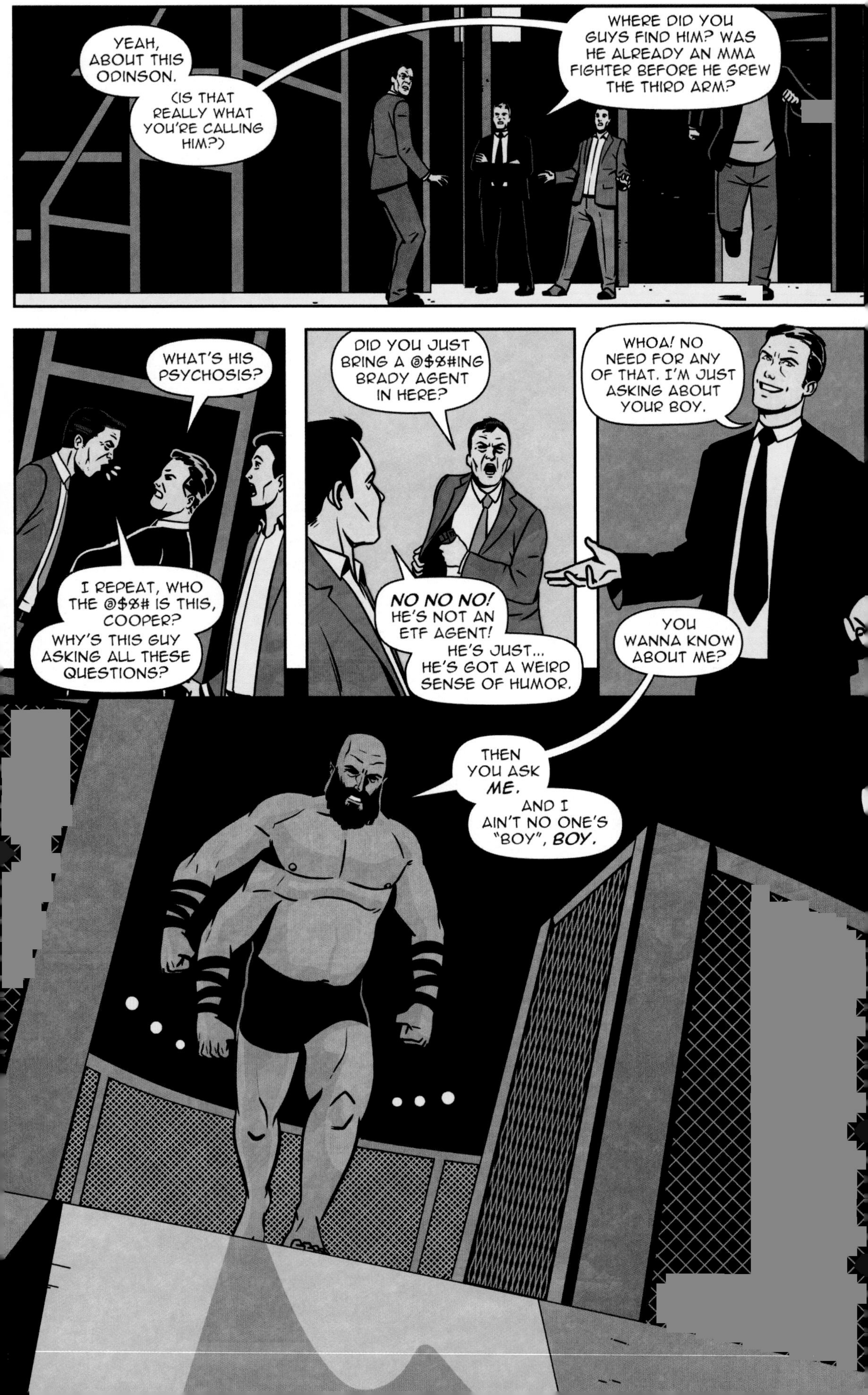
YEAH, ABOUT THIS ODINSON.
(IS THAT REALLY WHAT YOU'RE CALLING HIM?)
WHERE DID YOU GUYS FIND HIM? WAS HE ALREADY AN MMA FIGHTER BEFORE HE GREW THE THIRD ARM?
WHAT'S HIS PSYCHOSIS?
I REPEAT, WHO THE @$%# IS THIS, COOPER?
WHY'S THIS GUY ASKING ALL THESE QUESTIONS?
DID YOU JUST BRING A @$%#ING BRADY AGENT IN HERE?
NO NO NO! HE'S NOT AN ETF AGENT!
HE'S JUST... HE'S GOT A WEIRD SENSE OF HUMOR.
WHOA! NO NEED FOR ANY OF THAT. I'M JUST ASKING ABOUT YOUR BOY.
YOU WANNA KNOW ABOUT ME?
THEN YOU ASK ME.
AND I AIN'T NO ONE'S "BOY", BOY.

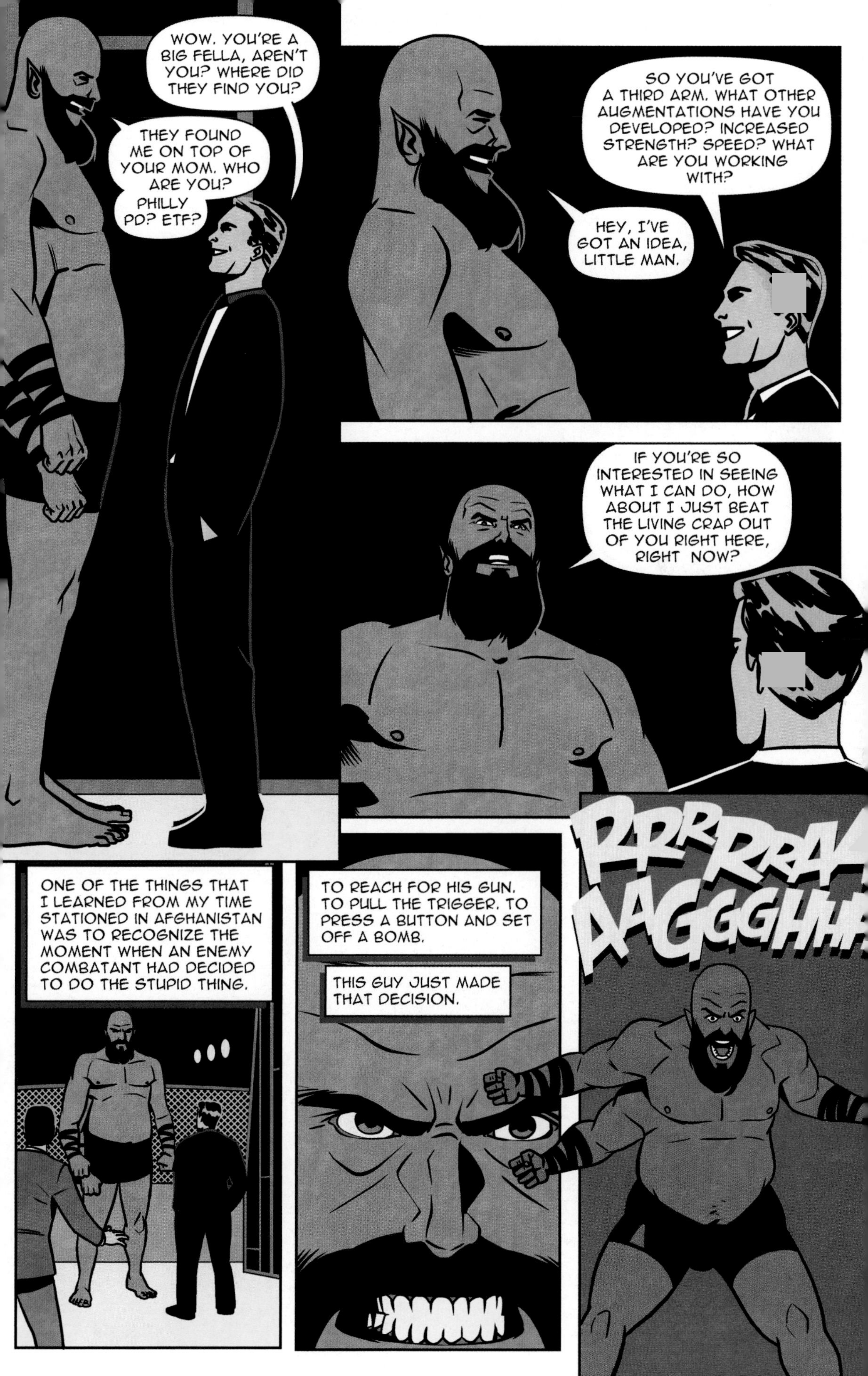
WOW. YOU'RE A BIG FELLA, AREN'T YOU? WHERE DID THEY FIND YOU?
THEY FOUND ME ON TOP OF YOUR MOM. WHO ARE YOU?
PHILLY PD? ETF?
SO YOU'VE GOT A THIRD ARM. WHAT OTHER AUGMENTATIONS HAVE YOU DEVELOPED? INCREASED STRENGTH? SPEED? WHAT ARE YOU WORKING WITH?
HEY, I'VE GOT AN IDEA, LITTLE MAN.
IF YOU'RE SO INTERESTED IN SEEING WHAT I CAN DO, HOW ABOUT I JUST BEAT THE LIVING CRAP OUT OF YOU RIGHT HERE, RIGHT NOW?
ONE OF THE THINGS THAT I LEARNED FROM MY TIME STATIONED IN AFGHANISTAN WAS TO RECOGNIZE THE MOMENT WHEN AN ENEMY COMBATANT HAD DECIDED TO DO THE STUPID THING.
TO REACH FOR HIS GUN. TO PULL THE TRIGGER. TO PRESS A BUTTON AND SET OFF A BOMB.
THIS GUY JUST MADE THAT DECISION.
RRRRRA
AAGGGHH

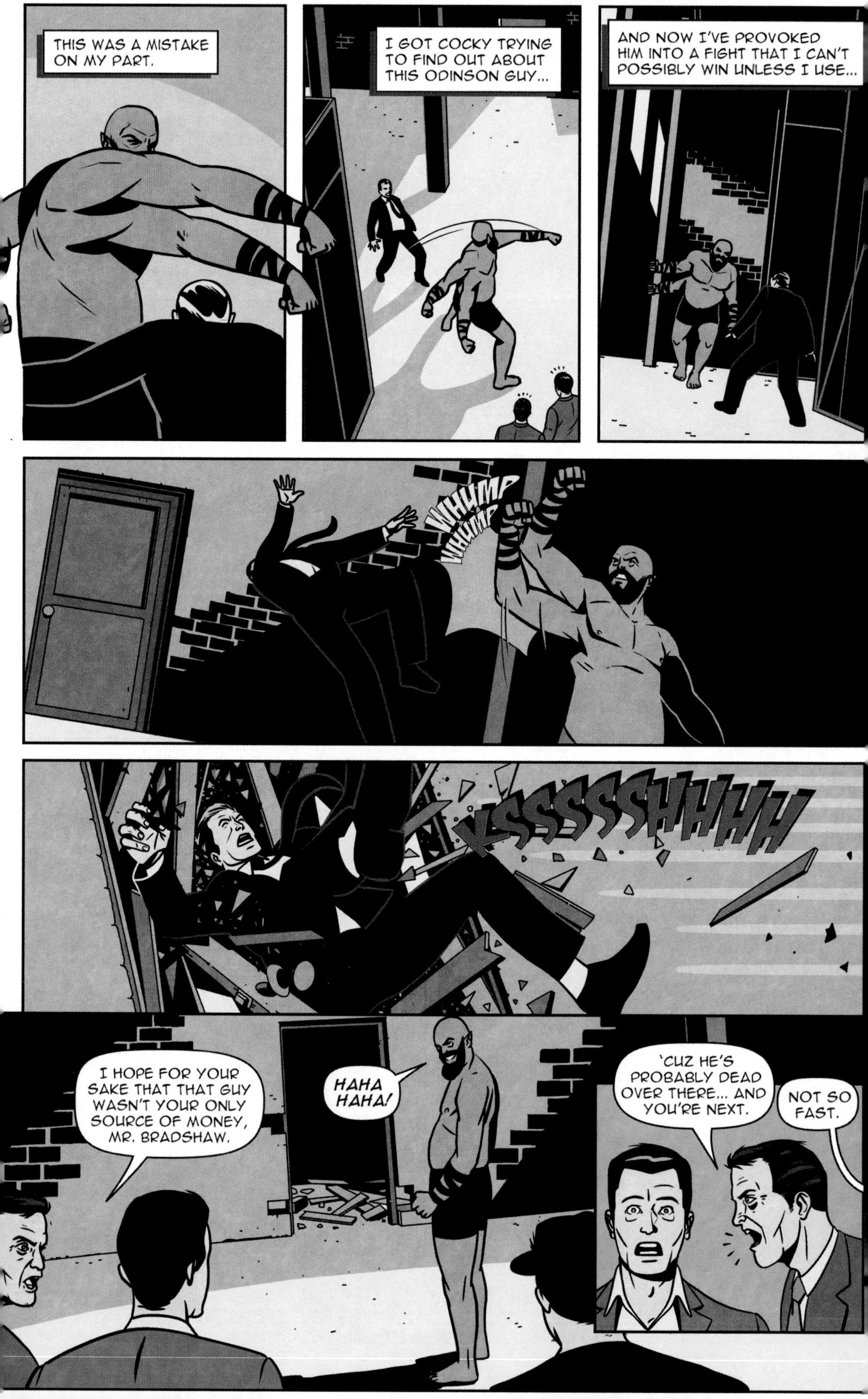
THIS WAS A MISTAKE ON MY PART.
I GOT COCKY TRYING TO FIND OUT ABOUT THIS ODINSON GUY...
AND NOW I'VE PROVOKED HIM INTO A FIGHT THAT I CAN'T POSSIBLY WIN UNLESS I USE...
WHUMP
WHUMP
KSSSSSHHHHH
I HOPE FOR YOUR SAKE THAT THAT GUY WASN'T YOUR ONLY SOURCE OF MONEY, MR. BRADSHAW.
HAHA HAHA!
'CUZ HE'S PROBABLY DEAD OVER THERE... AND YOU'RE NEXT.
NOT SO FAST.

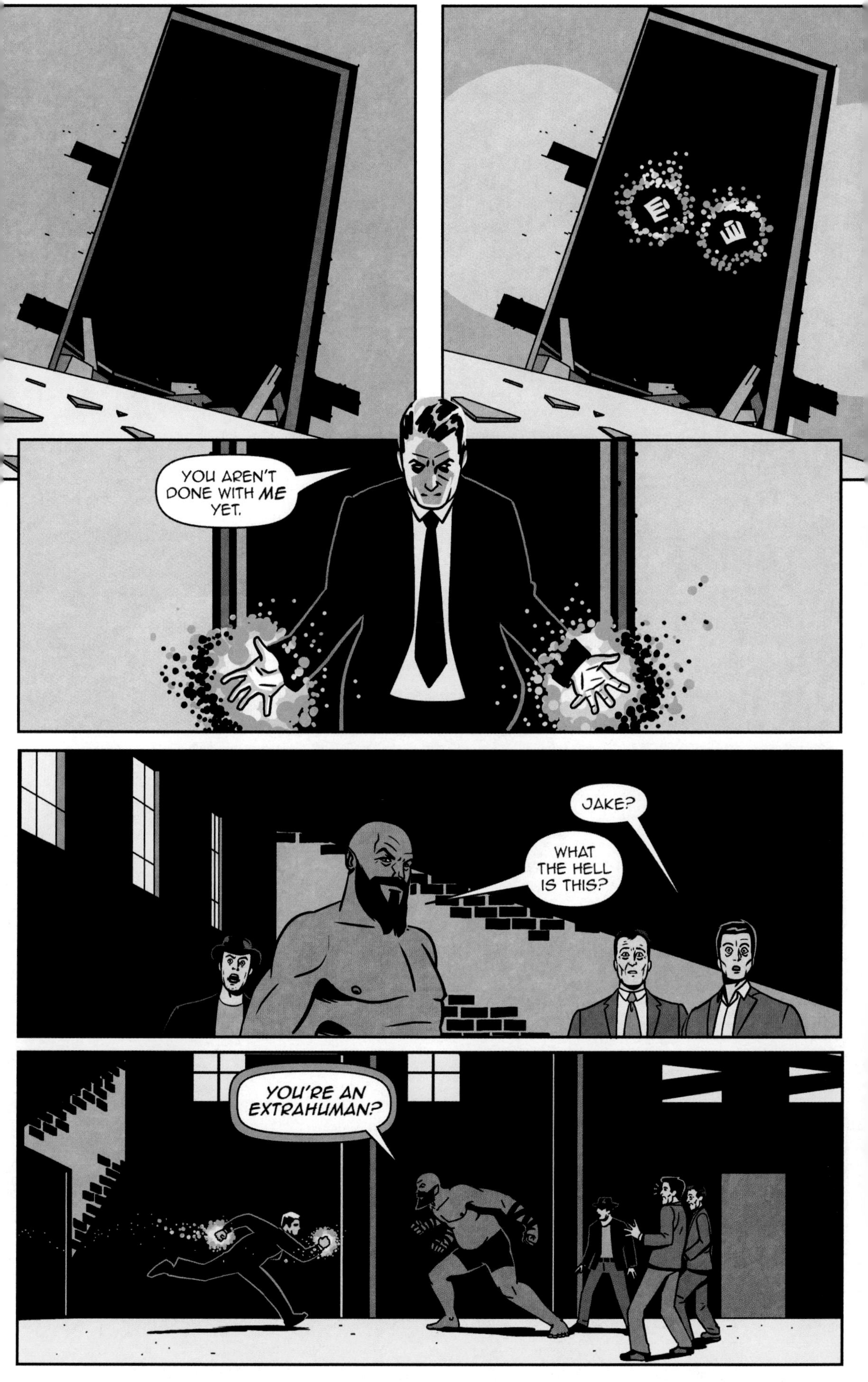
YOU AREN'T DONE WITH *ME* YET.
JAKE?
WHAT THE HELL IS THIS?
YOU'RE AN EXTRAHUMAN?

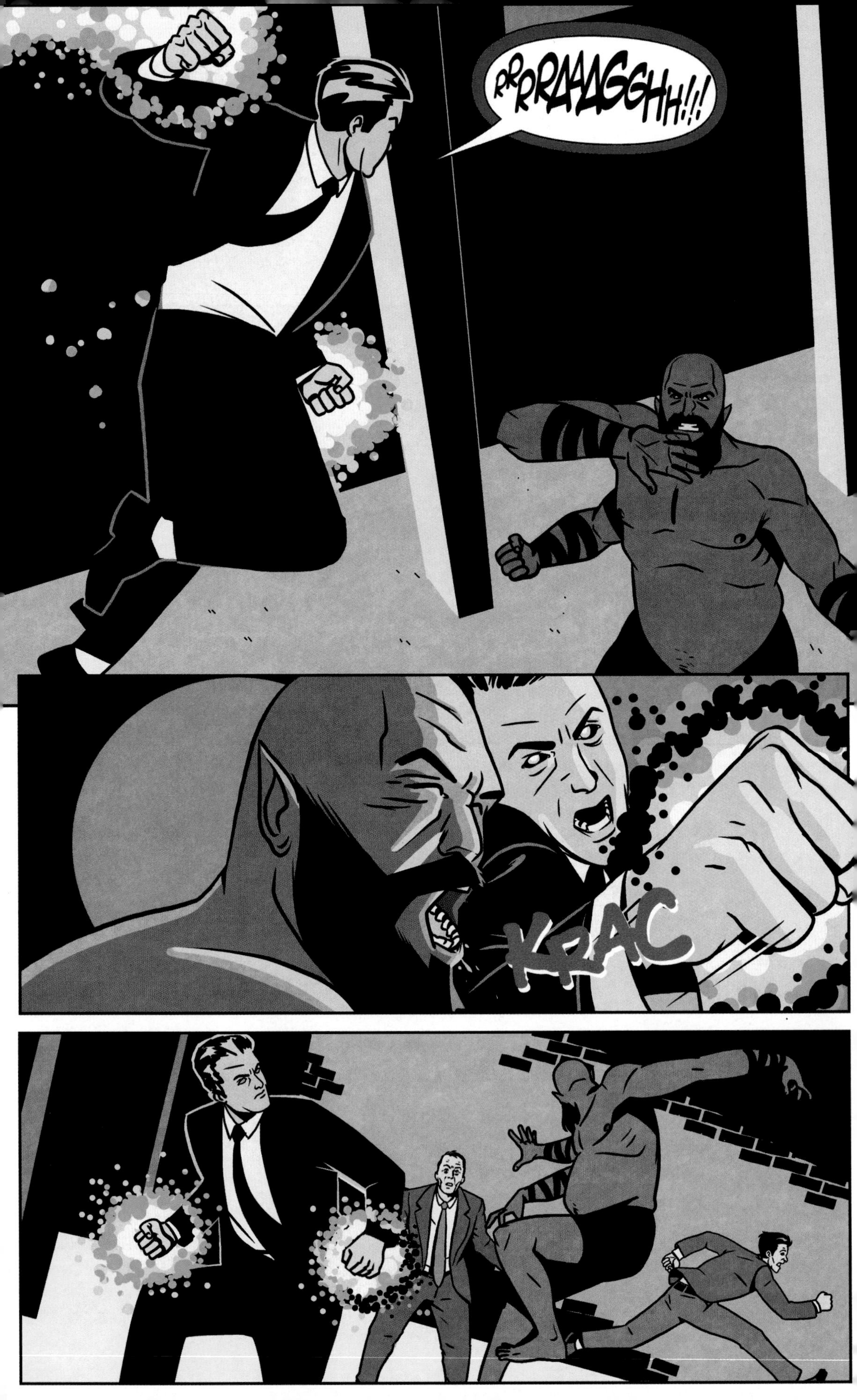
RRRRAAAGGHH!!!
KRAC

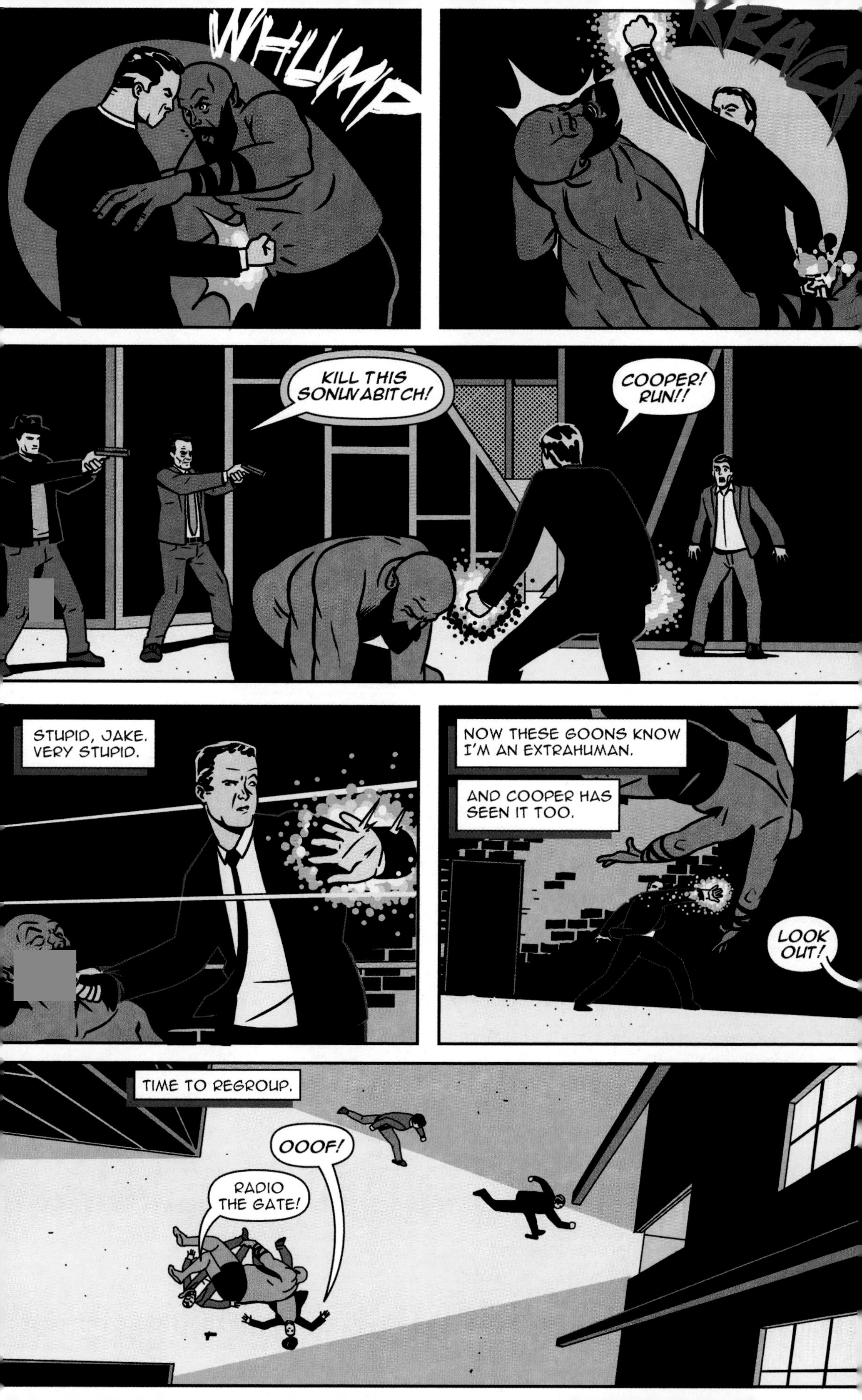
WHUMP
KRACK
KILL THIS SONUVABITCH!
COOPER! RUN!!
STUPID, JAKE. VERY STUPID.
NOW THESE GOONS KNOW I'M AN EXTRAHUMAN.
AND COOPER HAS SEEN IT TOO.
LOOK OUT!
TIME TO REGROUP.
OOOF!
RADIO THE GATE!

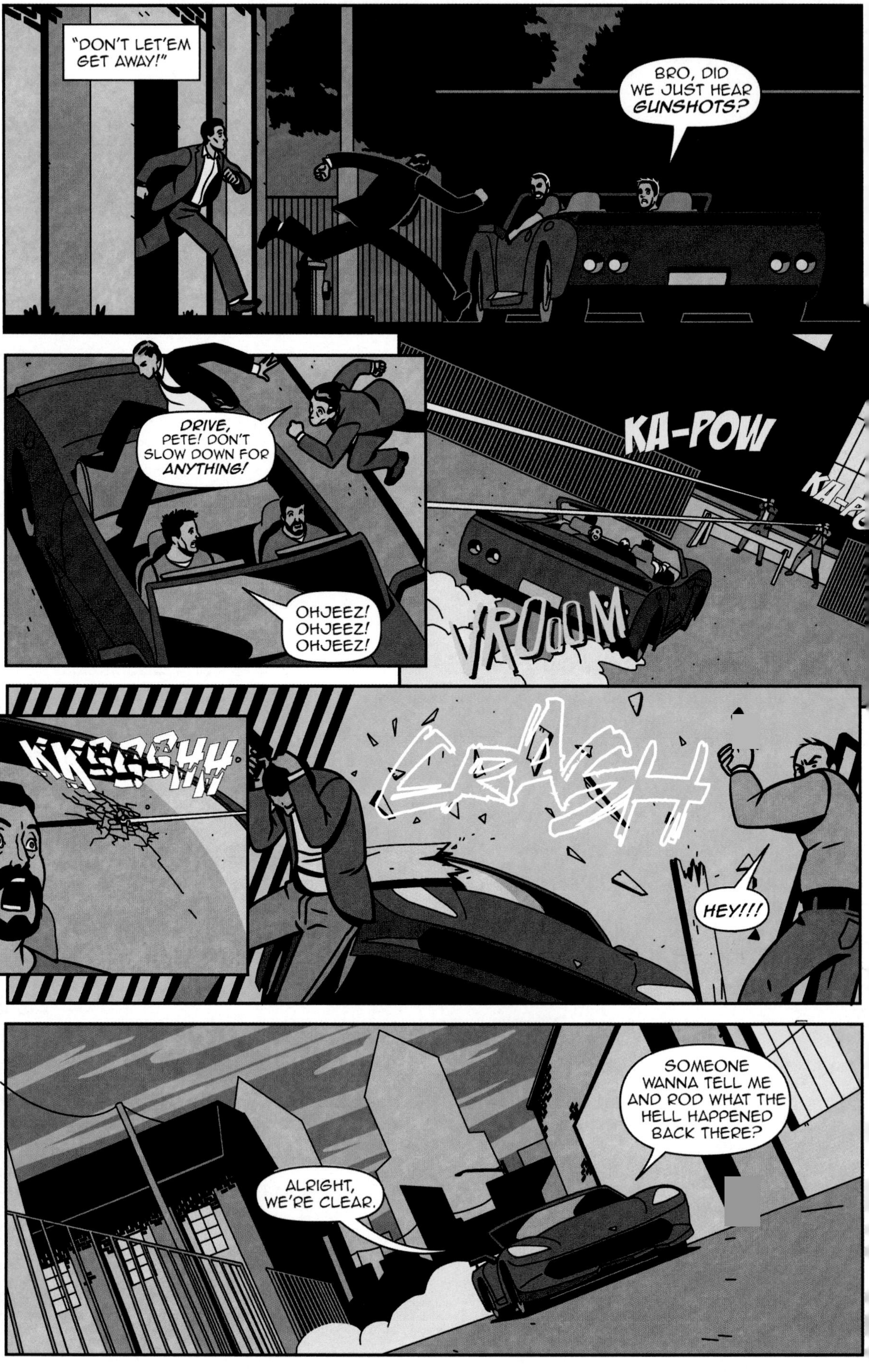

"DON'T LET'EM GET AWAY!"
BRO, DID WE JUST HEAR GUNSHOTS?
DRIVE, PETE! DON'T SLOW DOWN FOR ANYTHING!
OHJEEZ! OHJEEZ! OHJEEZ!
KA-POW
VROOOM
CRASH
HEY!!!
SOMEONE WANNA TELL ME AND ROD WHAT THE HELL HAPPENED BACK THERE?
ALRIGHT, WE'RE CLEAR.

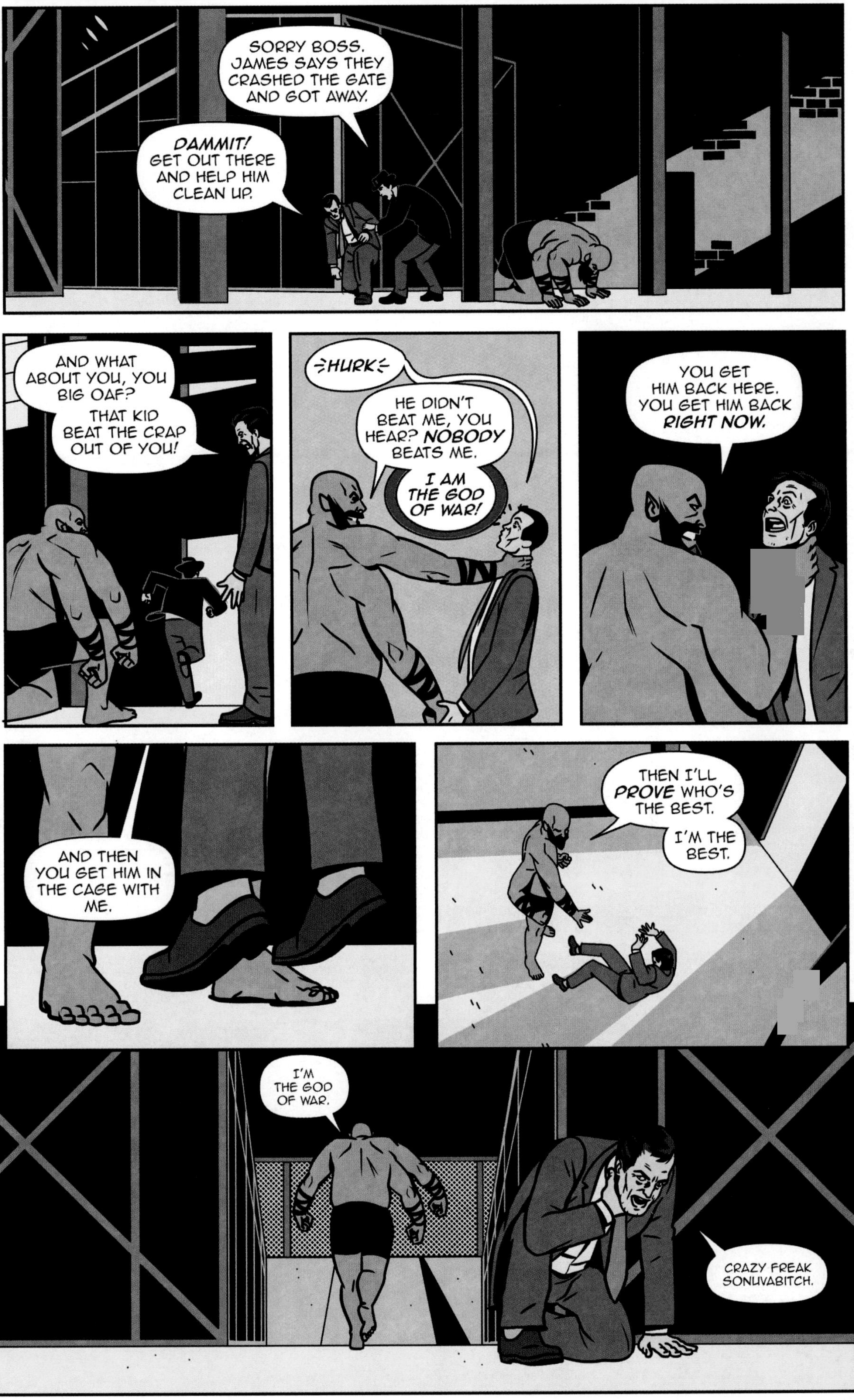
SORRY BOSS. JAMES SAYS THEY CRASHED THE GATE AND GOT AWAY.
DAMMIT! GET OUT THERE AND HELP HIM CLEAN UP.
AND WHAT ABOUT YOU, YOU BIG OAF?
THAT KID BEAT THE CRAP OUT OF YOU!
HURK
HE DIDN'T BEAT ME, YOU HEAR? NOBODY BEATS ME.
I AM THE GOD OF WAR!
YOU GET HIM BACK HERE. YOU GET HIM BACK RIGHT NOW.
AND THEN YOU GET HIM IN THE CAGE WITH ME.
THEN I'LL PROVE WHO'S THE BEST.
I'M THE BEST.
I'M THE GOD OF WAR.
CRAZY FREAK SONUVABITCH.

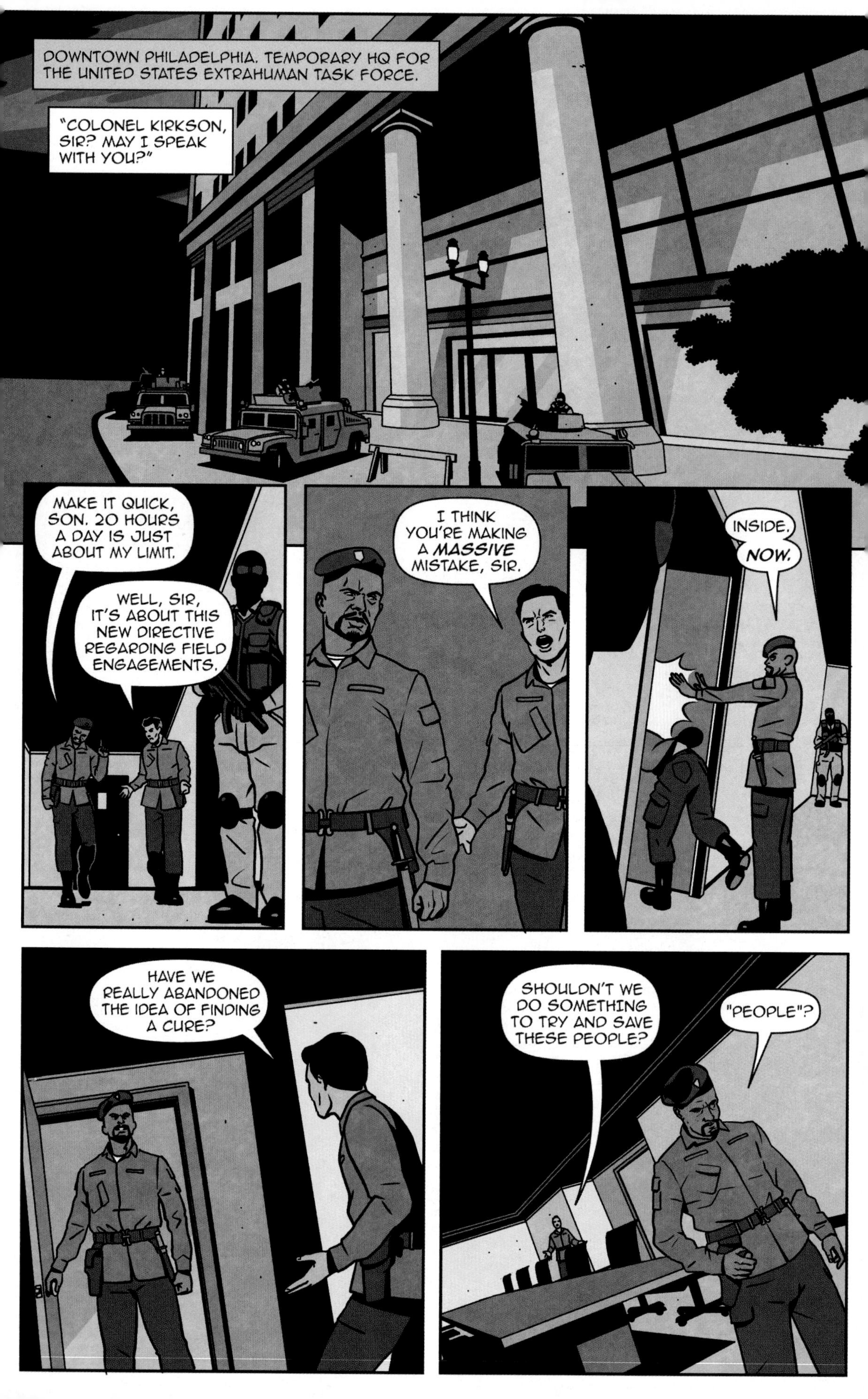
DOWNTOWN PHILADELPHIA. TEMPORARY HQ FOR THE UNITED STATES EXTRAHUMAN TASK FORCE.
"COLONEL KIRKSON, SIR? MAY I SPEAK WITH YOU?"
MAKE IT QUICK, SON. 20 HOURS A DAY IS JUST ABOUT MY LIMIT.
WELL, SIR, IT'S ABOUT THIS NEW DIRECTIVE REGARDING FIELD ENGAGEMENTS.
I THINK YOU'RE MAKING A *MASSIVE* MISTAKE, SIR.
INSIDE. *NOW.*
HAVE WE REALLY ABANDONED THE IDEA OF FINDING A CURE?
SHOULDN'T WE DO SOMETHING TO TRY AND SAVE THESE PEOPLE?
"PEOPLE"?

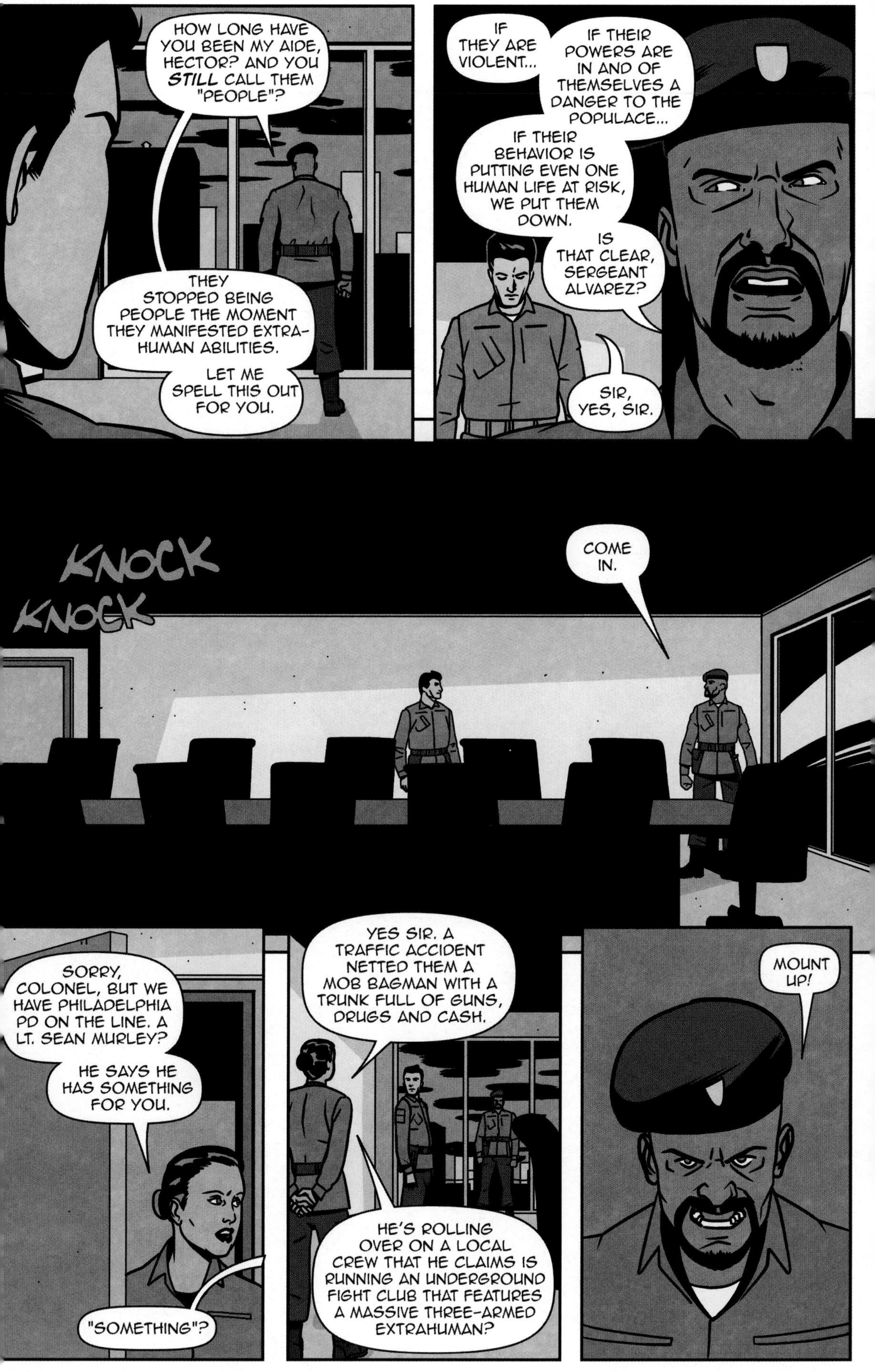
HOW LONG HAVE YOU BEEN MY AIDE, HECTOR? AND YOU *STILL* CALL THEM "PEOPLE"?
THEY STOPPED BEING PEOPLE THE MOMENT THEY MANIFESTED EXTRA-HUMAN ABILITIES.
LET ME SPELL THIS OUT FOR YOU.
IF THEY ARE VIOLENT...
IF THEIR POWERS ARE IN AND OF THEMSELVES A DANGER TO THE POPULACE...
IF THEIR BEHAVIOR IS PUTTING EVEN ONE HUMAN LIFE AT RISK, WE PUT THEM DOWN.
IS THAT CLEAR, SERGEANT ALVAREZ?
SIR, YES, SIR.
KNOCK
KNOCK
COME IN.
SORRY, COLONEL, BUT WE HAVE PHILADELPHIA PD ON THE LINE. A LT. SEAN MURLEY?
HE SAYS HE HAS SOMETHING FOR YOU.
"SOMETHING"?
YES SIR. A TRAFFIC ACCIDENT NETTED THEM A MOB BAGMAN WITH A TRUNK FULL OF GUNS, DRUGS AND CASH.
HE'S ROLLING OVER ON A LOCAL CREW THAT HE CLAIMS IS RUNNING AN UNDERGROUND FIGHT CLUB THAT FEATURES A MASSIVE THREE-ARMED EXTRAHUMAN?
MOUNT UP!

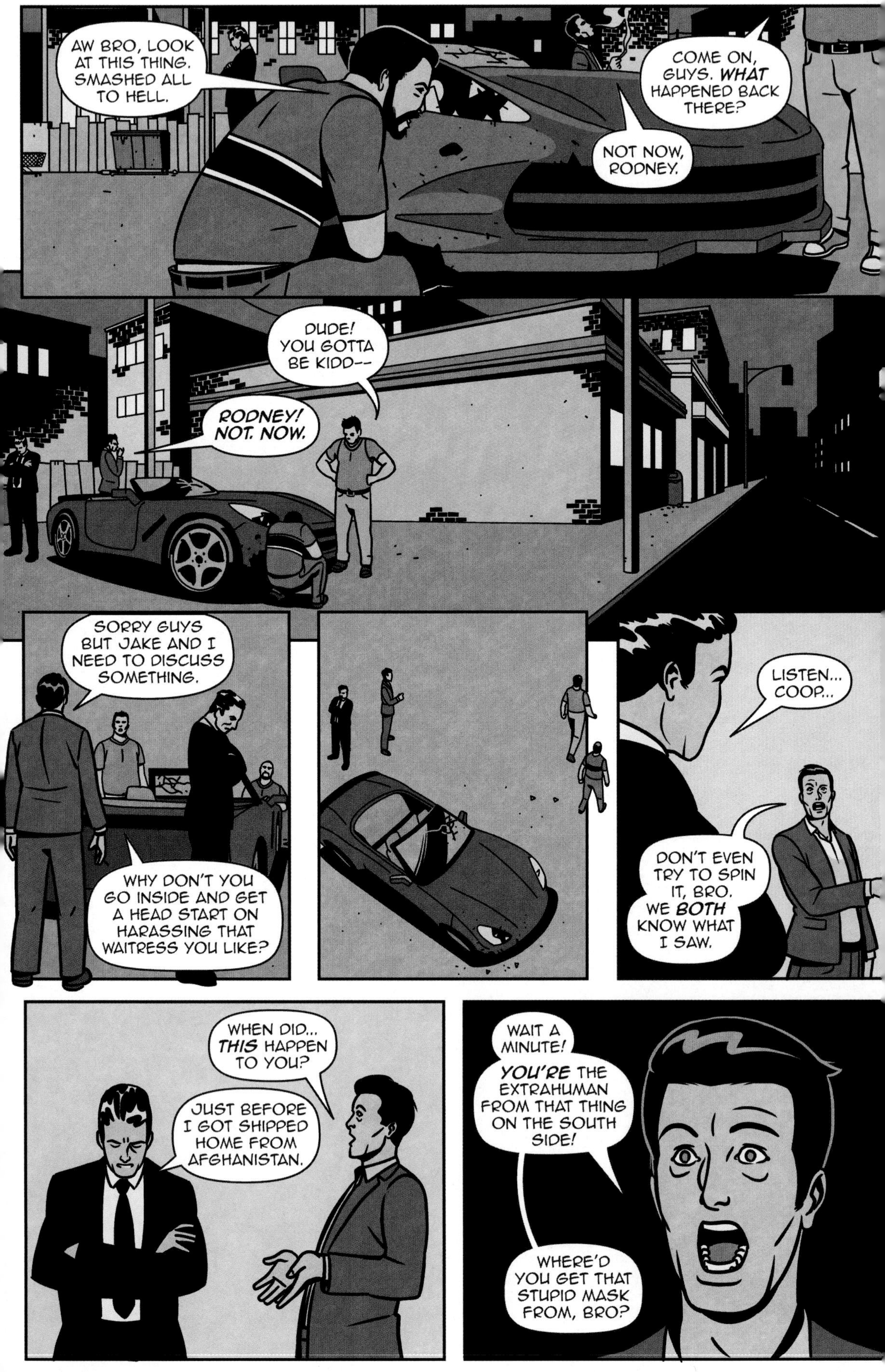
AW BRO, LOOK AT THIS THING. SMASHED ALL TO HELL.
COME ON, GUYS. WHAT HAPPENED BACK THERE?
NOT NOW, RODNEY.
DUDE! YOU GOTTA BE KIDD--
RODNEY! NOT. NOW.
SORRY GUYS BUT JAKE AND I NEED TO DISCUSS SOMETHING.
WHY DON'T YOU GO INSIDE AND GET A HEAD START ON HARASSING THAT WAITRESS YOU LIKE?
LISTEN... COOP...
DON'T EVEN TRY TO SPIN IT, BRO. WE BOTH KNOW WHAT I SAW.
WHEN DID... THIS HAPPEN TO YOU?
JUST BEFORE I GOT SHIPPED HOME FROM AFGHANISTAN.
WAIT A MINUTE!
YOU'RE THE EXTRAHUMAN FROM THAT THING ON THE SOUTH SIDE!
WHERE'D YOU GET THAT STUPID MASK FROM, BRO?

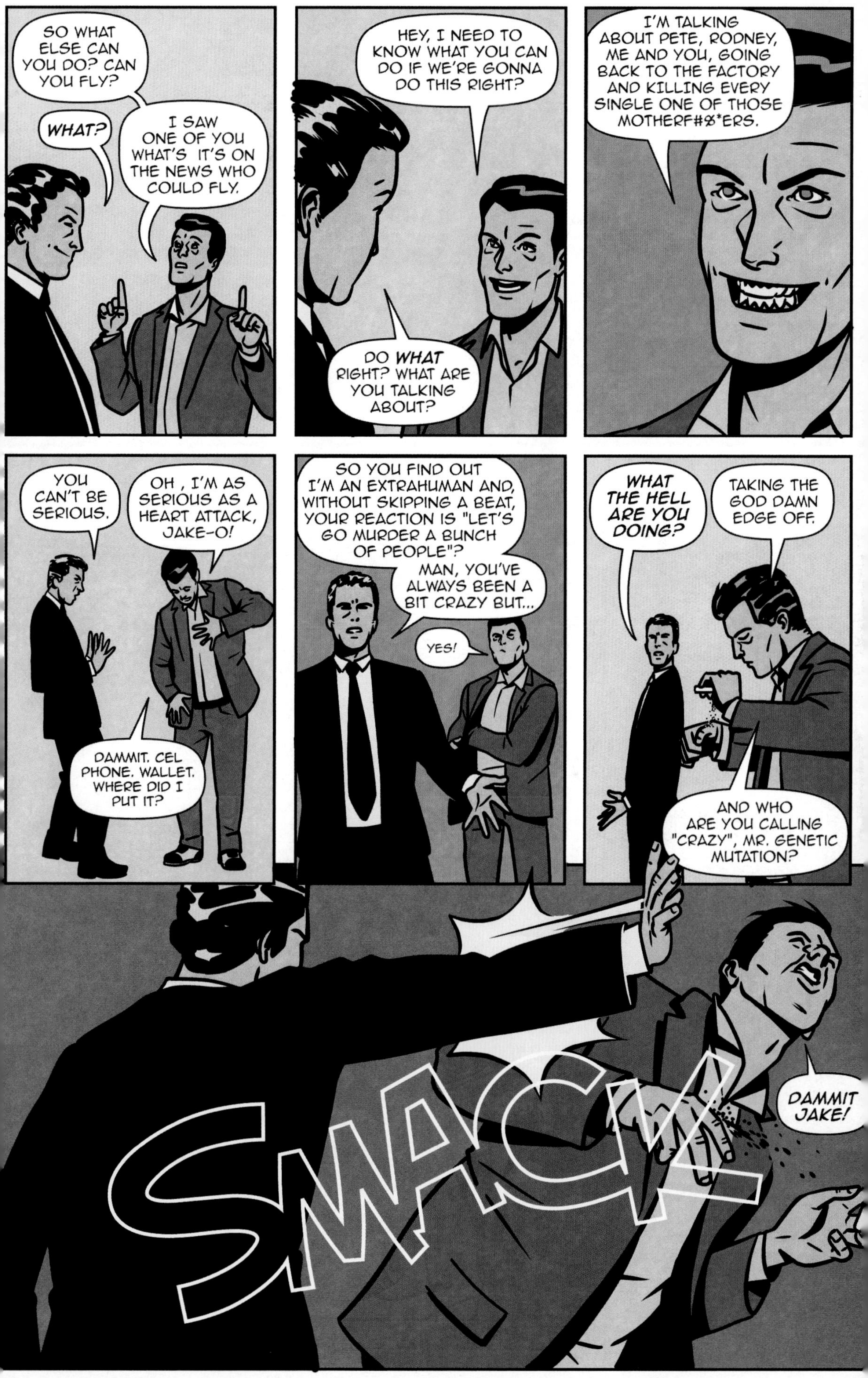
SO WHAT ELSE CAN YOU DO? CAN YOU FLY?
WHAT?
I SAW ONE OF YOU WHAT'S IT'S ON THE NEWS WHO COULD FLY.
HEY, I NEED TO KNOW WHAT YOU CAN DO IF WE'RE GONNA DO THIS RIGHT?
DO WHAT RIGHT? WHAT ARE YOU TALKING ABOUT?
I'M TALKING ABOUT PETE, RODNEY, ME AND YOU, GOING BACK TO THE FACTORY AND KILLING EVERY SINGLE ONE OF THOSE MOTHERF#%*ERS.
YOU CAN'T BE SERIOUS.
OH , I'M AS SERIOUS AS A HEART ATTACK, JAKE-O!
DAMMIT. CEL PHONE. WALLET. WHERE DID I PUT IT?
SO YOU FIND OUT I'M AN EXTRAHUMAN AND, WITHOUT SKIPPING A BEAT, YOUR REACTION IS "LET'S GO MURDER A BUNCH OF PEOPLE"?
MAN, YOU'VE ALWAYS BEEN A BIT CRAZY BUT...
YES!
WHAT THE HELL ARE YOU DOING?
TAKING THE GOD DAMN EDGE OFF.
AND WHO ARE YOU CALLING "CRAZY", MR. GENETIC MUTATION?
SMACK
DAMMIT JAKE!

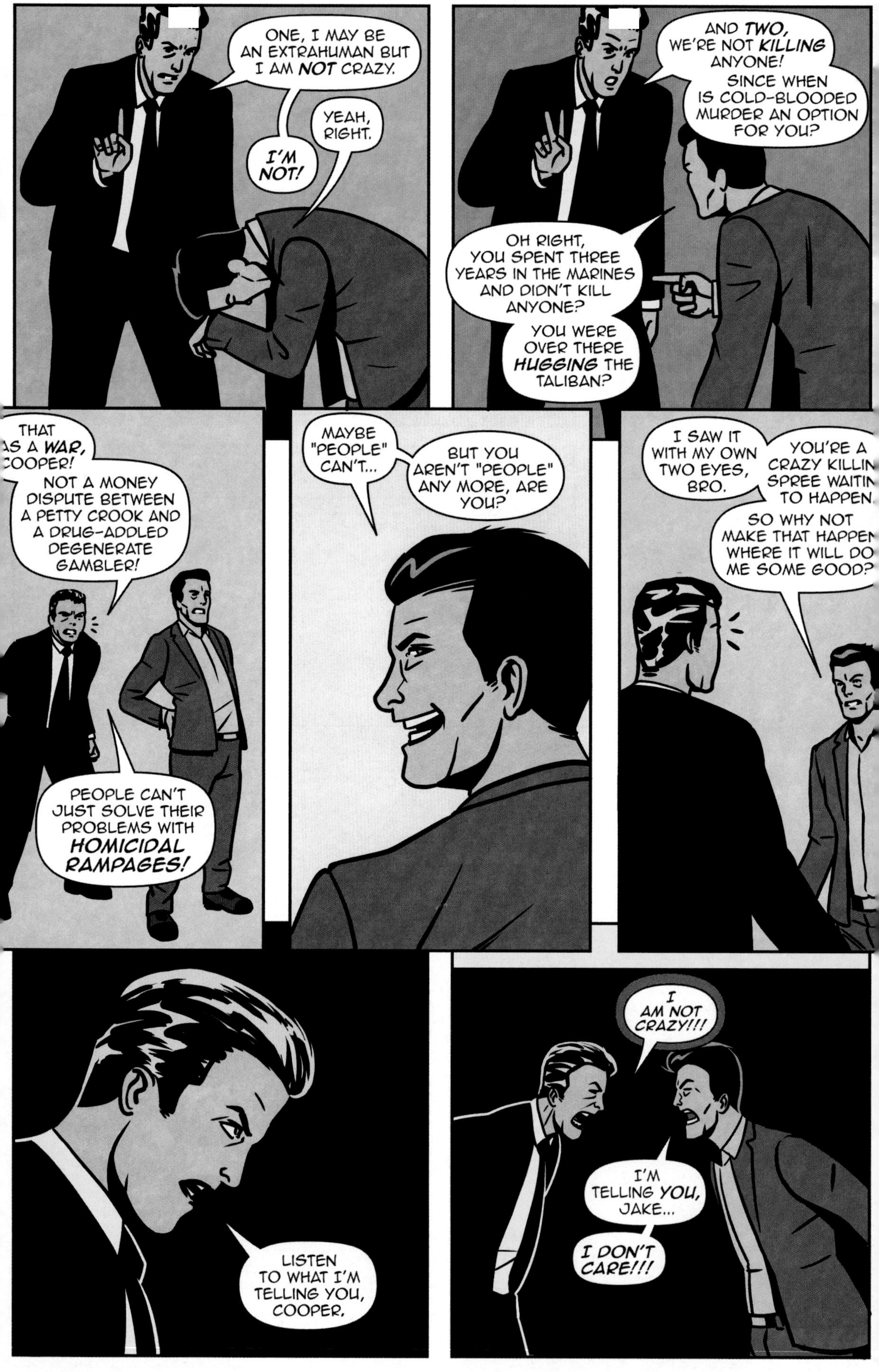
ONE, I MAY BE AN EXTRAHUMAN BUT I AM *NOT* CRAZY.
I'M NOT!
YEAH, RIGHT.
AND *TWO,* WE'RE NOT *KILLING* ANYONE!
SINCE WHEN IS COLD-BLOODED MURDER AN OPTION FOR YOU?
OH RIGHT, YOU SPENT THREE YEARS IN THE MARINES AND DIDN'T KILL ANYONE?
YOU WERE OVER THERE *HUGGING* THE TALIBAN?
THAT AS A *WAR,* OOPER!
NOT A MONEY DISPUTE BETWEEN A PETTY CROOK AND A DRUG-ADDLED DEGENERATE GAMBLER!
PEOPLE CAN'T JUST SOLVE THEIR PROBLEMS WITH ***HOMICIDAL RAMPAGES!***
MAYBE "PEOPLE" CAN'T...
BUT YOU AREN'T "PEOPLE" ANY MORE, ARE YOU?
I SAW IT WITH MY OWN TWO EYES, BRO.
YOU'RE A CRAZY KILLIN SPREE WAITIN TO HAPPEN.
SO WHY NOT MAKE THAT HAPPEN WHERE IT WILL DO ME SOME GOOD?
LISTEN TO WHAT I'M TELLING YOU, COOPER.
I AM NOT CRAZY!!!
I'M TELLING *YOU,* JAKE...
I DON'T CARE!!!

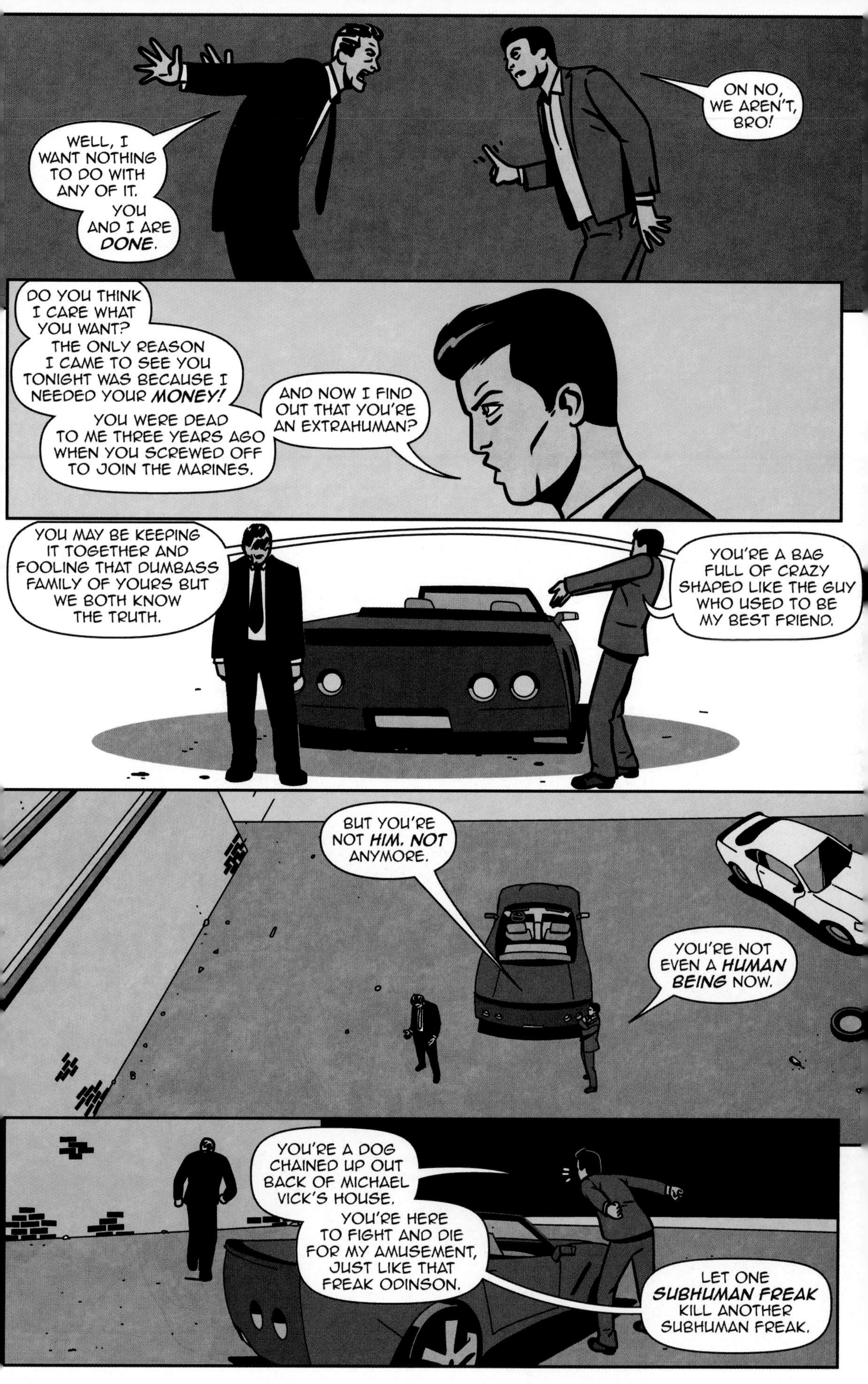
WELL, I WANT NOTHING TO DO WITH ANY OF IT.
YOU AND I ARE *DONE*.
ON NO, WE AREN'T, BRO!
DO YOU THINK I CARE WHAT YOU WANT?
THE ONLY REASON I CAME TO SEE YOU TONIGHT WAS BECAUSE I NEEDED YOUR *MONEY!*
YOU WERE DEAD TO ME THREE YEARS AGO WHEN YOU SCREWED OFF TO JOIN THE MARINES.
AND NOW I FIND OUT THAT YOU'RE AN EXTRAHUMAN?
YOU MAY BE KEEPING IT TOGETHER AND FOOLING THAT DUMBASS FAMILY OF YOURS BUT WE BOTH KNOW THE TRUTH.
YOU'RE A BAG FULL OF CRAZY SHAPED LIKE THE GUY WHO USED TO BE MY BEST FRIEND.
BUT YOU'RE NOT *HIM. NOT* ANYMORE.
YOU'RE NOT EVEN A *HUMAN BEING* NOW.
YOU'RE A DOG CHAINED UP OUT BACK OF MICHAEL VICK'S HOUSE.
YOU'RE HERE TO FIGHT AND DIE FOR MY AMUSEMENT, JUST LIKE THAT FREAK ODINSON.
LET ONE *SUBHUMAN FREAK* KILL ANOTHER SUBHUMAN FREAK.

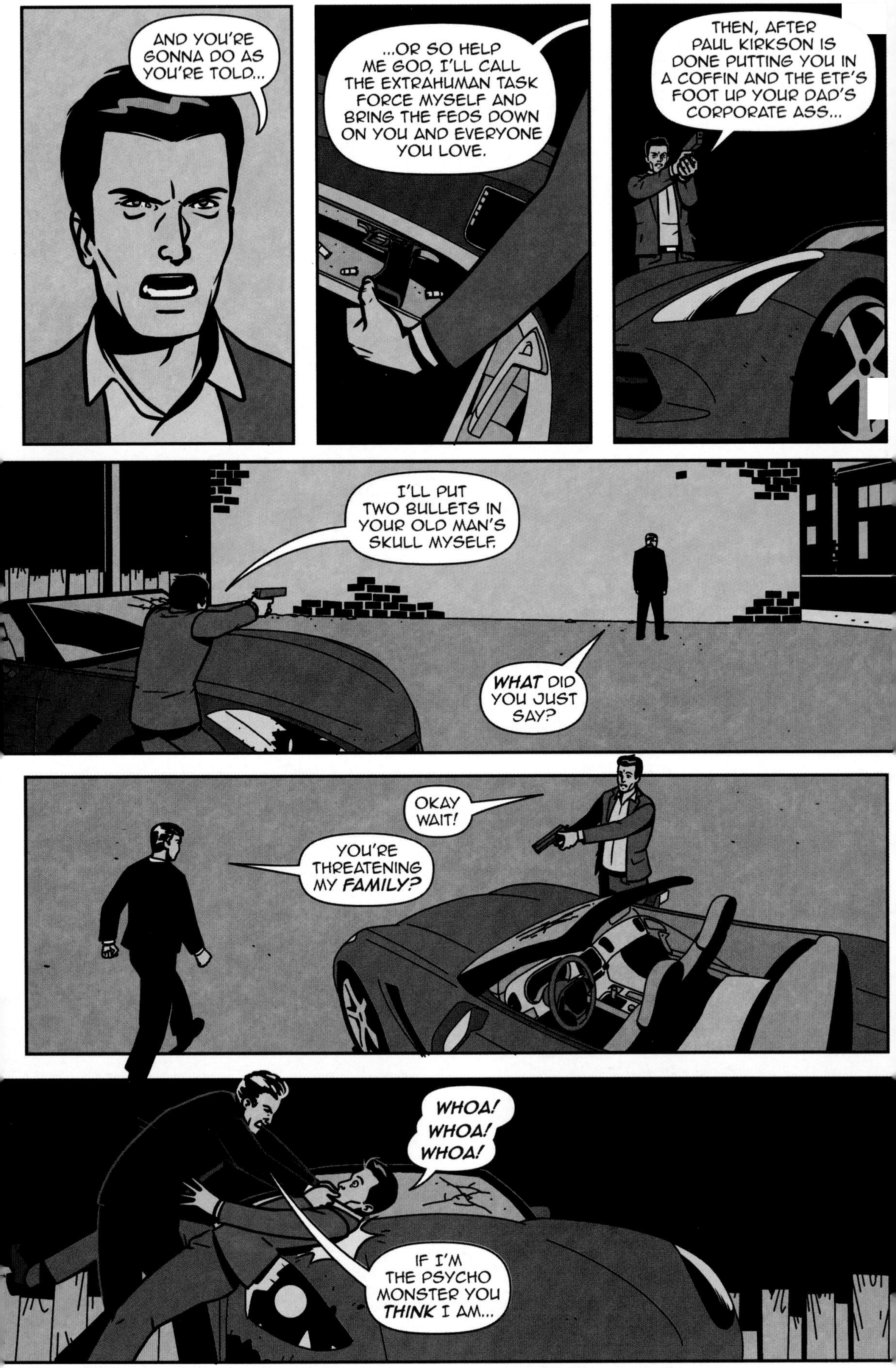
AND YOU'RE GONNA DO AS YOU'RE TOLD...
...OR SO HELP ME GOD, I'LL CALL THE EXTRAHUMAN TASK FORCE MYSELF AND BRING THE FEDS DOWN ON YOU AND EVERYONE YOU LOVE.
THEN, AFTER PAUL KIRKSON IS DONE PUTTING YOU IN A COFFIN AND THE ETF'S FOOT UP YOUR DAD'S CORPORATE ASS...
I'LL PUT TWO BULLETS IN YOUR OLD MAN'S SKULL MYSELF.
WHAT DID YOU JUST SAY?
OKAY WAIT!
YOU'RE THREATENING MY FAMILY?
WHOA! WHOA! WHOA!
IF I'M THE PSYCHO MONSTER YOU THINK I AM...

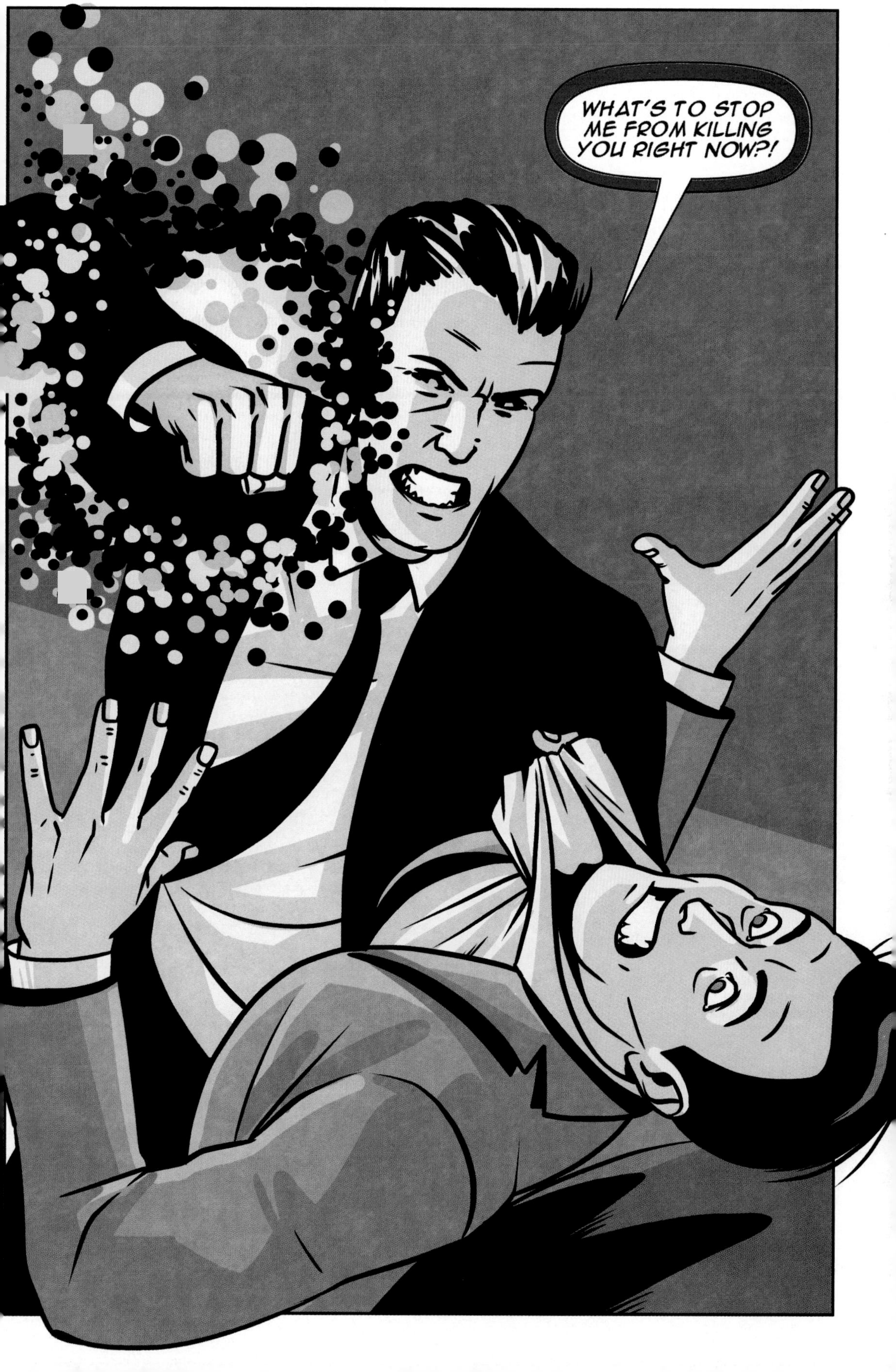
WHAT'S TO STOP ME FROM KILLING YOU RIGHT NOW?!

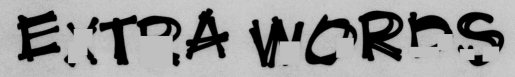

EXTRA WORDS

Website: theflrsthero.com / Twitter: 16Hectares / Instagram: SixteenHectares / Facebook: theflrsthero
Questions, comments, need some life advice? Contact us directly at sixteenhectares@gmail.com

"Just when they think they got the answers, I change the questions."
- "Rowdy" Roddy Piper (1954 - 2015)

* * *

I don't know if I have the words to express just how much I'm enjoying bringing TFH: FIGHT FOR YOUR LIKE to you all. Danny's ↕ gets better and stronger with each page and Fred's colour work in this volume is sublime. When Dan sent me his first pages f FIGHT FOR YOUR LIFE, Fred and I marvelled at how terrific they were. Fred and I discussed a palate and a tone for this story c and we immediately agreed that Richmond Lewis' amazing colour work on BATMAN: YEAR ONE should and would be an influence.

That story arc has actually been a huge influence on my comic book writing in general and on THE FIRST HERO, specifically. much as Frank Miller's THE DARK KNIGHT RETURNS helped redefine aspects the genre, it's BATMAN issues 404 through 407 that c possibly my favourite of all the writer's comic book work. Similarly, as solid as David Mazzucchelli's work was during his run DAREDEVIL and the small handful of other comics he drew, his art for YEAR ONE is... art. It's just SO beautiful. And of cour there's the aforementioned Ms. Lewis, whom I have since come to learn is Mazzucchelli's wife, which is how she got involved in ↕ comics industry to begin with.

I sometimes worry that I might be repeating myself in the content of these essay pages but here's something I am pretty confider am telling you all for the very first time. THE FIRST HERO is going to run no less than TWENTY-FIVE issues and encompass the fi (and possibly ONLY) year of Jacob Roth's life as an extrahuman. Jake will need to really get his act together for the increasin massive challenges that are heading his way. I hope what we are producing here does justice to the legacy of Miller, Mazzucch and Lewis' 1987 masterpiece.

* * *

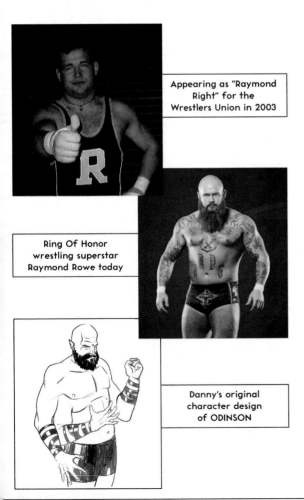

Appearing as "Raymond Right" for the Wrestlers Union in 2003

Ring Of Honor wrestling superstar Raymond Rowe today

Danny's original character design of ODINSON

Round One between Jake and the massive Odinson is in ↕ books. But never fear, kids! There's a big money rematch on ↕ horizon. I'm pretty sure that I've mentioned this before but, ↕ way it was originally envisioned, this series was basically just excuse for me to create a succession of crazy extrahum villains. As the idea for the series evolved, that desire to cre some seriously wacky and kick-ass villains remained stro That's why I'm so happy about the way Odinson has turned c He's a massive mutant monster and all he wants to do is fig And he looks SO damn cool.

Physically, Odinson is based on professional wrestler Raymc Rowe. I met Ray back in 2003 when I promoted my first f Union of Independent Professional Wrestlers events in Erie, ↕ My friend Lou Marconi called me and told me about this kid was training who was a surefire prospect and just needed to some experience under his belt. Lou's endorsement was a really needed and so, as part of my May 2003 event, a mos clean-shaven and yet-to-be-tattooed "Raymond Right" dan (yes, danced!) his way to the ring to fight "Mr. Insanity" Tc Cline. Lou was right. It was easy to see, right from the ste that Ray was special. He's a tremendous talent in the ring c an even more tremendous person outside of it. I'm proud to that we're still friends all these years later. I love this guy c I'm so happy that he agreed to let me turn him into Odinson.

If you've never seen Ray wrestle, do yourself a favour and ch out an episode of Ring of Honor's nationally syndicated televis show where Ray does battle as one half of the appropriat named tag team War Machine.

* * *

NEXT ISSUE: Jake Roth vs Odinson... ROUND TWO!!!

Thank y
Anthony Ruttgai
Toronto, 4 August 2

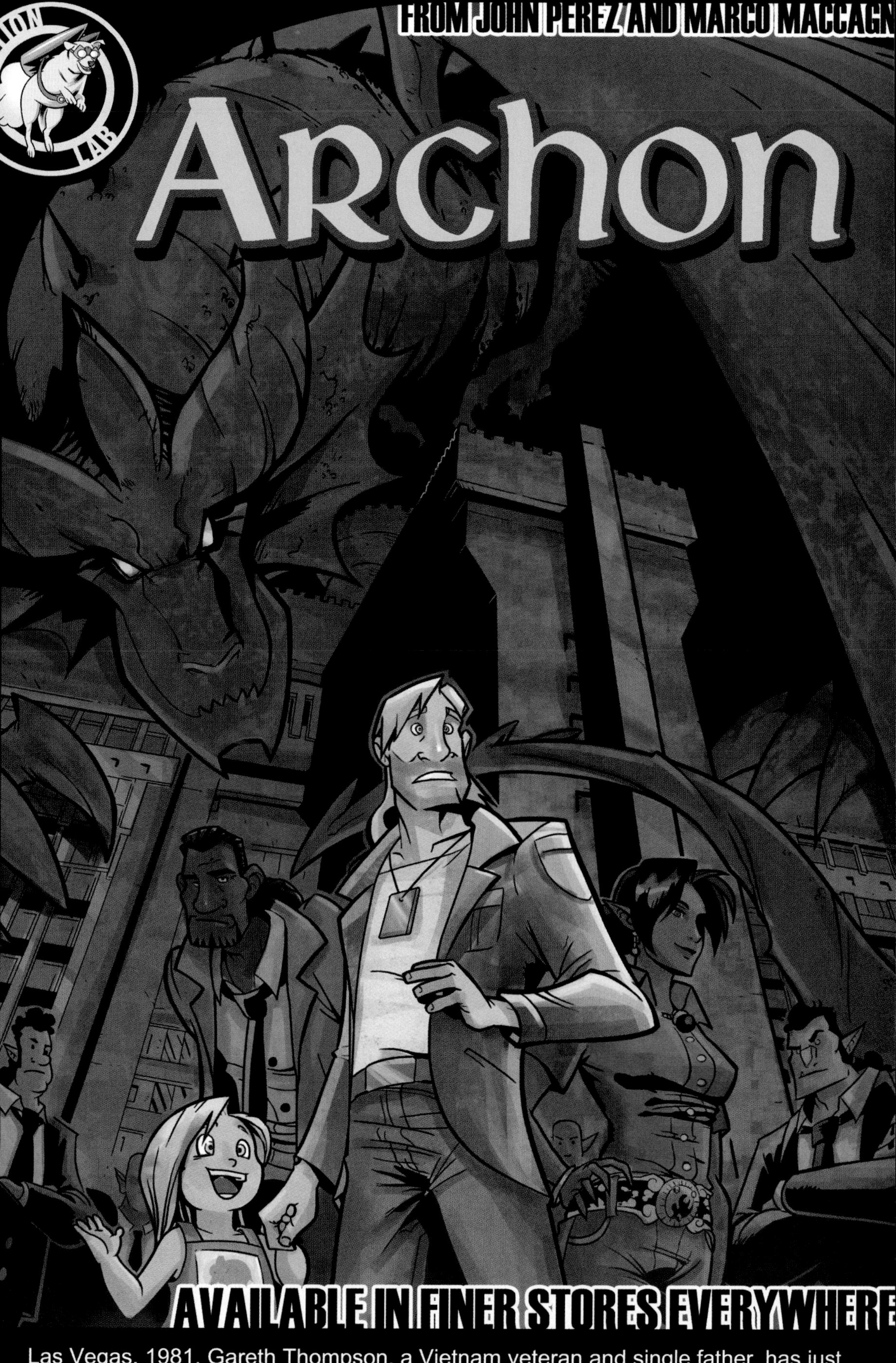

FROM JOHN PEREZ AND MARCO MACCAGN

Archon

AVAILABLE IN FINER STORES EVERYWHERE

Las Vegas, 1981. Gareth Thompson, a Vietnam veteran and single father, has just accepted a security job at the new fantasy-themed "Archon Hotel and Casino." However, he'll soon discover all the Orcs, Elves and Dragons at the Resort are not people in costumes, but actual creatures of myth and legend.

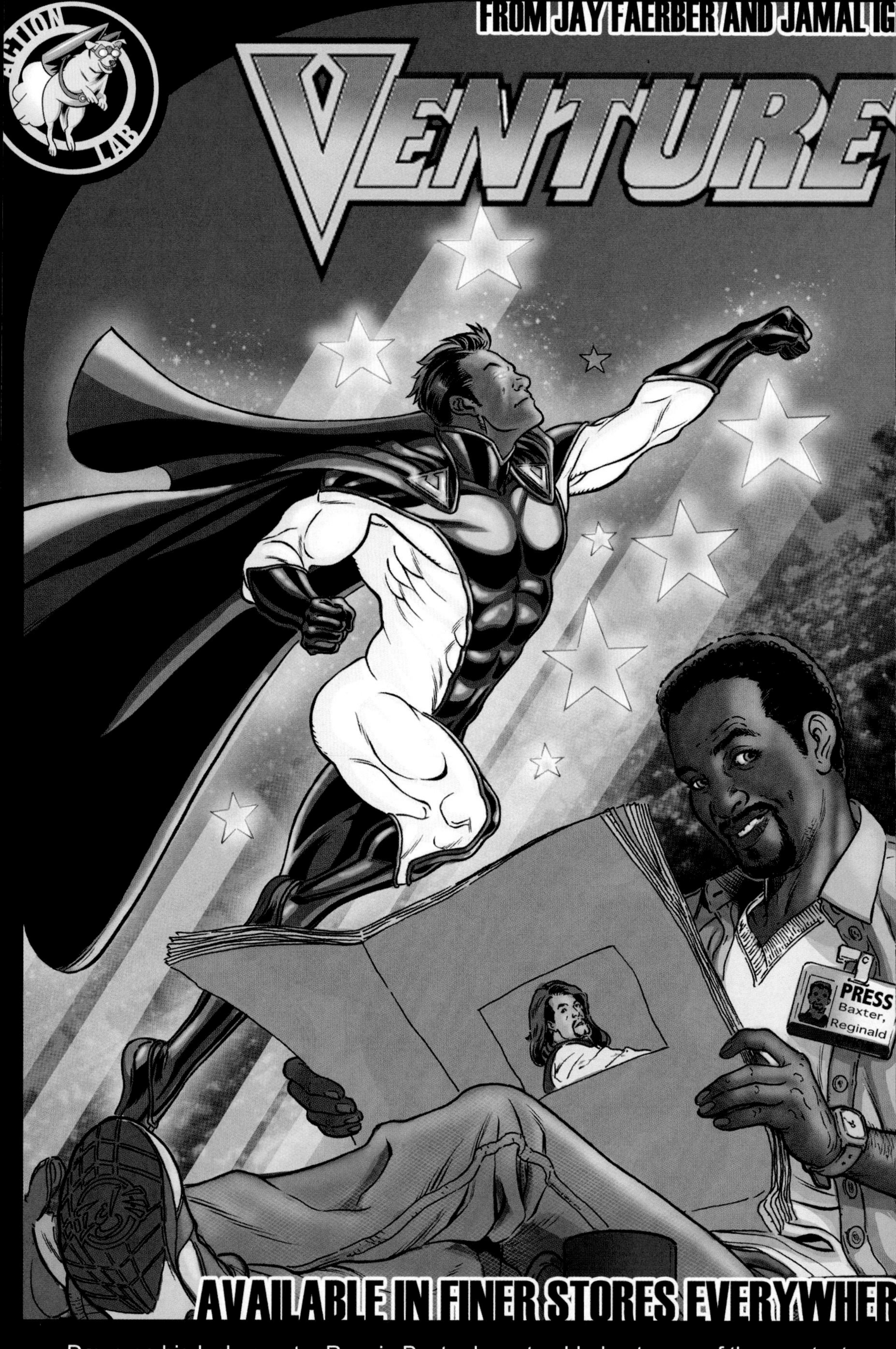
ACTION LAB
FROM JAY FAERBER AND JAMAL IG
VENTURE
PRESS
Baxter, Reginald
AVAILABLE IN FINER STORES EVERYWHER

Down-on-his-luck reporter Reggie Baxter has stumbled onto one of the greatest secrets of all time...superpowered high school history teacher Joe Campbell! But who is Joe Campbell and more importantly, how rich will Reggie become by blackmailing him?

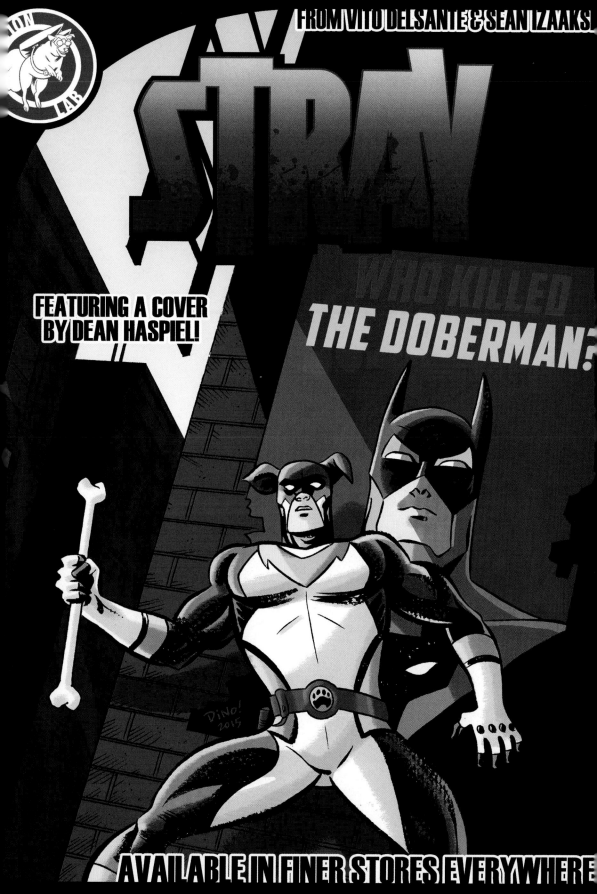

FROM VITO DELSANTE & SEAN IZAAKS!

STRAY

FEATURING A COVER BY DEAN HASPIEL!

WHO KILLED THE DOBERMAN?

AVAILABLE IN FINER STORES EVERYWHERE

Collecting the hit mini-series, STRAY tells the story of Rodney Weller, the former sidekick known as "the Rottweiler." When his mentor, the Doberman, is murdered, Rodney has to decide if he wants to come back to the world of capes and masks and, if he does, who he wants to be. Cover by Emmy Award winner, Dean Haspiel (The Fox)! Collects Stray #1-4.

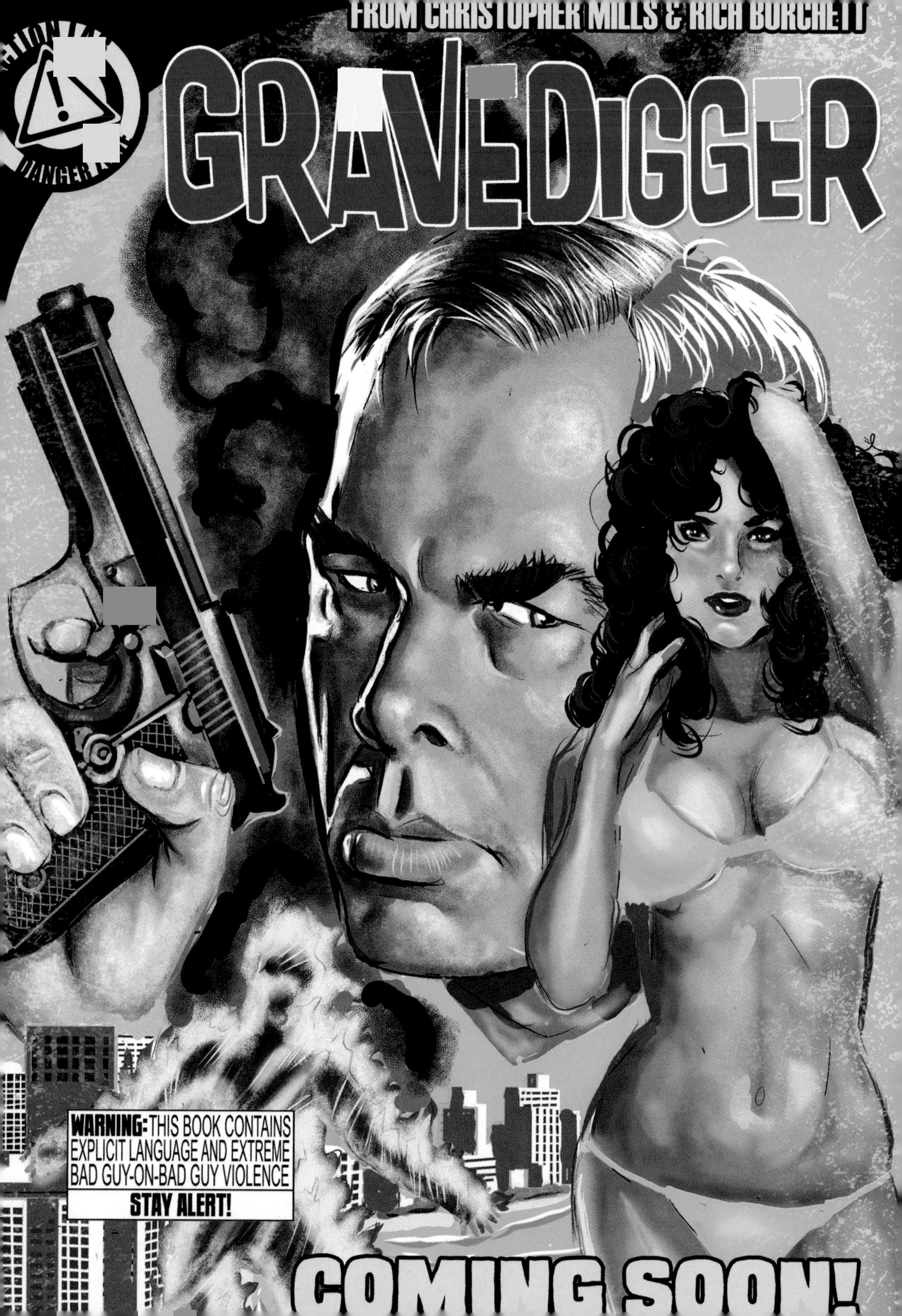
FROM CHRISTOPHER MILLS & RICH BURCHETT
GRAVEDIGGER
WARNING: THIS BOOK CONTAINS EXPLICIT LANGUAGE AND EXTREME BAD GUY-ON-BAD GUY VIOLENCE
STAY ALERT!
COMING SOON!

ACTION LAB

READ MORE NOW

F1rst Hero - Action Lab
www.actionlabcomics.com
00611

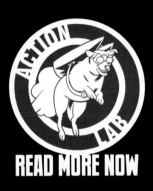

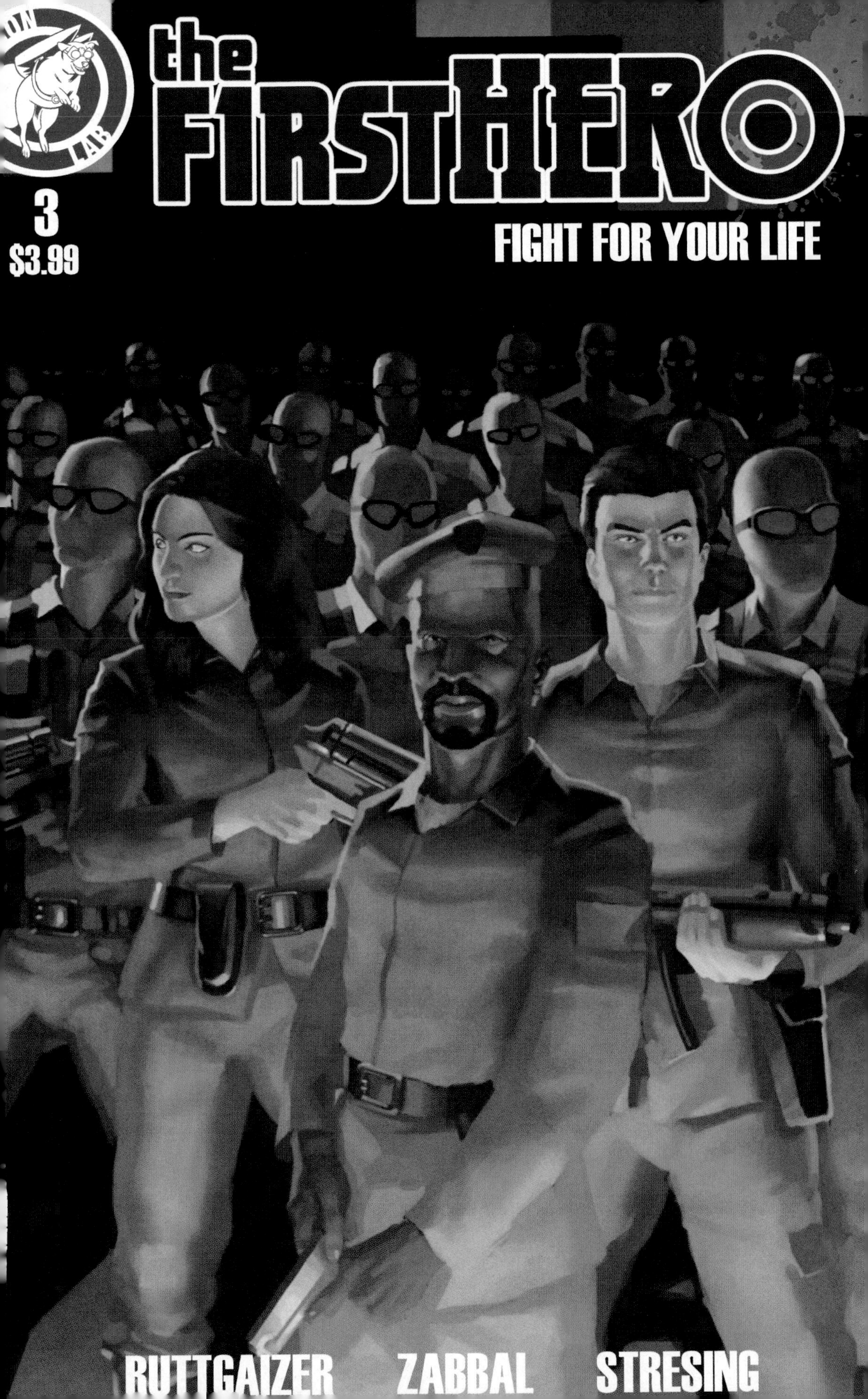
the FIRSTHERO
3
$3.99
FIGHT FOR YOUR LIFE
RUTTGAIZER
ZABBAL
STRESING

FROM ALL-AGES TO MATURE READERS
ACTION LAB HAS YOU COVERED.

 **Appropriate for everyone.**

 **Appropriate for age 9 and up. Absent of profanity or adult content.**

 **Suggested for 12 and Up. Comics with this rating are comparable to a PG-13 movie rating. Recommended for our teen and young adult readers.**

 **Appropriate for older teens. Similar to Teen, but featuring more mature themes and/or more graphic imagery.**

 **Contains extreme viloence and some nudity. Basically the Rated-R of comics.**

 FIND YOUR NEW FAVORITE COMICS.

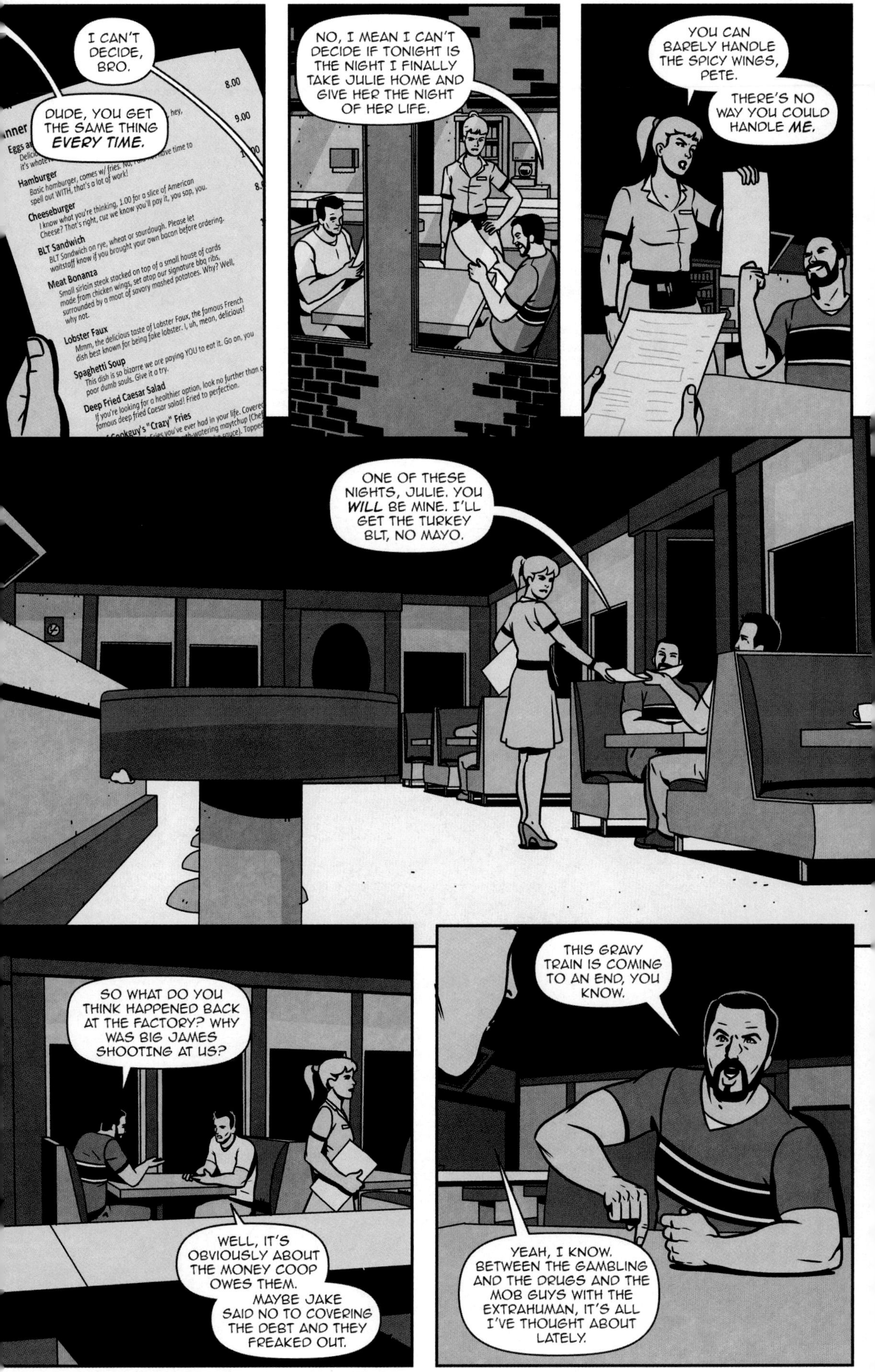
I CAN'T DECIDE, BRO.
DUDE, YOU GET THE SAME THING *EVERY TIME.*
8.00
9.00
Hamburger
Basic hamburger, comes w/ fries.
spell out WITH, that's a lot of work!
Cheeseburger
I know what you're thinking, 1.00 for a slice of American
Cheese? That's right, cuz we know you'll pay it, you sap, you.
BLT Sandwich
BLT Sandwich on rye, wheat or sourdough. Please let
waitstaff know if you brought your own bacon before ordering.
Meat Bonanza
Small sirloin steak stacked on top of a small house of cards
made from chicken wings, set atop our signature bbq ribs,
surrounded by a moat of savory mashed potatoes. Why? Well,
why not.
Lobster Faux
Mmm, the delicious taste of Lobster Faux, the famous French
dish best known for being fake lobster. I, uh, mean, delicious!
Spaghetti Soup
This dish is so bizarre we are paying YOU to eat it. Go on, you
poor dumb souls. Give it a try.
Deep Fried Caesar Salad
If you're looking for a healthier option, look no further than
famous deep fried Caesar salad! Fried to perfection.
NO, I MEAN I CAN'T DECIDE IF TONIGHT IS THE NIGHT I FINALLY TAKE JULIE HOME AND GIVE HER THE NIGHT OF HER LIFE.
YOU CAN BARELY HANDLE THE SPICY WINGS, PETE.
THERE'S NO WAY YOU COULD HANDLE *ME.*
ONE OF THESE NIGHTS, JULIE. YOU *WILL* BE MINE. I'LL GET THE TURKEY BLT, NO MAYO.
SO WHAT DO YOU THINK HAPPENED BACK AT THE FACTORY? WHY WAS BIG JAMES SHOOTING AT US?
WELL, IT'S OBVIOUSLY ABOUT THE MONEY COOP OWES THEM.
MAYBE JAKE SAID NO TO COVERING THE DEBT AND THEY FREAKED OUT.
THIS GRAVY TRAIN IS COMING TO AN END, YOU KNOW.
YEAH, I KNOW. BETWEEN THE GAMBLING AND THE DRUGS AND THE MOB GUYS WITH THE EXTRAHUMAN, IT'S ALL I'VE THOUGHT ABOUT LATELY.

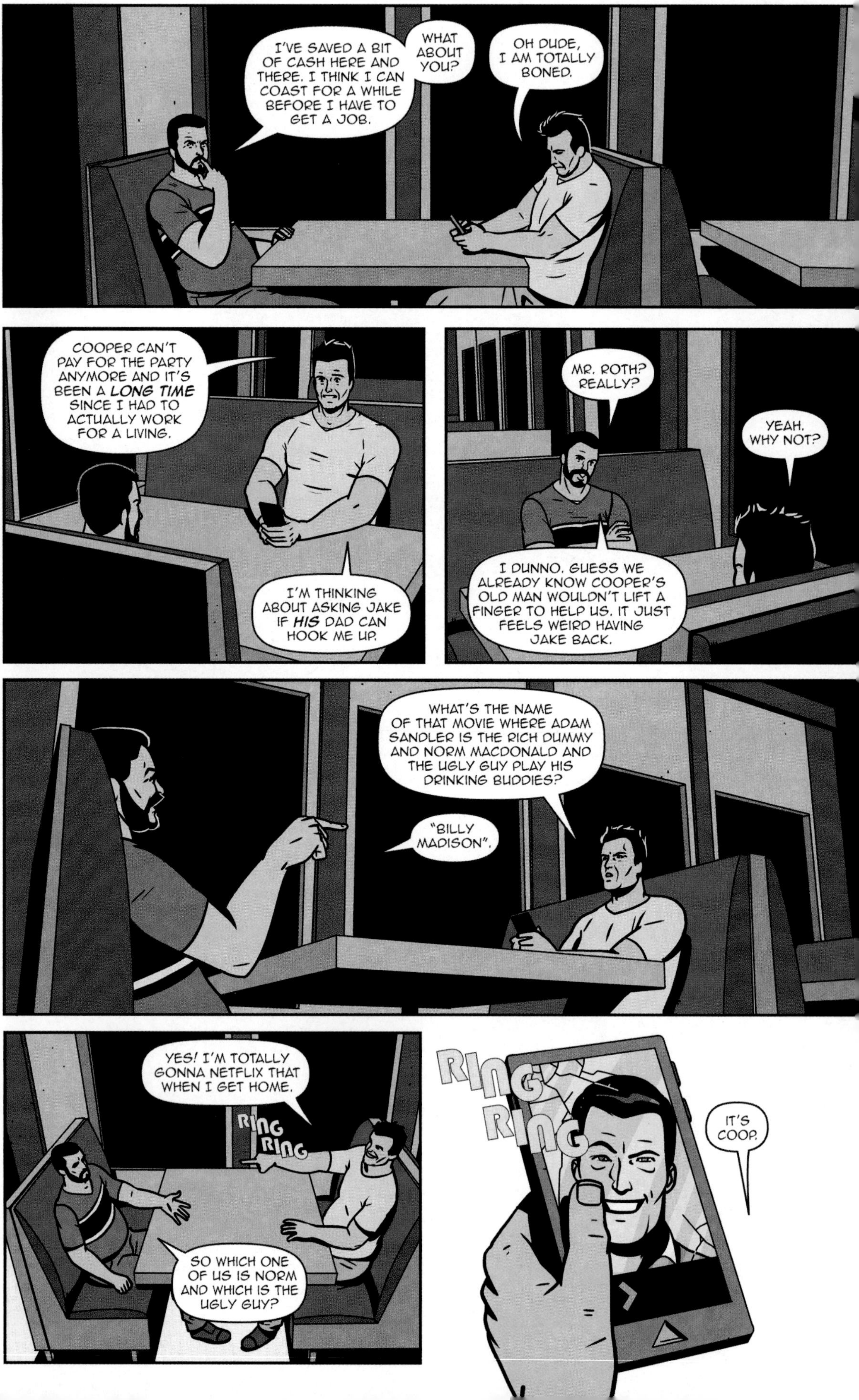
I'VE SAVED A BIT OF CASH HERE AND THERE. I THINK I CAN COAST FOR A WHILE BEFORE I HAVE TO GET A JOB.
WHAT ABOUT YOU?
OH DUDE, I AM TOTALLY BONED.
COOPER CAN'T PAY FOR THE PARTY ANYMORE AND IT'S BEEN A LONG TIME SINCE I HAD TO ACTUALLY WORK FOR A LIVING.
I'M THINKING ABOUT ASKING JAKE IF HIS DAD CAN HOOK ME UP.
MR. ROTH? REALLY?
YEAH. WHY NOT?
I DUNNO. GUESS WE ALREADY KNOW COOPER'S OLD MAN WOULDN'T LIFT A FINGER TO HELP US. IT JUST FEELS WEIRD HAVING JAKE BACK.
WHAT'S THE NAME OF THAT MOVIE WHERE ADAM SANDLER IS THE RICH DUMMY AND NORM MACDONALD AND THE UGLY GUY PLAY HIS DRINKING BUDDIES?
"BILLY MADISON".
YES! I'M TOTALLY GONNA NETFLIX THAT WHEN I GET HOME.
RING RING
SO WHICH ONE OF US IS NORM AND WHICH IS THE UGLY GUY?
RING RING
IT'S COOP.

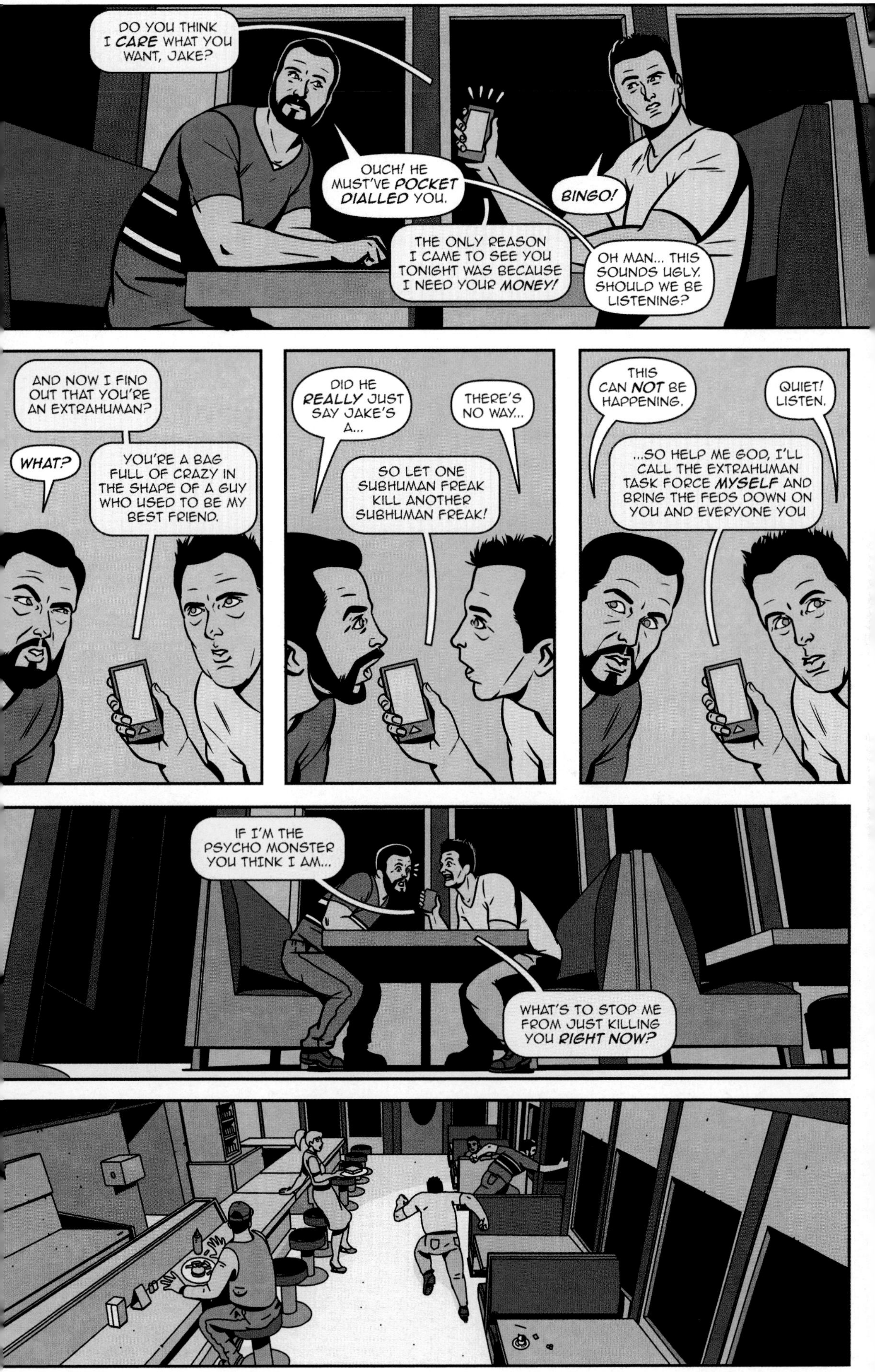
DO YOU THINK I CARE WHAT YOU WANT, JAKE?
OUCH! HE MUST'VE POCKET DIALLED YOU.
BINGO!
THE ONLY REASON I CAME TO SEE YOU TONIGHT WAS BECAUSE I NEED YOUR MONEY!
OH MAN... THIS SOUNDS UGLY. SHOULD WE BE LISTENING?
AND NOW I FIND OUT THAT YOU'RE AN EXTRAHUMAN?
WHAT?
YOU'RE A BAG FULL OF CRAZY IN THE SHAPE OF A GUY WHO USED TO BE MY BEST FRIEND.
DID HE REALLY JUST SAY JAKE'S A...
THERE'S NO WAY...
SO LET ONE SUBHUMAN FREAK KILL ANOTHER SUBHUMAN FREAK!
THIS CAN NOT BE HAPPENING.
QUIET! LISTEN.
...SO HELP ME GOD, I'LL CALL THE EXTRAHUMAN TASK FORCE MYSELF AND BRING THE FEDS DOWN ON YOU AND EVERYONE YOU
IF I'M THE PSYCHO MONSTER YOU THINK I AM...
WHAT'S TO STOP ME FROM JUST KILLING YOU RIGHT NOW?

ACTION LAB ENTERTAINMENT PROUDLY PRESENTS

the FIRSTHERO

VOLUME 2: FIGHT FOR YOUR LIFE

CHAPTER SEVEN: LET'S MAKE A DEAL

for SIXTEEN HECTARES AND A MOOSE, INK.

Created/Written by ANTHONY RUTTGAIZER
Cover/Interior Art by DANNY ZABBAL
Letters/Colors by FRED C. STRESING

For More Info, visit SixteenHectares.com

for ACTION LAB ENTERTAINMENT

BRYAN SEATON Publisher
KEVIN FREEMAN President
SHAWN GABBORIN Editor-in-Chief
DAVE DWONCH Creative Driector
JIM DIETZ Social Media Director
JAMAL IGLE Director of Marketing
VITO DELSANTE Director of Marketing
COLLEEN BOYD Associate Editor
CHAD CICCONI Three-Armed Psychopath

Read More Now at ActionLabComics.com

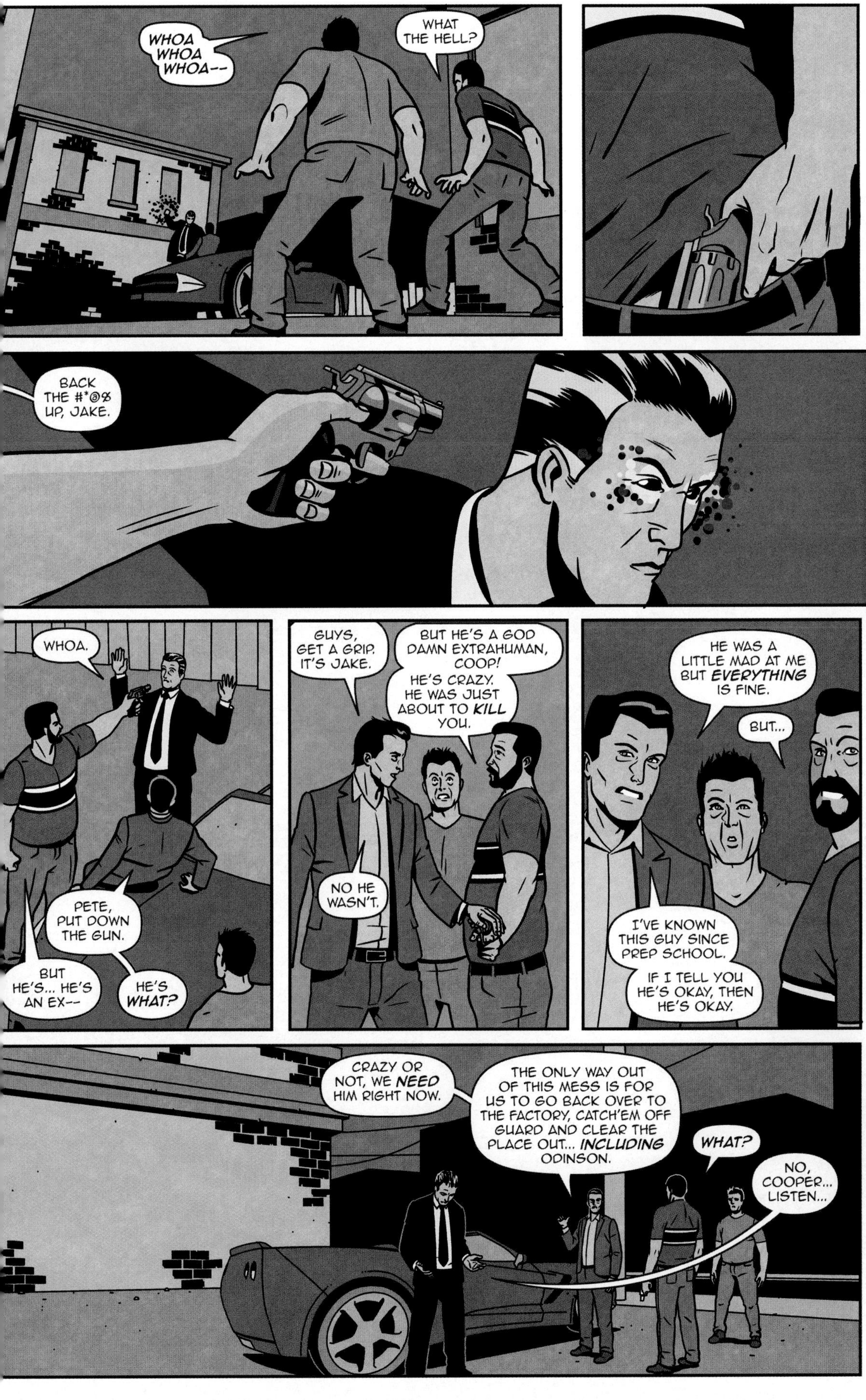

WHOA WHOA WHOA--
WHAT THE HELL?
BACK THE #*@% UP, JAKE.
WHOA.
PETE, PUT DOWN THE GUN.
BUT HE'S... HE'S AN EX--
HE'S *WHAT?*
GUYS, GET A GRIP. IT'S JAKE.
BUT HE'S A GOD DAMN EXTRAHUMAN, COOP!
HE'S CRAZY. HE WAS JUST ABOUT TO **KILL** YOU.
NO HE WASN'T.
HE WAS A LITTLE MAD AT ME BUT ***EVERYTHING*** IS FINE.
BUT...
I'VE KNOWN THIS GUY SINCE PREP SCHOOL.
IF I TELL YOU HE'S OKAY, THEN HE'S OKAY.
CRAZY OR NOT, WE ***NEED*** HIM RIGHT NOW.
THE ONLY WAY OUT OF THIS MESS IS FOR US TO GO BACK OVER TO THE FACTORY, CATCH'EM OFF GUARD AND CLEAR THE PLACE OUT... ***INCLUDING*** ODINSON.
WHAT?
NO, COOPER... LISTEN...

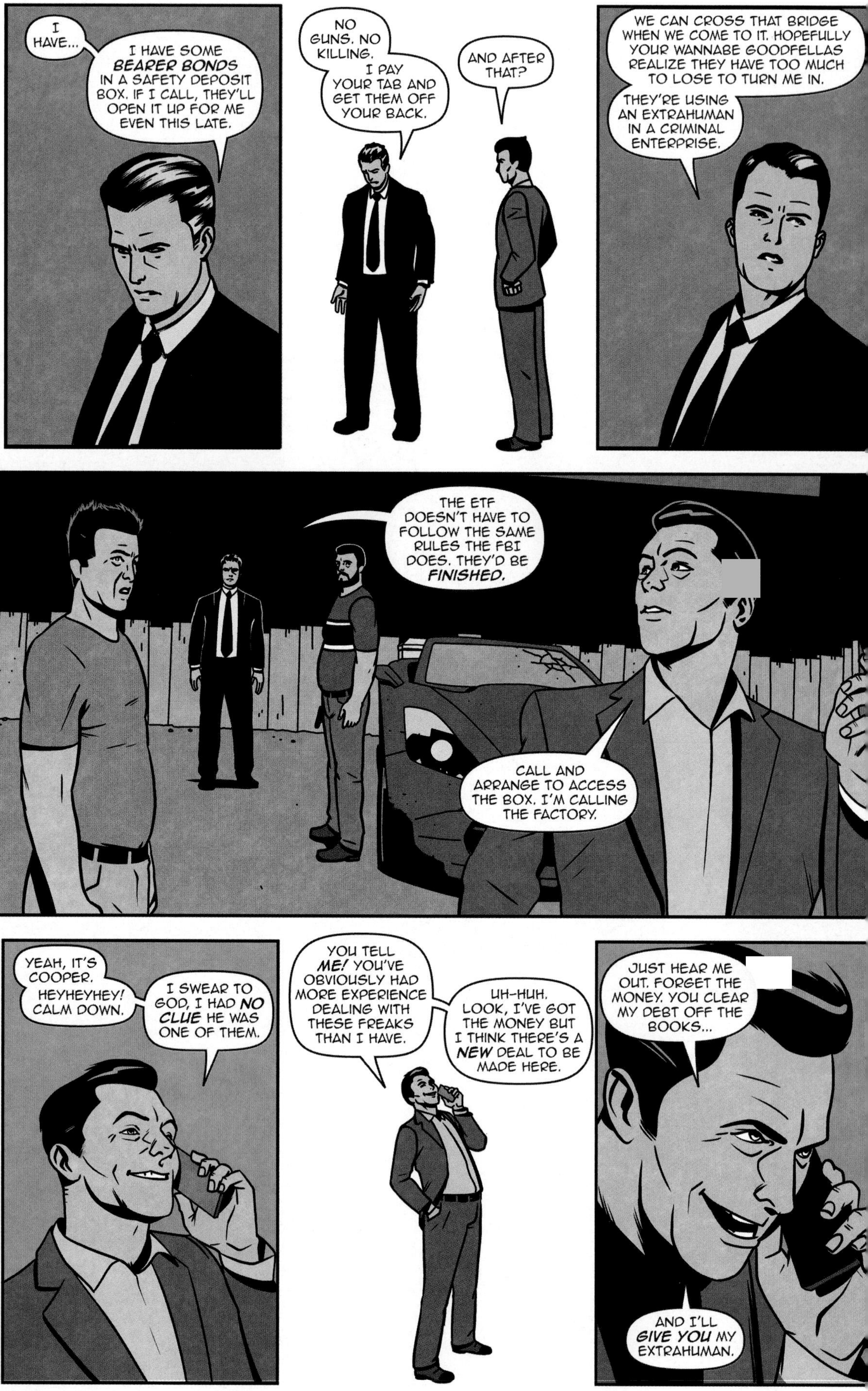
I HAVE...
I HAVE SOME BEARER BONDS IN A SAFETY DEPOSIT BOX. IF I CALL, THEY'LL OPEN IT UP FOR ME EVEN THIS LATE.
NO GUNS. NO KILLING.
I PAY YOUR TAB AND GET THEM OFF YOUR BACK.
AND AFTER THAT?
WE CAN CROSS THAT BRIDGE WHEN WE COME TO IT. HOPEFULLY YOUR WANNABE GOODFELLAS REALIZE THEY HAVE TOO MUCH TO LOSE TO TURN ME IN.
THEY'RE USING AN EXTRAHUMAN IN A CRIMINAL ENTERPRISE.
THE ETF DOESN'T HAVE TO FOLLOW THE SAME RULES THE FBI DOES. THEY'D BE FINISHED.
CALL AND ARRANGE TO ACCESS THE BOX. I'M CALLING THE FACTORY.
YEAH, IT'S COOPER.
HEYHEYHEY! CALM DOWN.
I SWEAR TO GOD, I HAD NO CLUE HE WAS ONE OF THEM.
YOU TELL ME! YOU'VE OBVIOUSLY HAD MORE EXPERIENCE DEALING WITH THESE FREAKS THAN I HAVE.
UH-HUH. LOOK, I'VE GOT THE MONEY BUT I THINK THERE'S A NEW DEAL TO BE MADE HERE.
JUST HEAR ME OUT. FORGET THE MONEY. YOU CLEAR MY DEBT OFF THE BOOKS...
AND I'LL GIVE YOU MY EXTRAHUMAN.

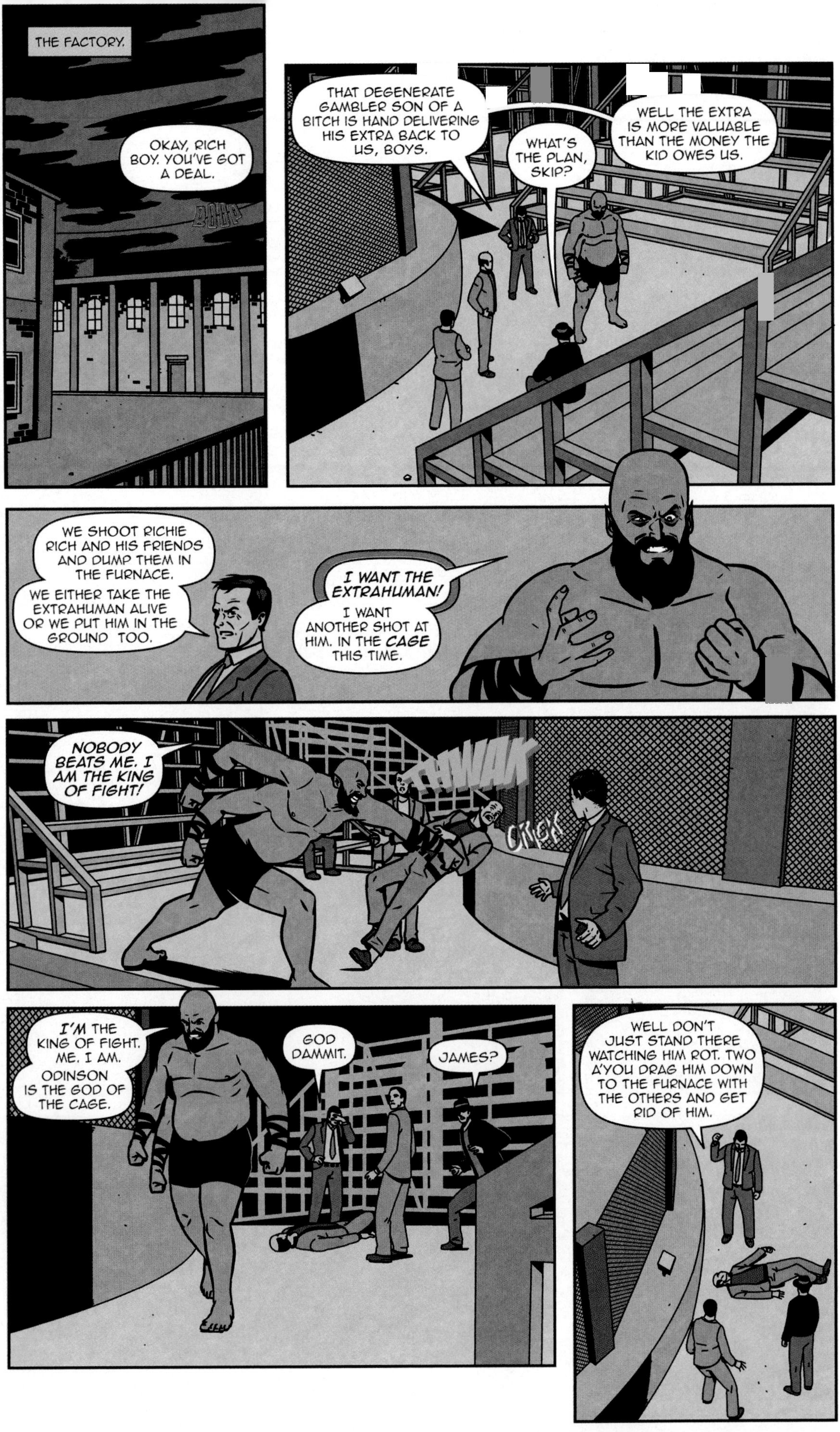
THE FACTORY.
OKAY, RICH BOY. YOU'VE GOT A DEAL.
BOOP
THAT DEGENERATE GAMBLER SON OF A BITCH IS HAND DELIVERING HIS EXTRA BACK TO US, BOYS.
WHAT'S THE PLAN, SKIP?
WELL THE EXTRA IS MORE VALUABLE THAN THE MONEY THE KID OWES US.
WE SHOOT RICHIE RICH AND HIS FRIENDS AND DUMP THEM IN THE FURNACE.
WE EITHER TAKE THE EXTRAHUMAN ALIVE OR WE PUT HIM IN THE GROUND TOO.
I WANT THE EXTRAHUMAN!
I WANT ANOTHER SHOT AT HIM. IN THE CAGE THIS TIME.
NOBODY BEATS ME. I AM THE KING OF FIGHT!
THWAK
CRACK
I'M THE KING OF FIGHT. ME. I AM.
ODINSON IS THE GOD OF THE CAGE.
GOD DAMMIT.
JAMES?
WELL DON'T JUST STAND THERE WATCHING HIM ROT. TWO A'YOU DRAG HIM DOWN TO THE FURNACE WITH THE OTHERS AND GET RID OF HIM.

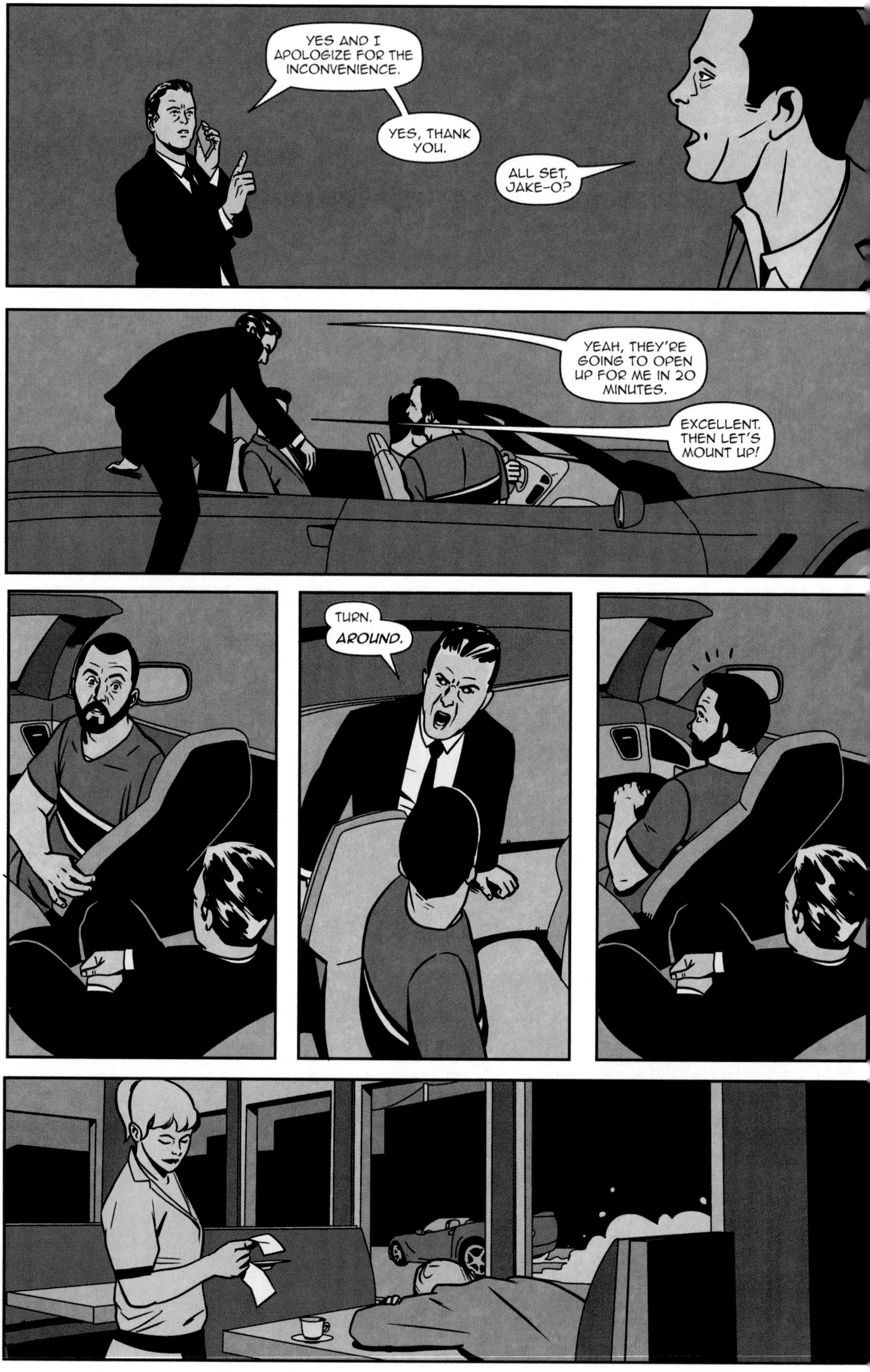
YES AND I APOLOGIZE FOR THE INCONVENIENCE.
YES, THANK YOU.
ALL SET, JAKE-O?
YEAH, THEY'RE GOING TO OPEN UP FOR ME IN 20 MINUTES.
EXCELLENT. THEN LET'S MOUNT UP!
TURN.
AROUND.

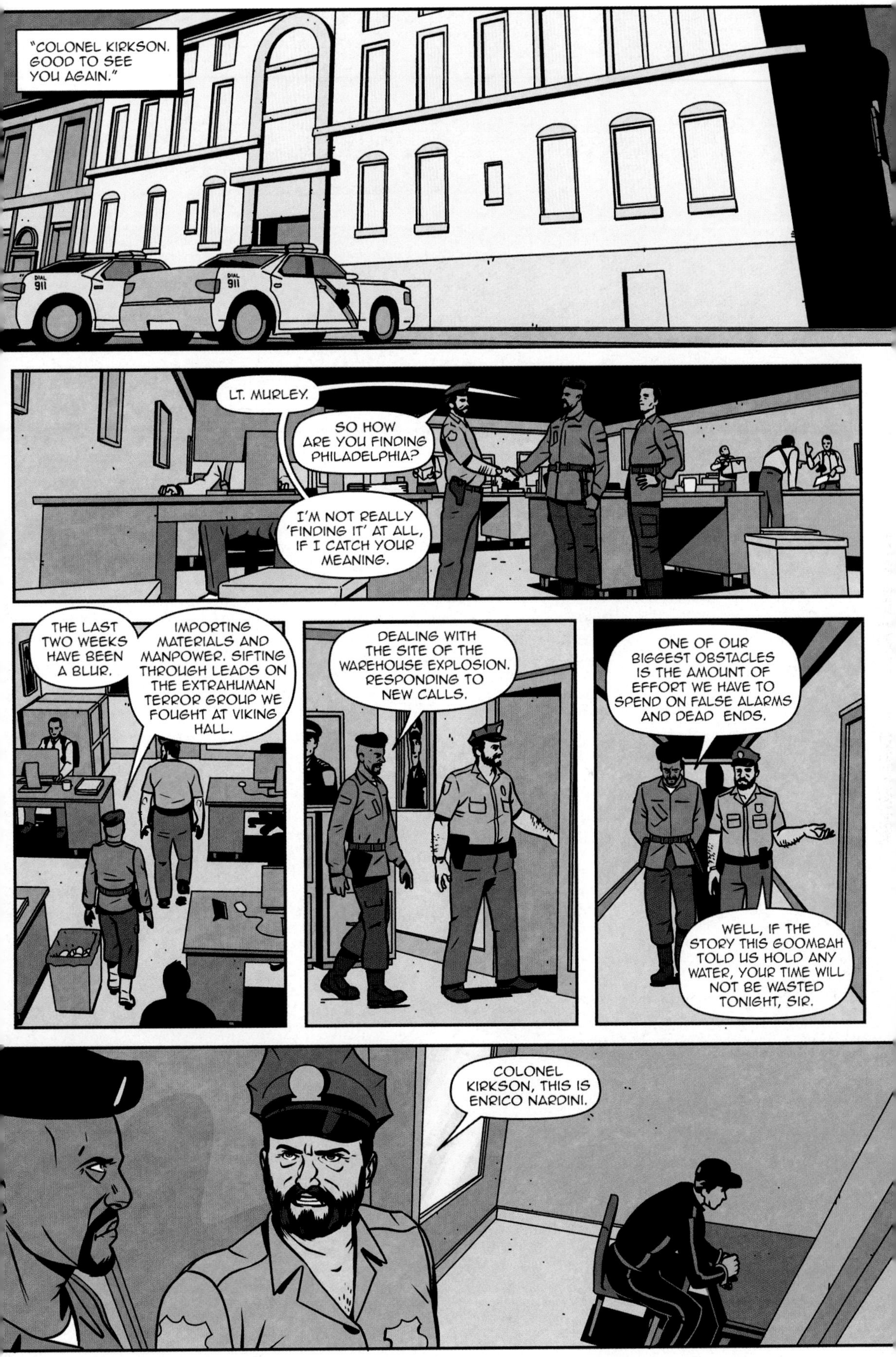
"COLONEL KIRKSON. GOOD TO SEE YOU AGAIN."
DIAL 911
DIAL 911
LT. MURLEY.
SO HOW ARE YOU FINDING PHILADELPHIA?
I'M NOT REALLY 'FINDING IT' AT ALL, IF I CATCH YOUR MEANING.
THE LAST TWO WEEKS HAVE BEEN A BLUR.
IMPORTING MATERIALS AND MANPOWER. SIFTING THROUGH LEADS ON THE EXTRAHUMAN TERROR GROUP WE FOUGHT AT VIKING HALL.
DEALING WITH THE SITE OF THE WAREHOUSE EXPLOSION. RESPONDING TO NEW CALLS.
ONE OF OUR BIGGEST OBSTACLES IS THE AMOUNT OF EFFORT WE HAVE TO SPEND ON FALSE ALARMS AND DEAD ENDS.
WELL, IF THE STORY THIS GOOMBAH TOLD US HOLD ANY WATER, YOUR TIME WILL NOT BE WASTED TONIGHT, SIR.
COLONEL KIRKSON, THIS IS ENRICO NARDINI.

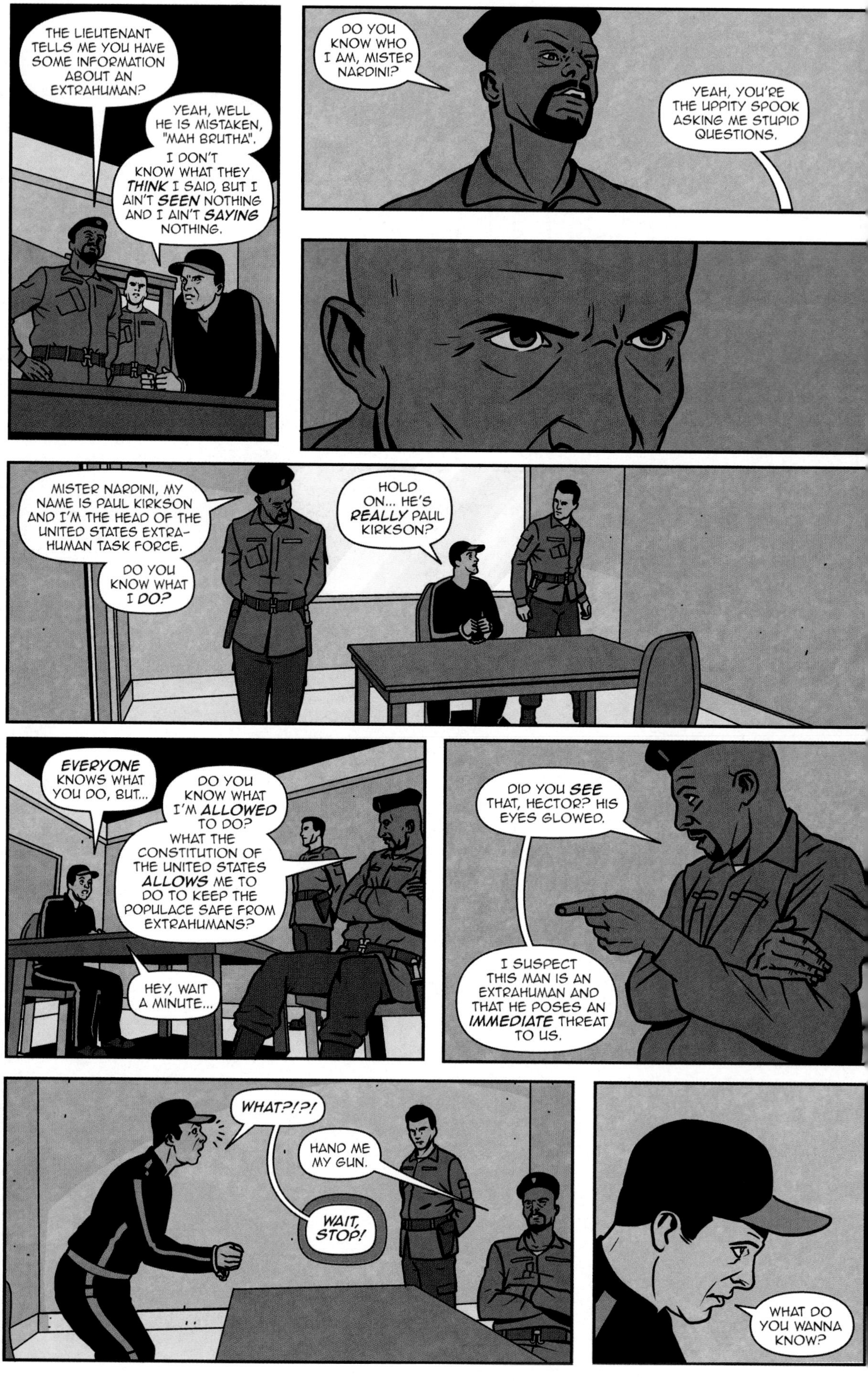
THE LIEUTENANT TELLS ME YOU HAVE SOME INFORMATION ABOUT AN EXTRAHUMAN?
YEAH, WELL HE IS MISTAKEN, "MAH BRUTHA".
I DON'T KNOW WHAT THEY *THINK* I SAID, BUT I AIN'T *SEEN* NOTHING AND I AIN'T *SAYING* NOTHING.
DO YOU KNOW WHO I AM, MISTER NARDINI?
YEAH, YOU'RE THE UPPITY SPOOK ASKING ME STUPID QUESTIONS.
MISTER NARDINI, MY NAME IS PAUL KIRKSON AND I'M THE HEAD OF THE UNITED STATES EXTRA-HUMAN TASK FORCE.
DO YOU KNOW WHAT I *DO?*
HOLD ON... HE'S *REALLY* PAUL KIRKSON?
EVERYONE KNOWS WHAT YOU DO, BUT...
DO YOU KNOW WHAT I'M *ALLOWED* TO DO? WHAT THE CONSTITUTION OF THE UNITED STATES *ALLOWS* ME TO DO TO KEEP THE POPULACE SAFE FROM EXTRAHUMANS?
HEY, WAIT A MINUTE...
DID YOU *SEE* THAT, HECTOR? HIS EYES GLOWED.
I SUSPECT THIS MAN IS AN EXTRAHUMAN AND THAT HE POSES AN *IMMEDIATE* THREAT TO US.
WHAT?!?!
HAND ME MY GUN.
WAIT, STOP!
WHAT DO YOU WANNA KNOW?

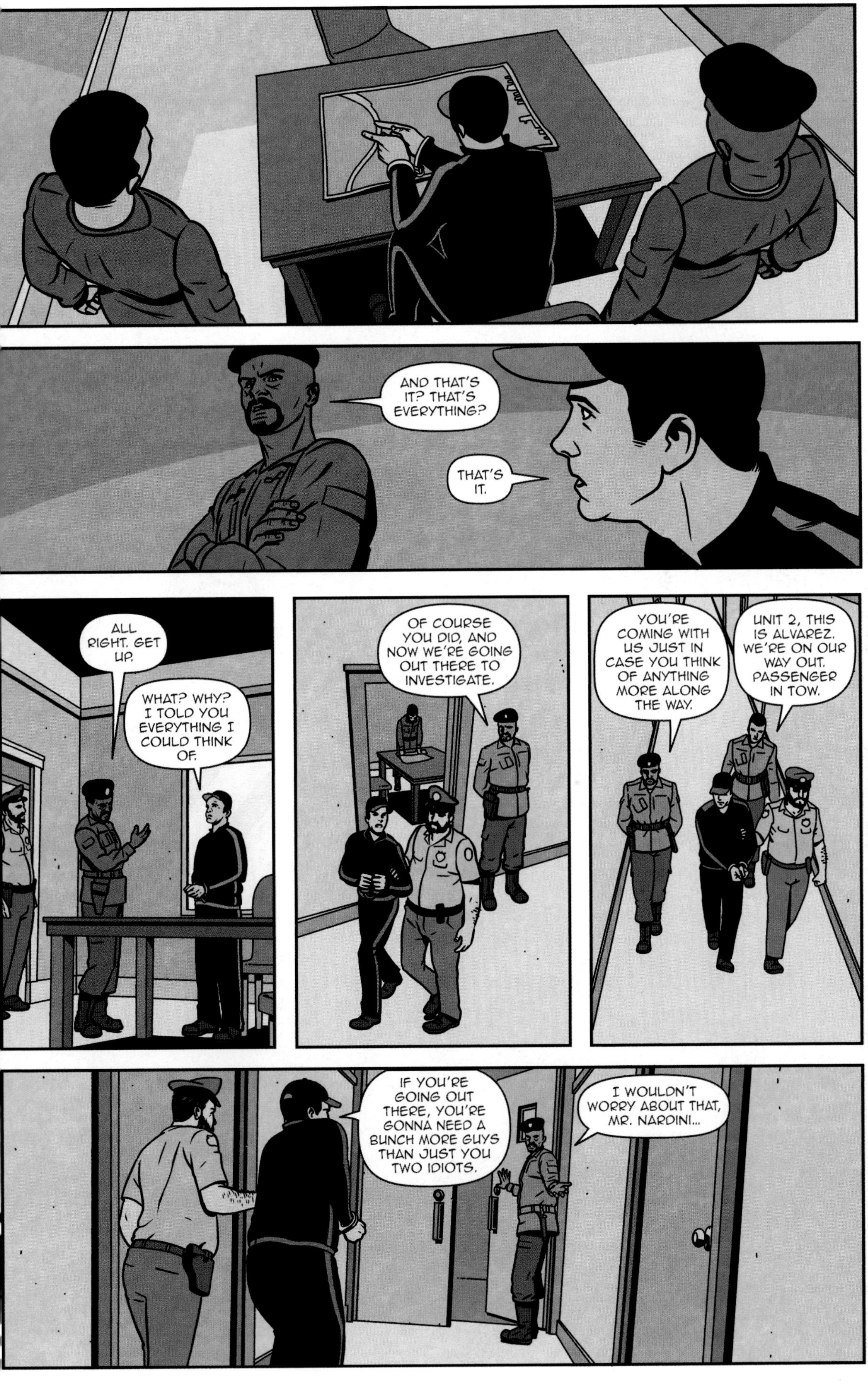
AND THAT'S IT? THAT'S EVERYTHING?
THAT'S IT.
ALL RIGHT. GET UP.
WHAT? WHY? I TOLD YOU EVERYTHING I COULD THINK OF.
OF COURSE YOU DID, AND NOW WE'RE GOING OUT THERE TO INVESTIGATE.
YOU'RE COMING WITH US JUST IN CASE YOU THINK OF ANYTHING MORE ALONG THE WAY.
UNIT 2, THIS IS ALVAREZ. WE'RE ON OUR WAY OUT. PASSENGER IN TOW.
IF YOU'RE GOING OUT THERE, YOU'RE GONNA NEED A BUNCH MORE GUYS THAN JUST YOU TWO IDIOTS.
I WOULDN'T WORRY ABOUT THAT, MR. NARDINI...

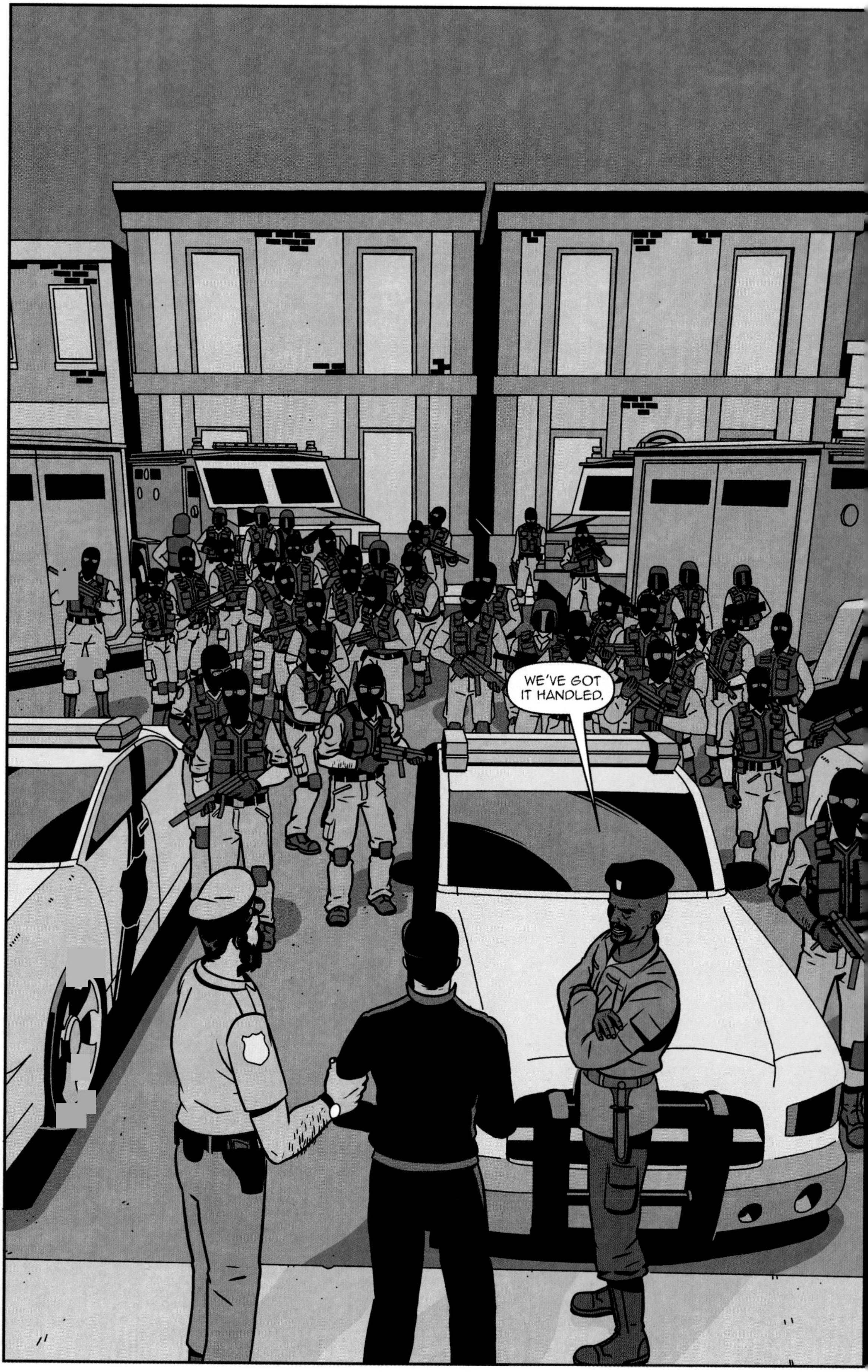
WE'VE GOT IT HANDLED.

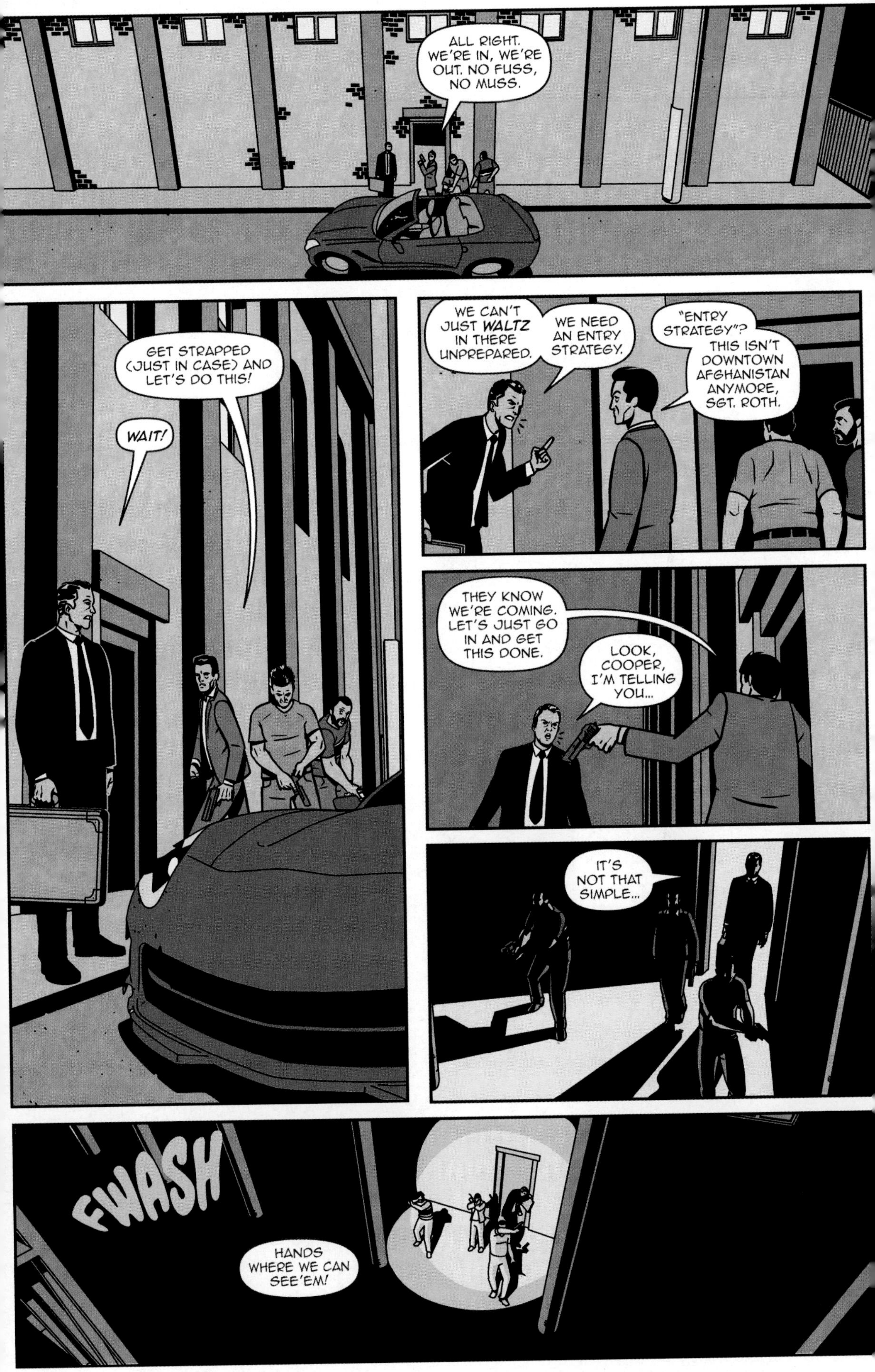

ALL RIGHT. WE'RE IN, WE'RE OUT. NO FUSS, NO MUSS.
GET STRAPPED (JUST IN CASE) AND LET'S DO THIS!
WAIT!
WE CAN'T JUST WALTZ IN THERE UNPREPARED.
WE NEED AN ENTRY STRATEGY.
"ENTRY STRATEGY"? THIS ISN'T DOWNTOWN AFGHANISTAN ANYMORE, SGT. ROTH.
THEY KNOW WE'RE COMING. LET'S JUST GO IN AND GET THIS DONE.
LOOK, COOPER, I'M TELLING YOU...
IT'S NOT THAT SIMPLE...
FWASH
HANDS WHERE WE CAN SEE'EM!

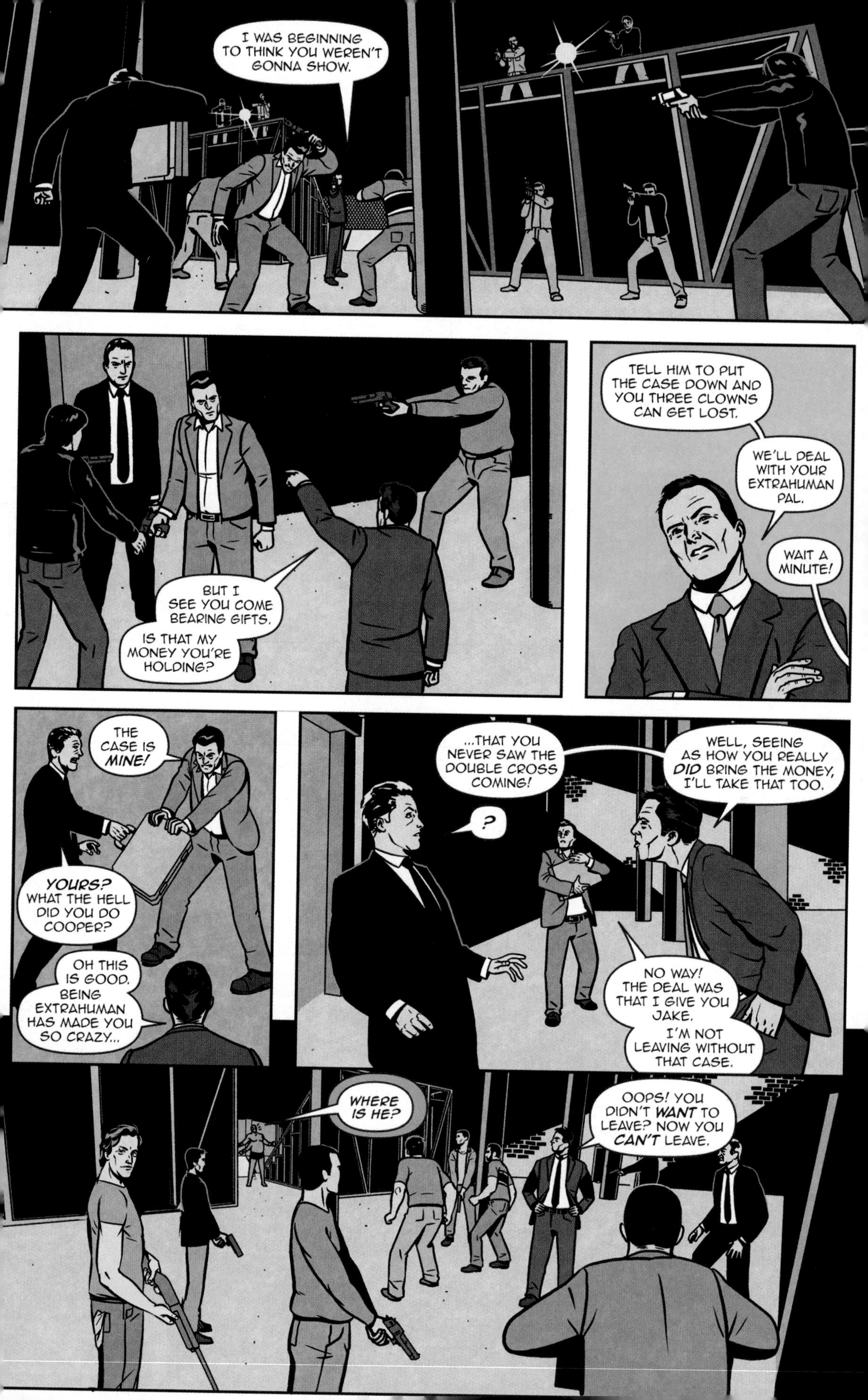
I WAS BEGINNING TO THINK YOU WEREN'T GONNA SHOW.
BUT I SEE YOU COME BEARING GIFTS.
IS THAT MY MONEY YOU'RE HOLDING?
TELL HIM TO PUT THE CASE DOWN AND YOU THREE CLOWNS CAN GET LOST.
WE'LL DEAL WITH YOUR EXTRAHUMAN PAL.
WAIT A MINUTE!
THE CASE IS MINE!
YOURS? WHAT THE HELL DID YOU DO COOPER?
OH THIS IS GOOD. BEING EXTRAHUMAN HAS MADE YOU SO CRAZY...
...THAT YOU NEVER SAW THE DOUBLE CROSS COMING!
WELL, SEEING AS HOW YOU REALLY DID BRING THE MONEY, I'LL TAKE THAT TOO.
?
NO WAY! THE DEAL WAS THAT I GIVE YOU JAKE.
I'M NOT LEAVING WITHOUT THAT CASE.
WHERE IS HE?
OOPS! YOU DIDN'T WANT TO LEAVE? NOW YOU CAN'T LEAVE.

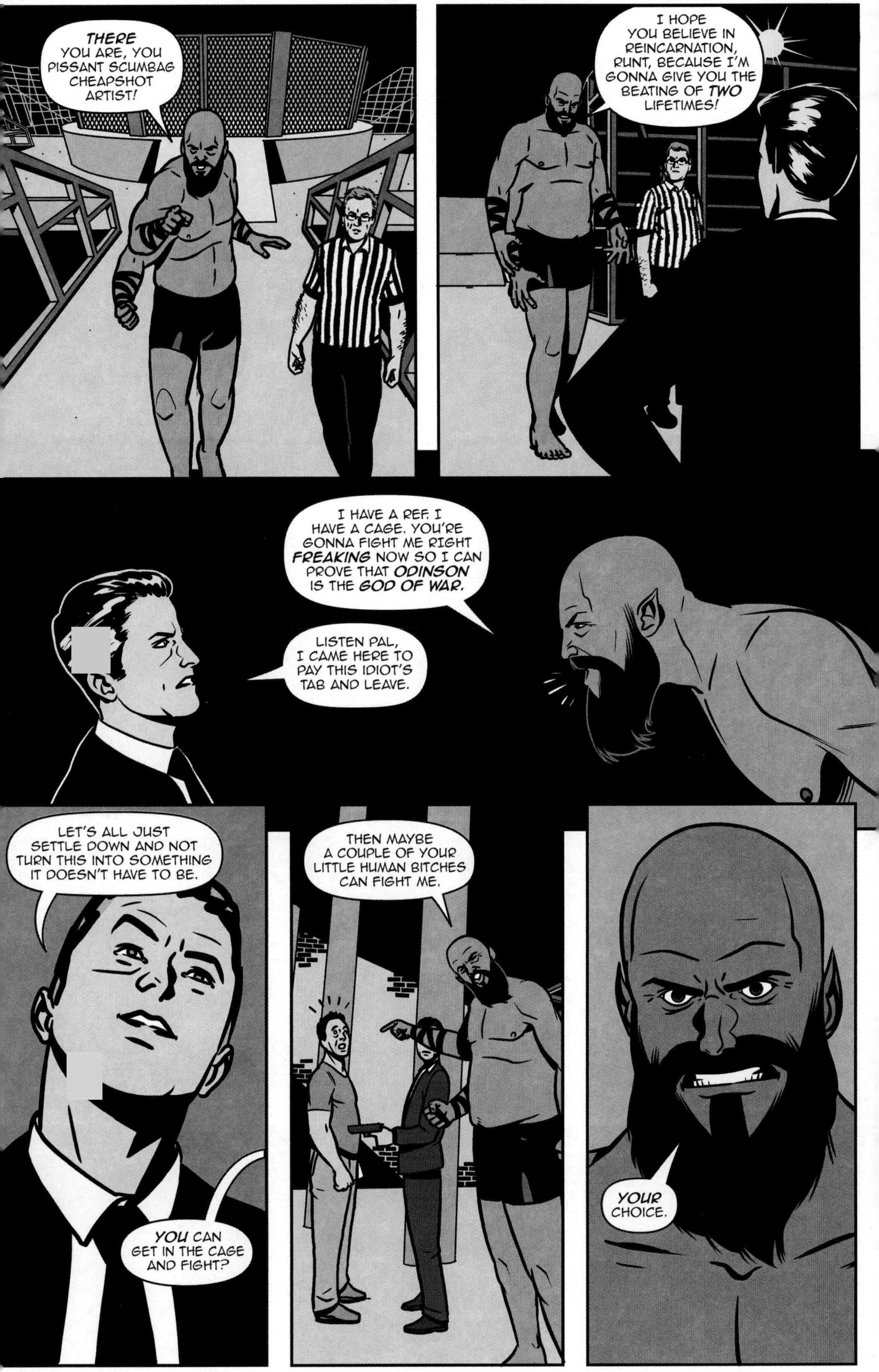
THERE YOU ARE, YOU PISSANT SCUMBAG CHEAPSHOT ARTIST!
I HOPE YOU BELIEVE IN REINCARNATION, RUNT, BECAUSE I'M GONNA GIVE YOU THE BEATING OF TWO LIFETIMES!
I HAVE A REF. I HAVE A CAGE. YOU'RE GONNA FIGHT ME RIGHT FREAKING NOW SO I CAN PROVE THAT ODINSON IS THE GOD OF WAR.
LISTEN PAL, I CAME HERE TO PAY THIS IDIOT'S TAB AND LEAVE.
LET'S ALL JUST SETTLE DOWN AND NOT TURN THIS INTO SOMETHING IT DOESN'T HAVE TO BE.
YOU CAN GET IN THE CAGE AND FIGHT?
THEN MAYBE A COUPLE OF YOUR LITTLE HUMAN BITCHES CAN FIGHT ME.
YOUR CHOICE.

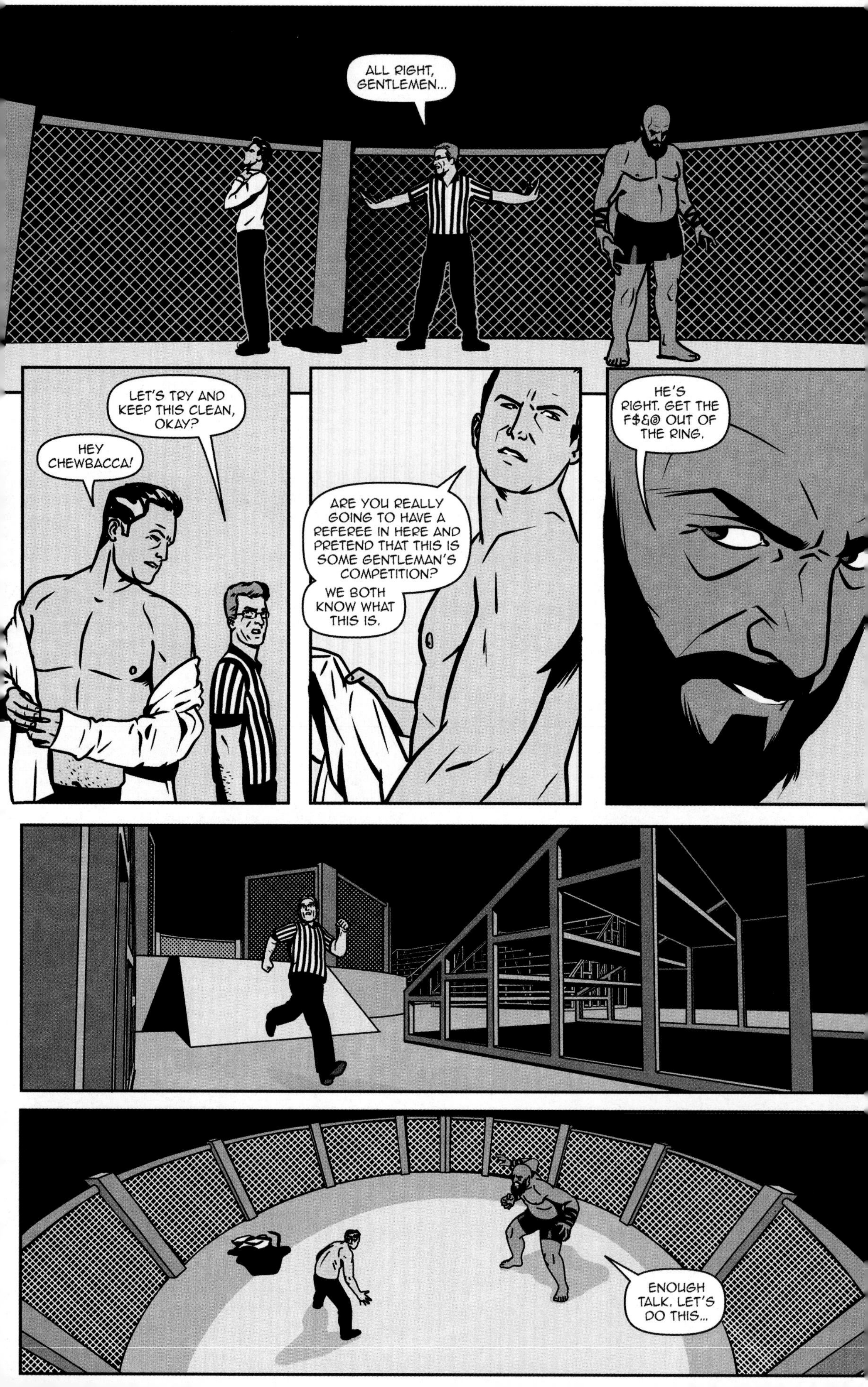
ALL RIGHT, GENTLEMEN...
LET'S TRY AND KEEP THIS CLEAN, OKAY?
HEY CHEWBACCA!
ARE YOU REALLY GOING TO HAVE A REFEREE IN HERE AND PRETEND THAT THIS IS SOME GENTLEMAN'S COMPETITION?
WE BOTH KNOW WHAT THIS IS.
HE'S RIGHT. GET THE F$&@ OUT OF THE RING.
ENOUGH TALK. LET'S DO THIS...

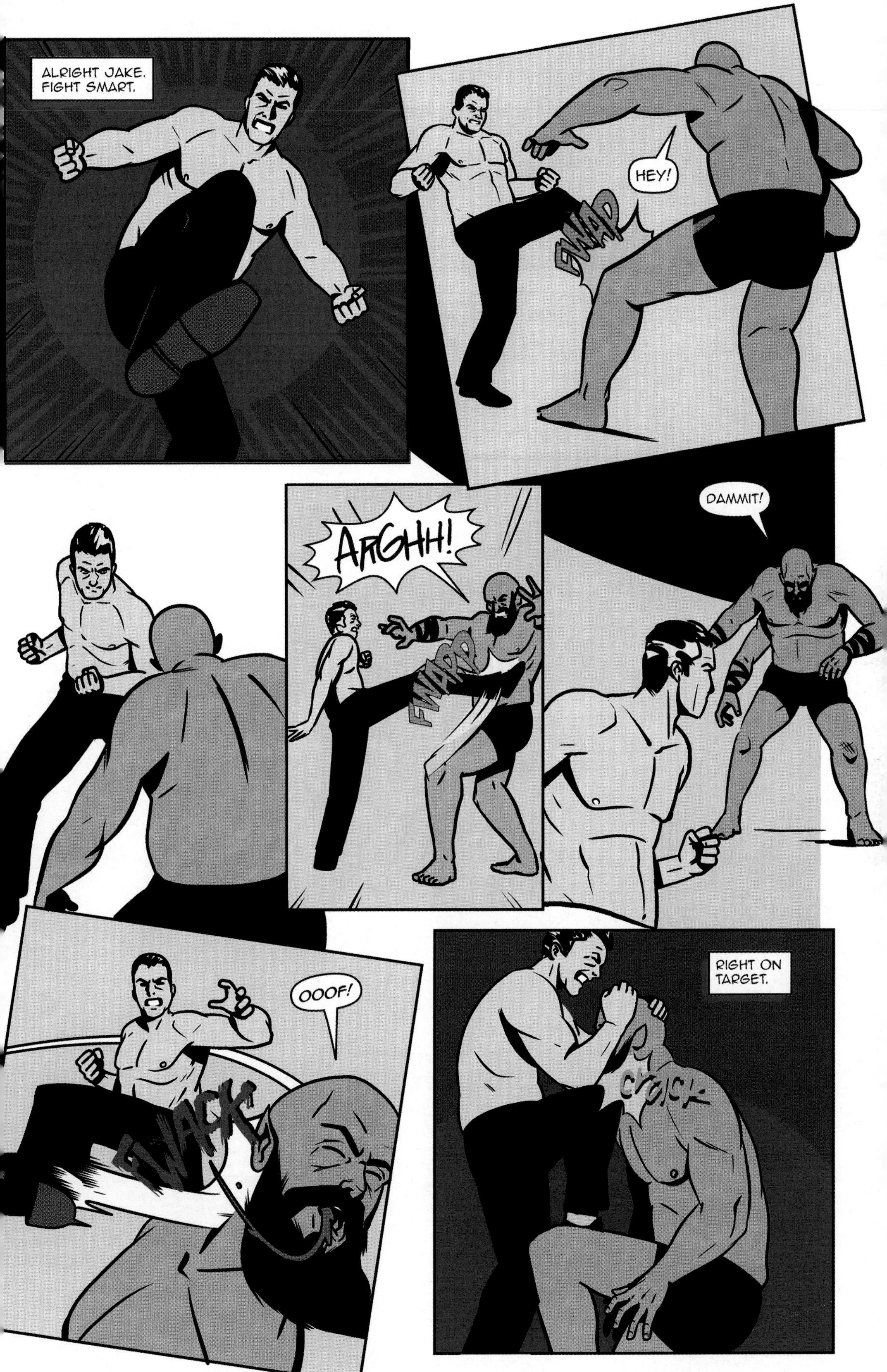
ALRIGHT JAKE. FIGHT SMART.
HEY!
FWAP
ARGHH!
FWAPP
DAMMIT!
OOOF!
FWACK
RIGHT ON TARGET.
CRACK

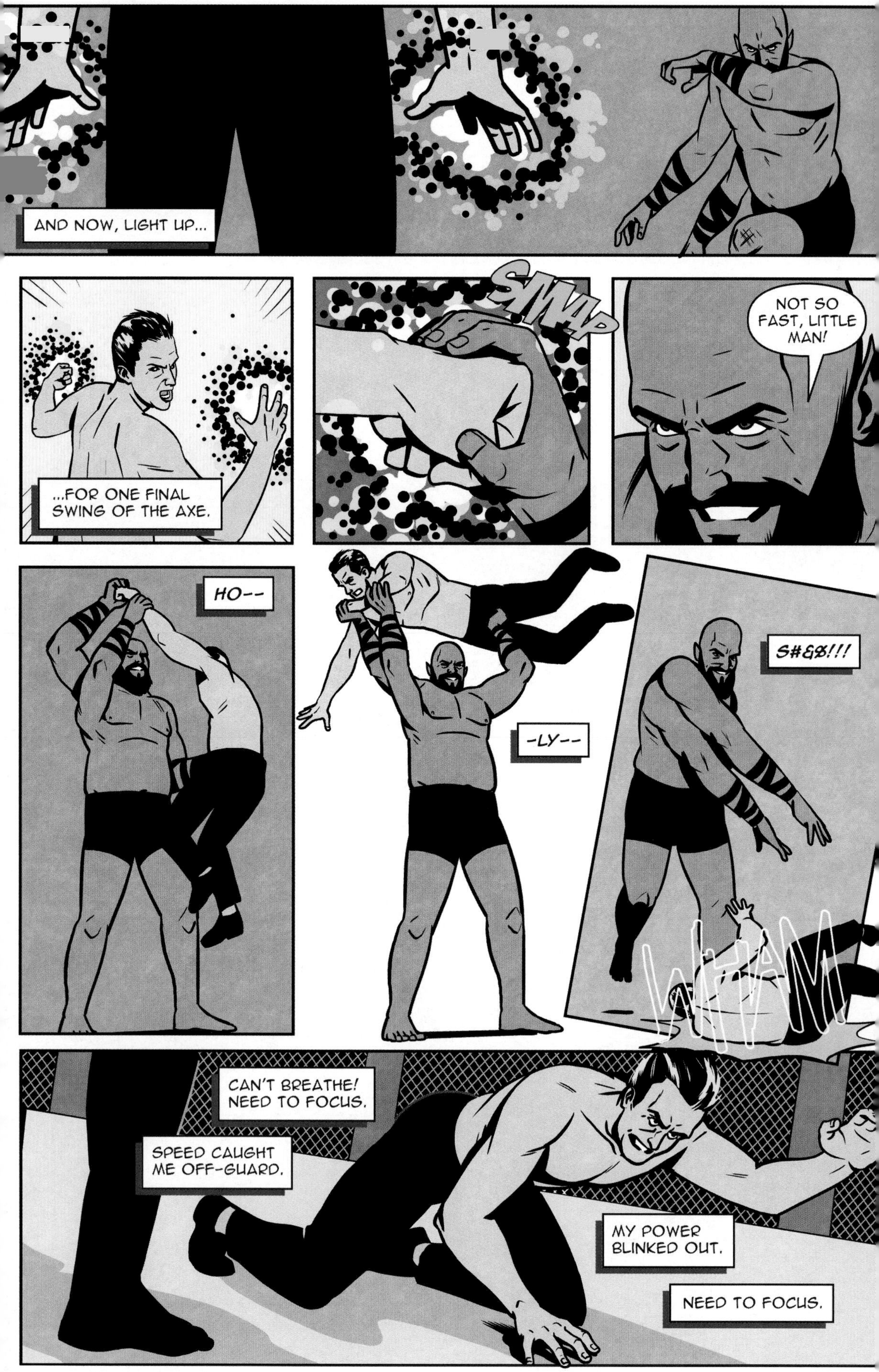
AND NOW, LIGHT UP...
...FOR ONE FINAL SWING OF THE AXE.
SNAP
NOT SO FAST, LITTLE MAN!
HO--
-LY--
S#&%!!!
WHAM
CAN'T BREATHE! NEED TO FOCUS.
SPEED CAUGHT ME OFF-GUARD.
MY POWER BLINKED OUT.
NEED TO FOCUS.

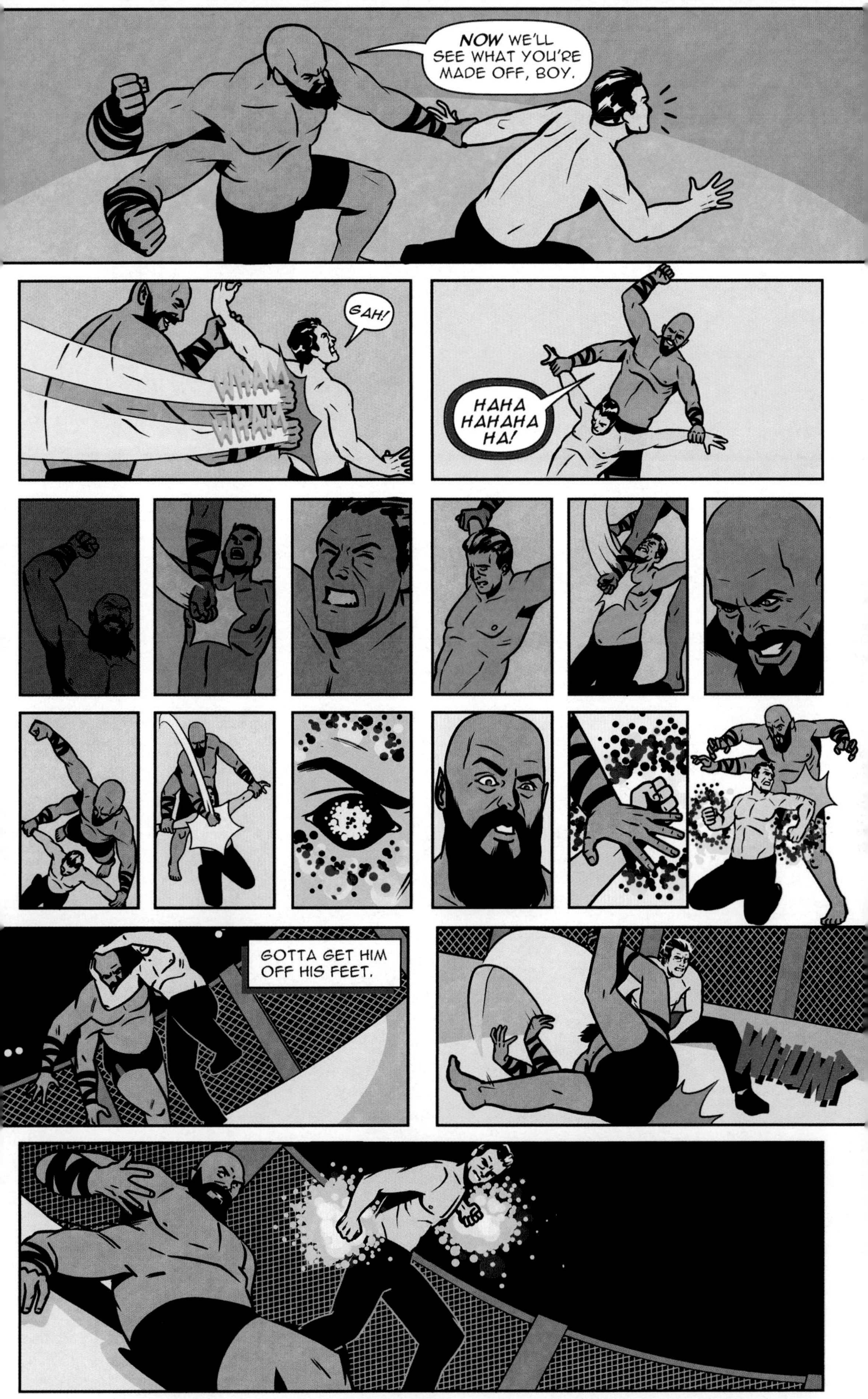
NOW WE'LL SEE WHAT YOU'RE MADE OFF, BOY.
GAH!
WHAM
WHAM
HAHA HAHAHA HA!
GOTTA GET HIM OFF HIS FEET.
WHUMP

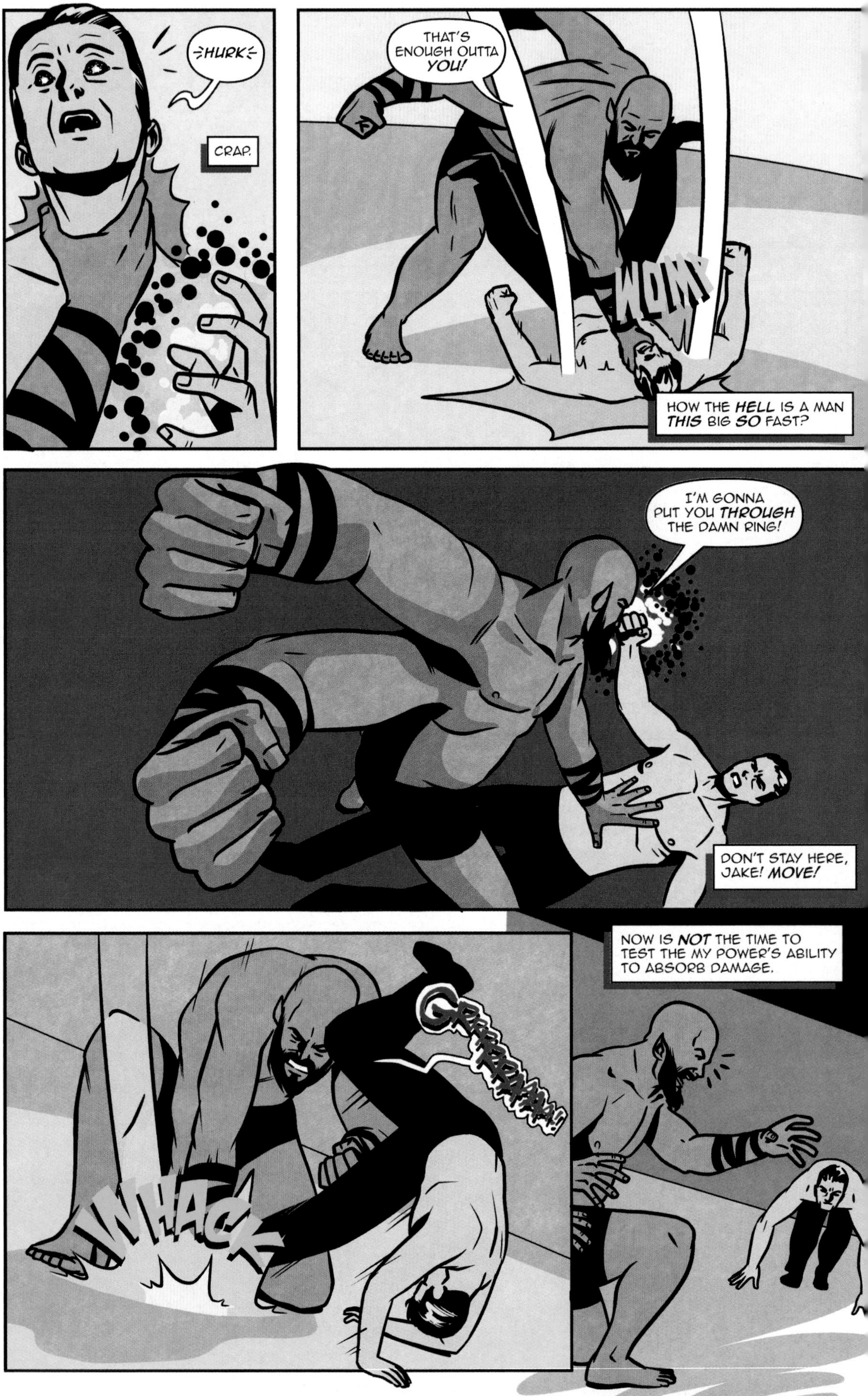
HURK
CRAP.
THAT'S ENOUGH OUTTA YOU!
WOMP
HOW THE HELL IS A MAN THIS BIG SO FAST?
I'M GONNA PUT YOU THROUGH THE DAMN RING!
DON'T STAY HERE, JAKE! MOVE!
NOW IS NOT THE TIME TO TEST THE MY POWER'S ABILITY TO ABSORB DAMAGE.
WHACK

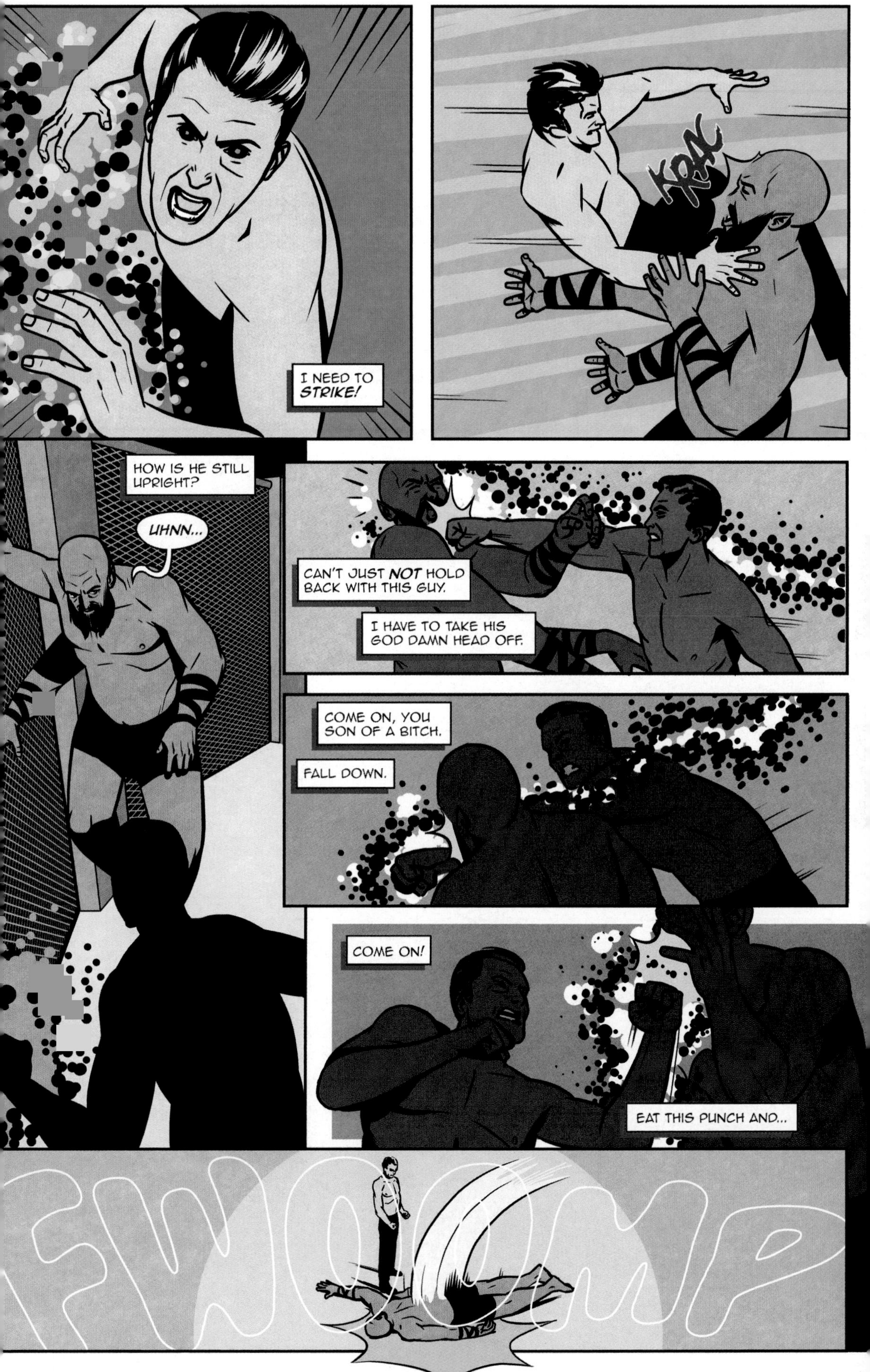
I NEED TO STRIKE!
KRAC
HOW IS HE STILL UPRIGHT?
UHNN...
CAN'T JUST NOT HOLD BACK WITH THIS GUY.
I HAVE TO TAKE HIS GOD DAMN HEAD OFF.
COME ON, YOU SON OF A BITCH.
FALL DOWN.
COME ON!
EAT THIS PUNCH AND...
FWOOMP

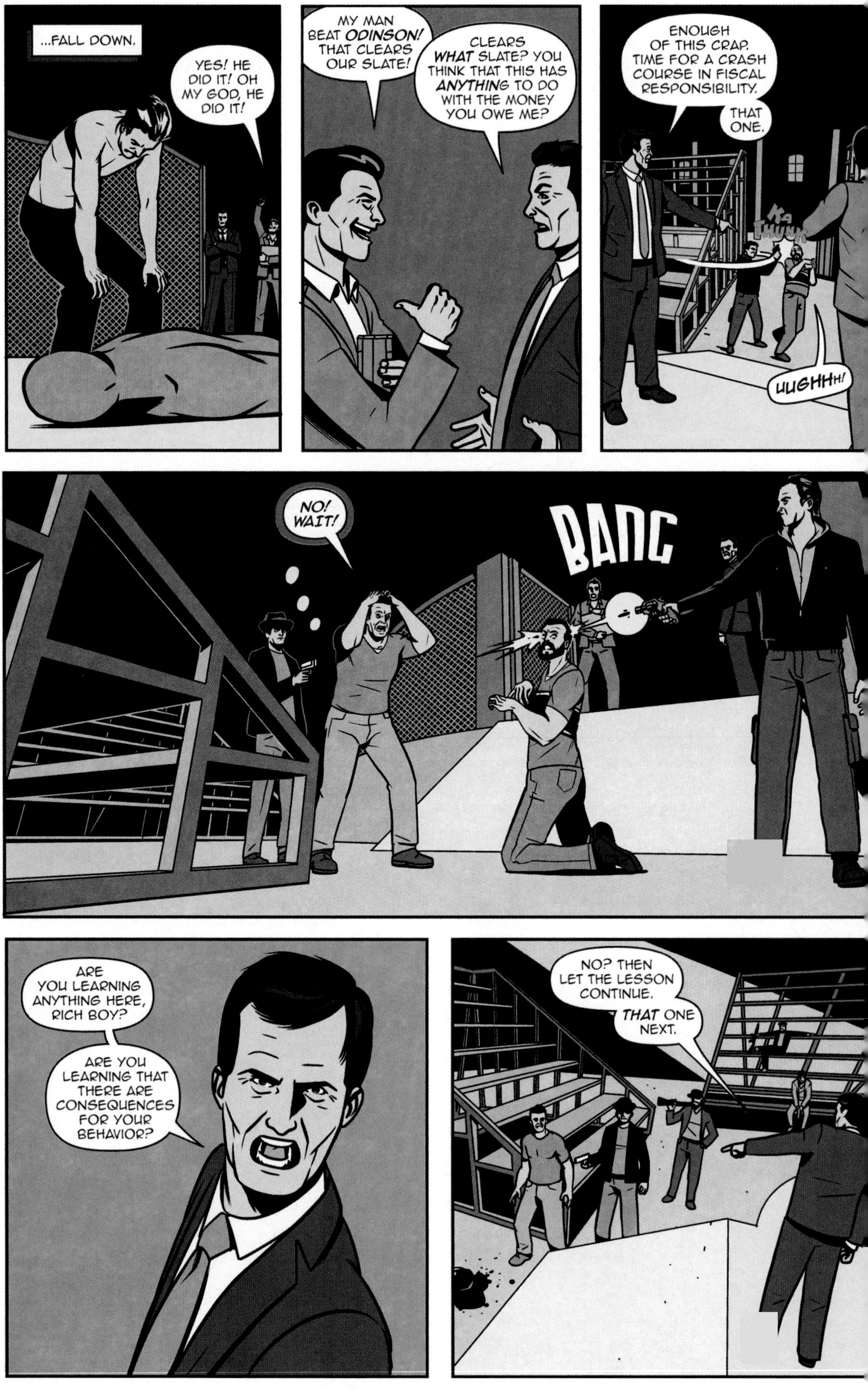
...FALL DOWN.
YES! HE DID IT! OH MY GOD, HE DID IT!
MY MAN BEAT ODINSON! THAT CLEARS OUR SLATE!
CLEARS WHAT SLATE? YOU THINK THAT THIS HAS ANYTHING TO DO WITH THE MONEY YOU OWE ME?
ENOUGH OF THIS CRAP. TIME FOR A CRASH COURSE IN FISCAL RESPONSIBILITY.
THAT ONE.
KA THUNK
UUGHHH!
NO! WAIT!
BANG
ARE YOU LEARNING ANYTHING HERE, RICH BOY?
ARE YOU LEARNING THAT THERE ARE CONSEQUENCES FOR YOUR BEHAVIOR?
NO? THEN LET THE LESSON CONTINUE.
THAT ONE NEXT.

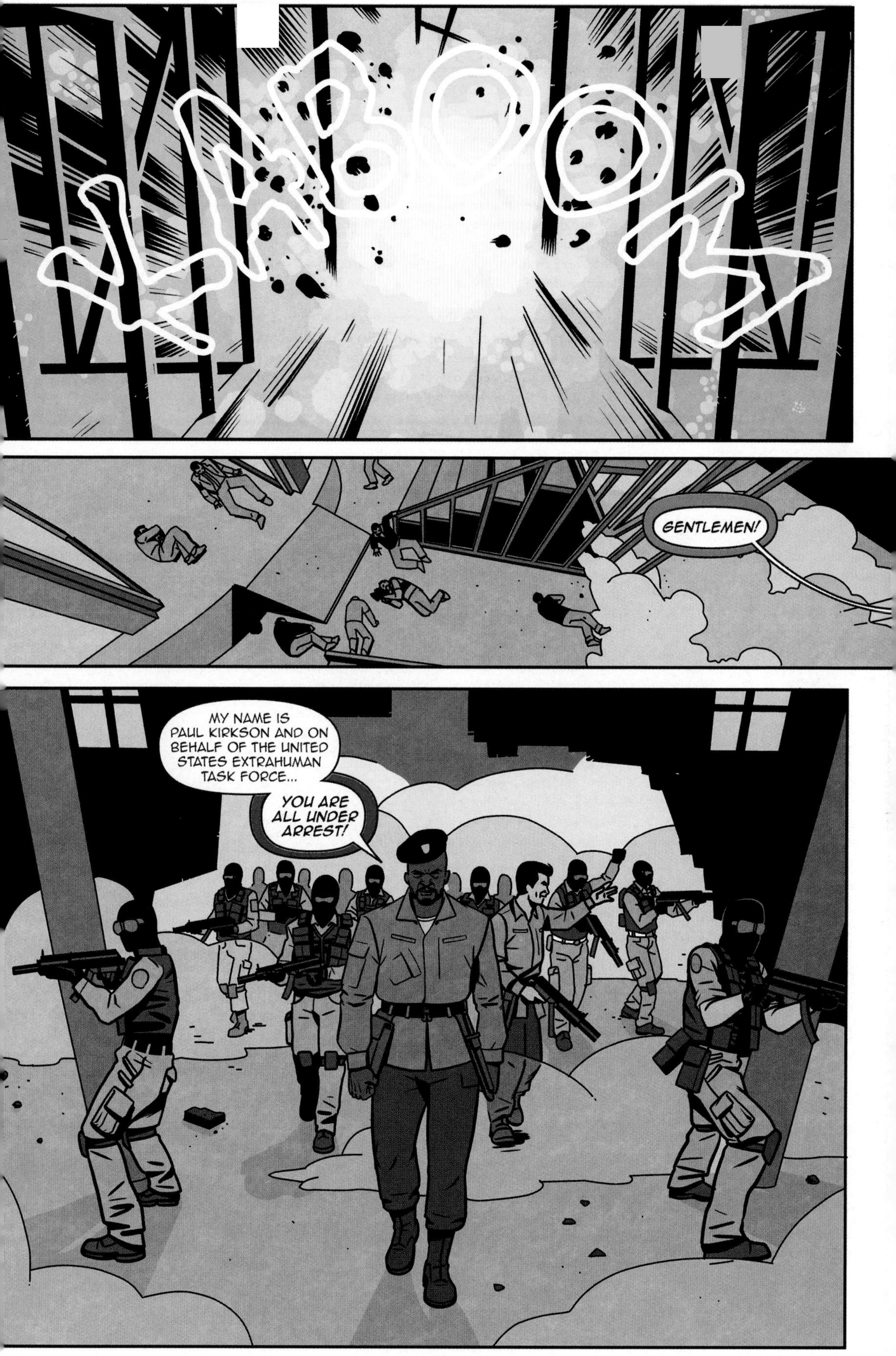
KABOOM
GENTLEMEN!
MY NAME IS PAUL KIRKSON AND ON BEHALF OF THE UNITED STATES EXTRAHUMAN TASK FORCE...
YOU ARE ALL UNDER ARREST!

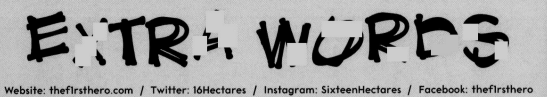

EXTRA WORDS

Website: thef1rsthero.com / Twitter: 16Hectares / Instagram: SixteenHectares / Facebook: thef1rsthero
Questions, comments, need some life advice? Contact us directly at sixteenhectares@gmail.com

Writing comics is not a hobby for me. It's not something I'm doing in my free time as a lark. I very much want to make writing
full-time career. I've read articles from people I respect and heard good friends say that comics aren't something you earn a liv
at outside of working for Marvel or DC. Can that be right? Jim Zubkavich, in particular, has posted some well-written, w
informed material on the economic realities of making comics on his website, www.jimzub.com. The numbers are daunting.
struggle is real, folks. But, and please dear reader, forgive me this cliche... I'm in it to win it.

For me, that means creating more and varied new ideas and then shopping them to and making deals with a variety of publish
Climbing the industry ladder and maybe earning a shot at a deal with Marvel or DC. (Can I own up to something? I tried trol
Marvel Comics' E-I-C Axel Alonso on Twitter a couple of weeks as a response to an assertion in a Comic Book Resources interv
that Marvel had a "noticeable lack of Black creators... specifically Black writers...") But, it also means cultivating a loyal audience
my creator-owned properties in hopes that one or two or three on-going series do well enough financially to provide that income

THE F1RST HERO is my passion project. It is also my foot in the industry's front door. Over the next few months, I'll be working h
with the lovely and talented Mr. Fred C Stresing and a number of exciting new artists to force that industry door wide open, bo
inside and steal the silverware. (Yes, I actually am looking at the start of my writing career as smash-and-grab caper.) And,
course, everything I do to garner attention for my other projects should help bring more attention to THE F1RST HERO as well.

* * *

On Wednesday August 12th, the Silver Snail Comic Shop in
downtown Toronto played host to a very nice little in-store
signing session, featuring yours truly, in honour of the
release of THE FIRST HERO: FIGHT FOR YOUR LIFE #1. My
thanks, as always to George, Mark, Kody and Cameron and
the store staff for their friendship and constant support of
my efforts in the field of professional comic bookery.

* * *

Speaking of signings and appearances, my "convention
season" is about to begin. This year's schedule includes Fan
Expo Canada here in Toronto, Wizard World in Pittsburgh and
my now-annual trip to New York Comic Con. This will be my
fourth year attending NYCC, my eighth or ninth at Fan Expo
and my first time attending any of Wizard World's events
anywhere.

ANTHONY'S AUTOGRAPH TABLE AT THE SILVER SNAIL

I've likely mentioned before that attending conventions as a guest is actually one of the things I was most looking forward to e
before signing with Action Lab to publish THE FIRST HERO. My friend Steve Corino playfully refers to this type of thing as "bein
merch table hell" but I love it. In fact, I want to do MORE of it. Attend more conventions, meet more fans, be a speaker on m
discussion panels (I am GREAT on panels, by the way!) and, hopefully, get my work into the hands of more and more readers.

As I type this, Fan Expo is only four days away. I've been working hard to get myself ready for the show, as has Danny Zab
This will be Danny's first ever convention as more than a ticket-buying customer and I'm excited for him to have this experie
Next issue, I promise to have some photos from the show to share with you. Danny will also be attending NYCC with me as a g
of Action Lab.

* * *

Current Listening: Committed to the Crime by Chaos Chaos, Royal Blood by Royal Blood and Run The Jewels 2 by Killer Mike & El-
Current Viewing: Rick & Morty: Season 2, Mr. Robot, Last Week Tonight with John Oliver, Kevin From Work and Coronation Stree
Current Doings: Lego Modular Buildings. (How much Lego? All. Bring me ALL THE LEGO.)

* * *

Next month: The exciting conclusion of THE F1RST HERO: FIGHT FOR YOUR LIFE. Jake has survived his battle with the monstrous
killer, Odinson, but can he and the Horsemen escape when Col. Paul Kirkson brings the full weight of the United States Extrahum
Task Force down on the scene? Come back in 30 days to find out!

Thank
Anthony Ruttga
Toronto, 30 August

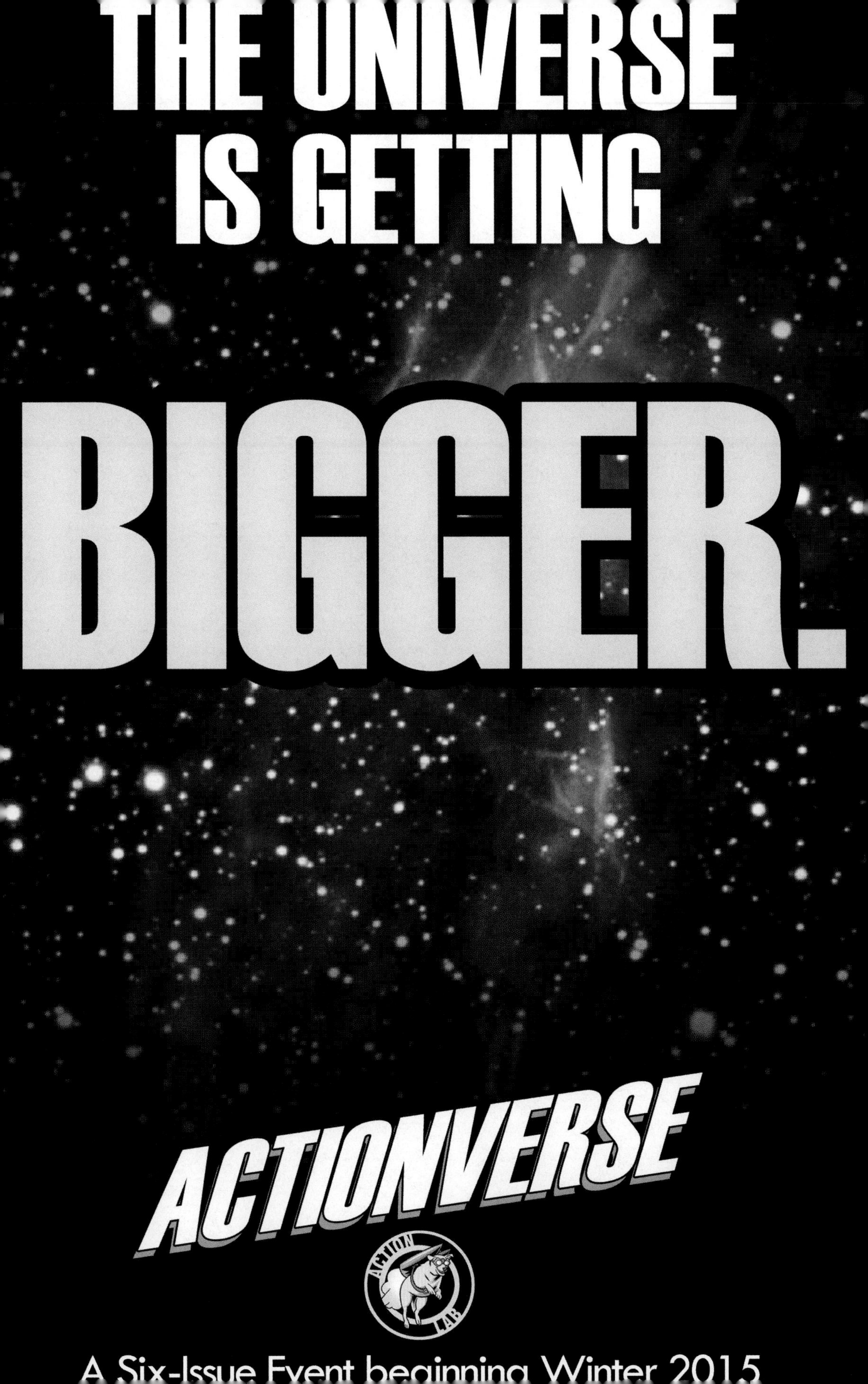
THE UNIVERSE
IS GETTING
BIGGER.
ACTIONVERSE
ACTION LAB
A Six-Issue Event beginning Winter 2015

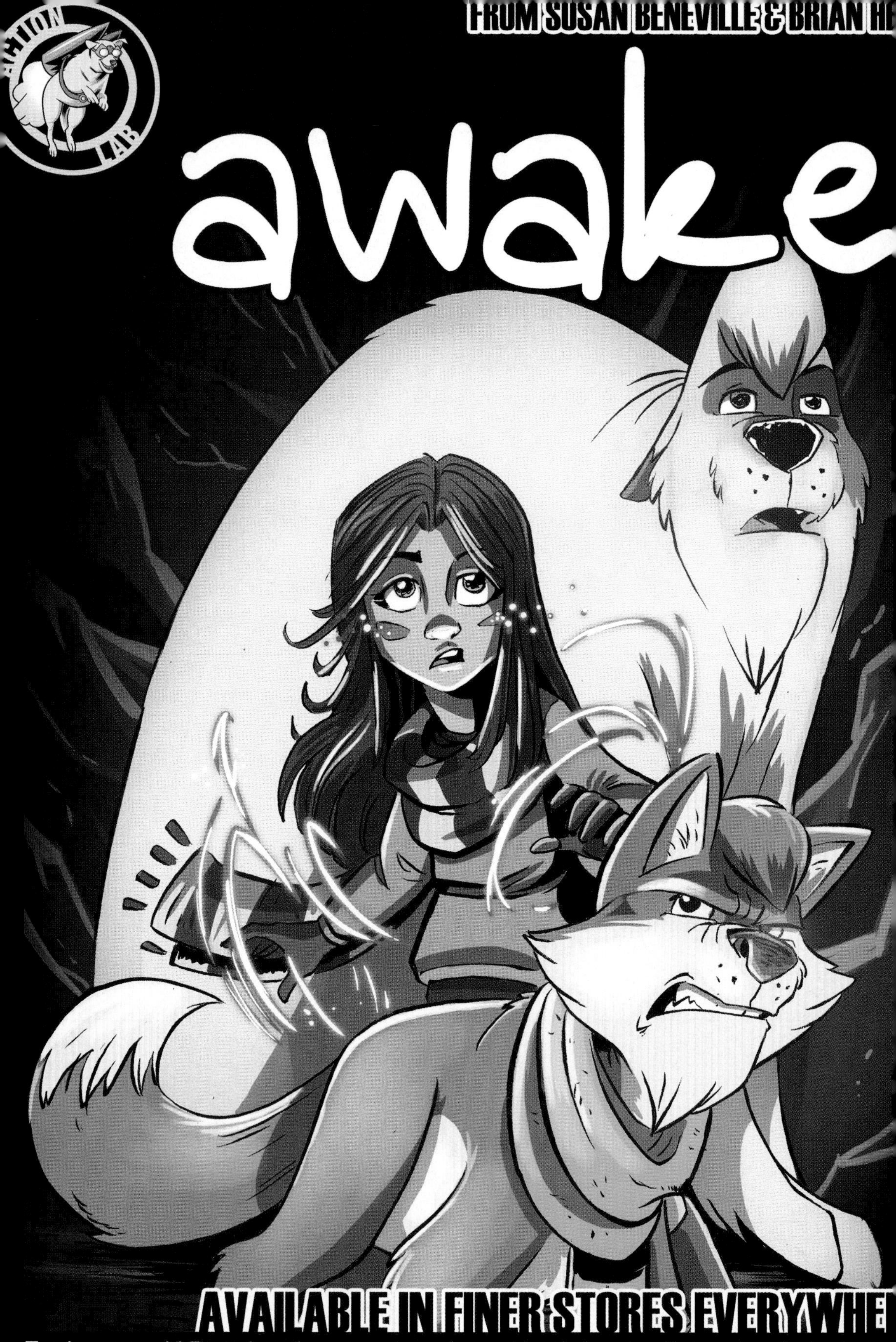

ACTION LAB
FROM SUSAN BENEVILLE & BRIAN HE
awake
AVAILABLE IN FINER STORES EVERYWHE

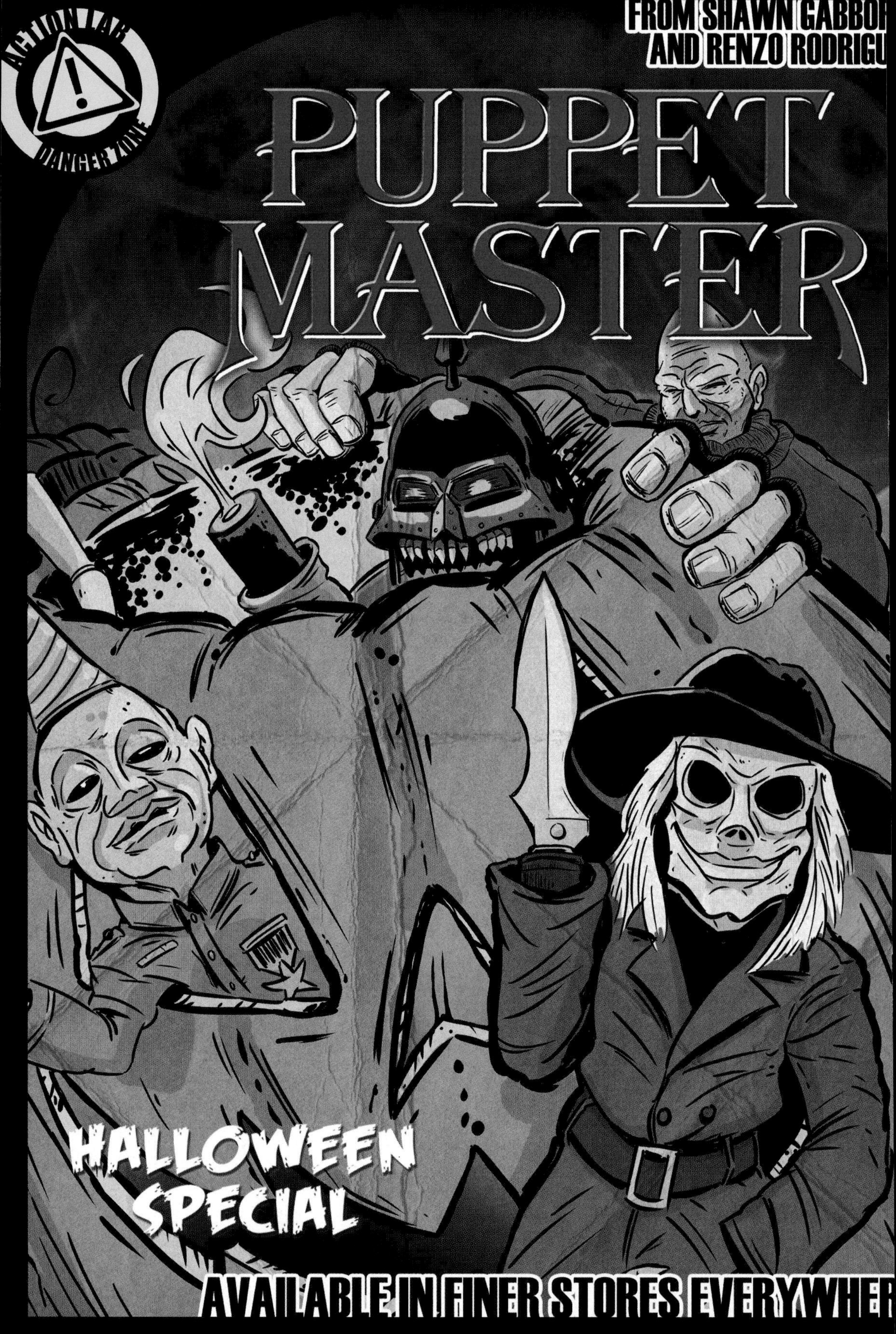

ACTION LAB
DANGER ZONE
FROM SHAWN GABBOR
AND RENZO RODRIGU
PUPPET MASTER
HALLOWEEN SPECIAL
AVAILABLE IN FINER STORES EVERYWHER

Halloween, 1988. The girls of Pi Kappa Sig are preparing for the annual Halloween bash when a late trick-or-treater brings their plans to a screeching halt. Now the Puppets are loose in the sorority house! Blood, guts and babes! Happy Halloween, Puppet Master sorority style!

F1rst Hero - Action Lab
www.actionlabcomics.com
00711
7 00465 77238 1

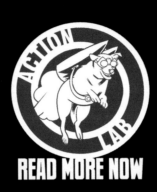

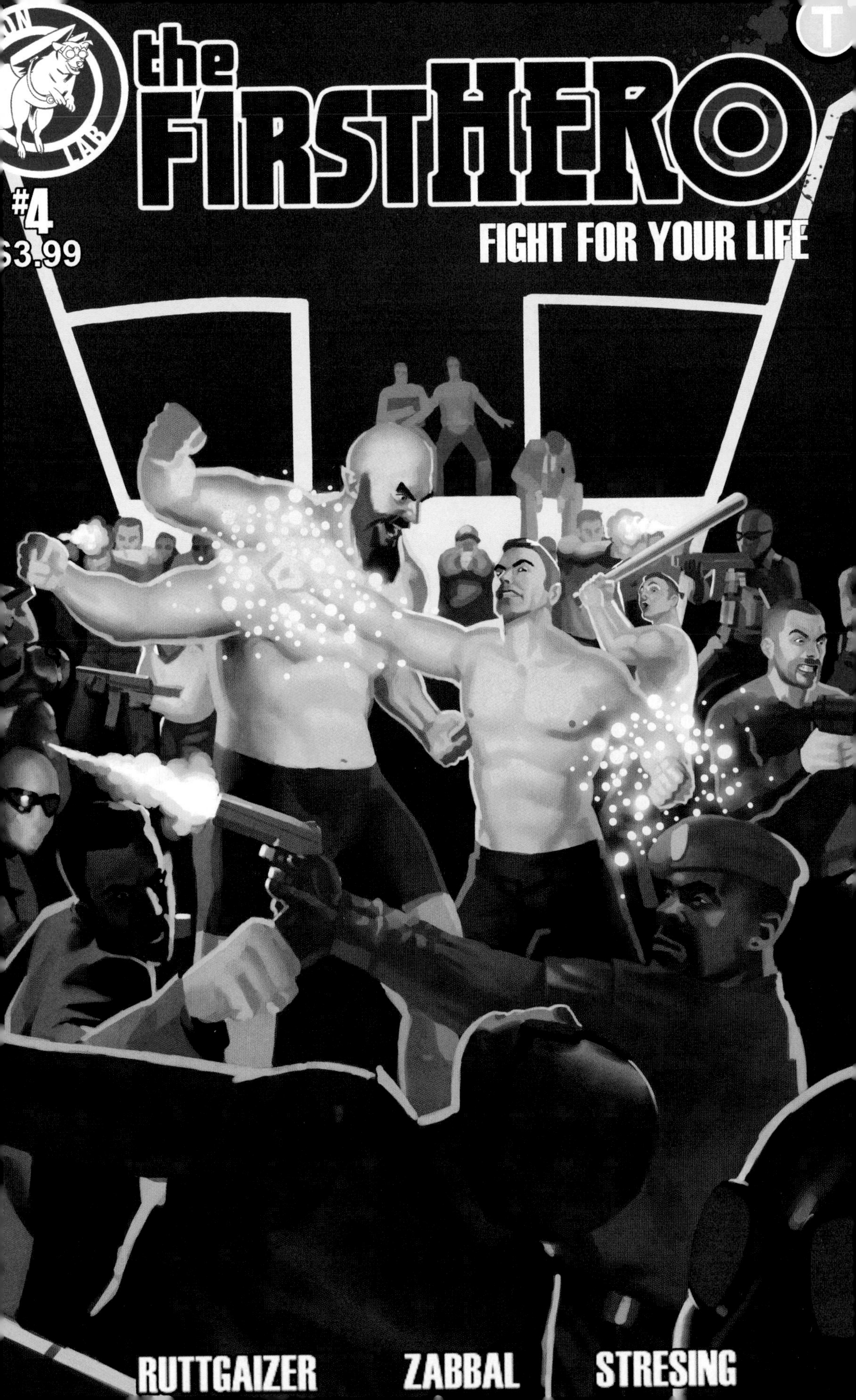the FIRSTHERO
T
#4
$3.99
FIGHT FOR YOUR LIFE
RUTTGAIZER
ZABBAL
STRESING

FROM ALL-AGES TO MATURE READERS
ACTION LAB HAS YOU COVERED.

 **Appropriate for everyone.**

 **Appropriate for age 9 and up. Absent of profanity or adult content.**

 **Suggested for 12 and Up. Comics with this rating are comparable to a PG-13 movie rating. Recommended for our teen and young adult readers.**

 **Appropriate for older teens. Similar to Teen, but featuring more mature themes and/or more graphic imagery.**

 **Contains extreme viloence and some nudity. Basically the Rated-R of comics.**

FIND YOUR NEW FAVORITE COMICS.

ACTION LAB ENTERTAINMENT PROUDLY PRESENTS

the FIRSTHERO

VOLUME 2: FIGHT FOR YOUR LIFE

CHAPTER EIGHT: CRAZY PLANS AND SCHEMES

for SIXTEEN HECTARES AND A MOOSE, INK.

Created/Written by **ANTHONY RUTTGAIZER**
Cover/Interior Art by **DANNY ZABBAL**
Letters/Colors by **FRED C. STRESING**

for ACTION LAB ENTERTAINMENT

BRYAN SEATON Publisher
KEVIN FREEMAN President
SHAWN GABBORIN Editor-in-Chief
DAVE DWONCH Creative Driector
JIM DIETZ Social Media Director
JAMAL IGLE Director of Marketing
VITO DELSANTE Director of Marketing
COLLEEN BOYD Associate Editor
CHAD CICCONI Three-Armed Psychopath

For More Info, visit SixteenHectares.com
Read More Now at ActionLabComics.com

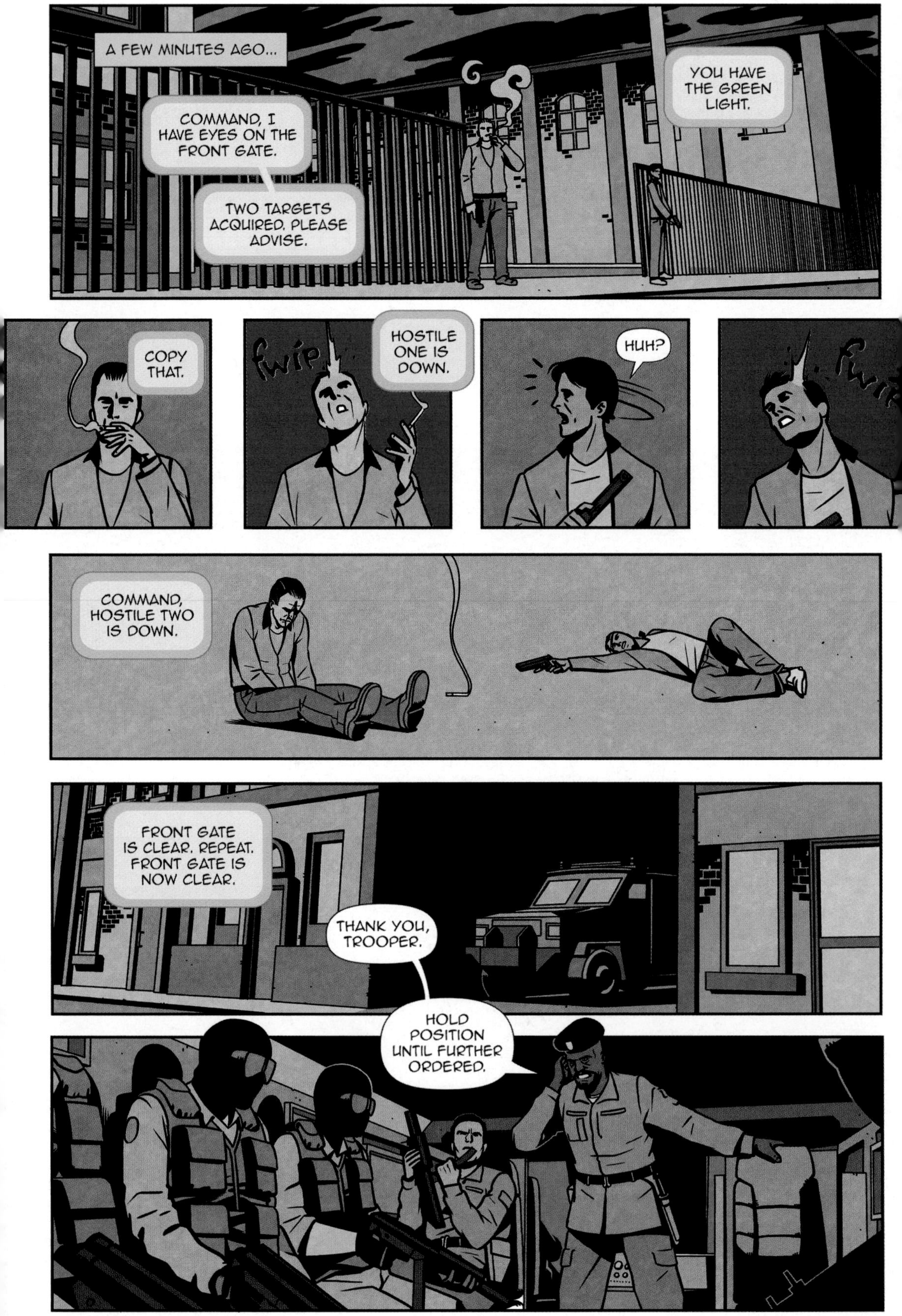
A FEW MINUTES AGO...
COMMAND, I HAVE EYES ON THE FRONT GATE.
TWO TARGETS ACQUIRED. PLEASE ADVISE.
YOU HAVE THE GREEN LIGHT.
COPY THAT.
fwip
HOSTILE ONE IS DOWN.
HUH?
fwip
COMMAND, HOSTILE TWO IS DOWN.
FRONT GATE IS CLEAR. REPEAT. FRONT GATE IS NOW CLEAR.
THANK YOU, TROOPER.
HOLD POSITION UNTIL FURTHER ORDERED.

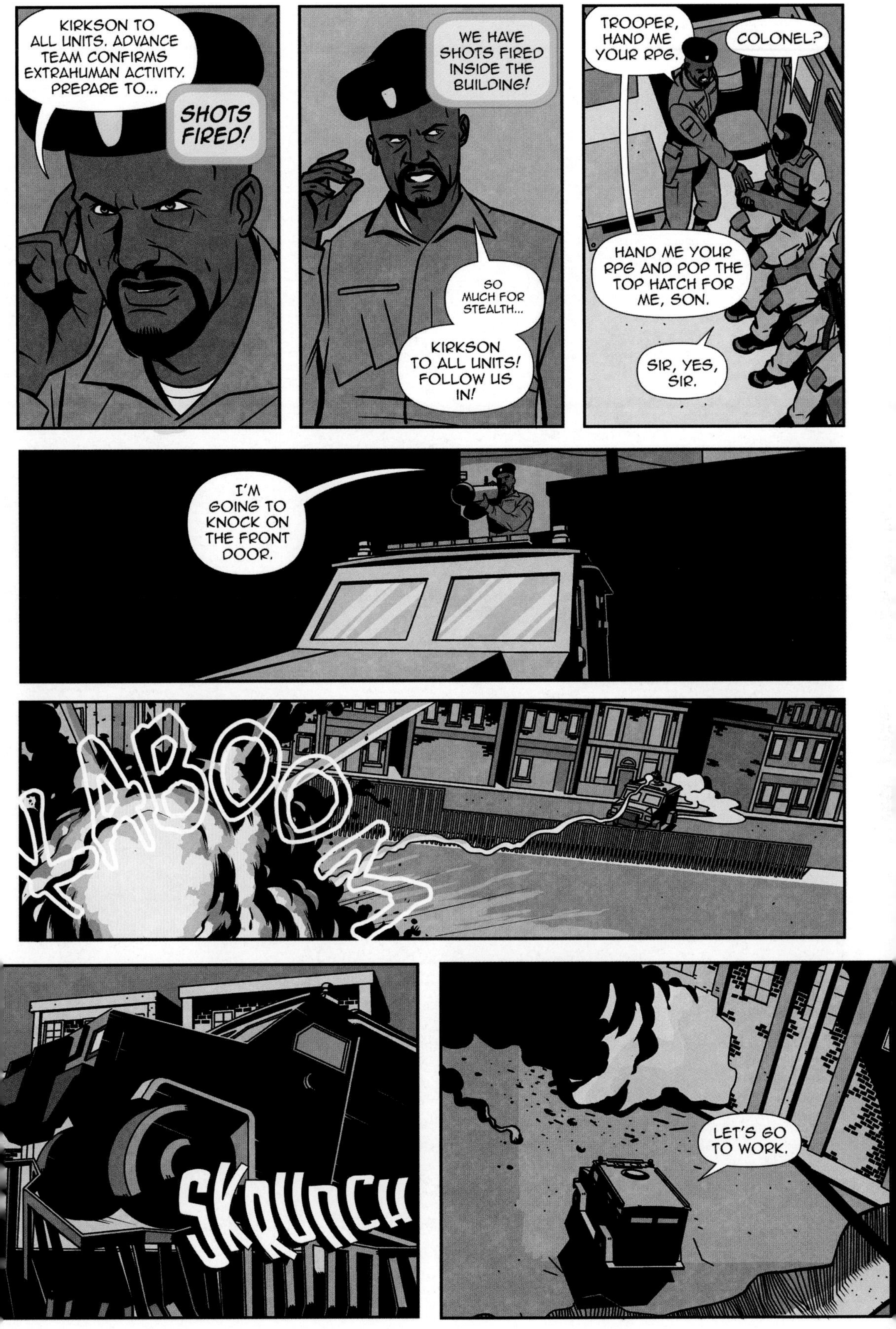
KIRKSON TO ALL UNITS. ADVANCE TEAM CONFIRMS EXTRAHUMAN ACTIVITY. PREPARE TO...
SHOTS FIRED!
WE HAVE SHOTS FIRED INSIDE THE BUILDING!
SO MUCH FOR STEALTH...
KIRKSON TO ALL UNITS! FOLLOW US IN!
TROOPER, HAND ME YOUR RPG.
COLONEL?
HAND ME YOUR RPG AND POP THE TOP HATCH FOR ME, SON.
SIR, YES, SIR.
I'M GOING TO KNOCK ON THE FRONT DOOR.
SKRUNCH
LET'S GO TO WORK.

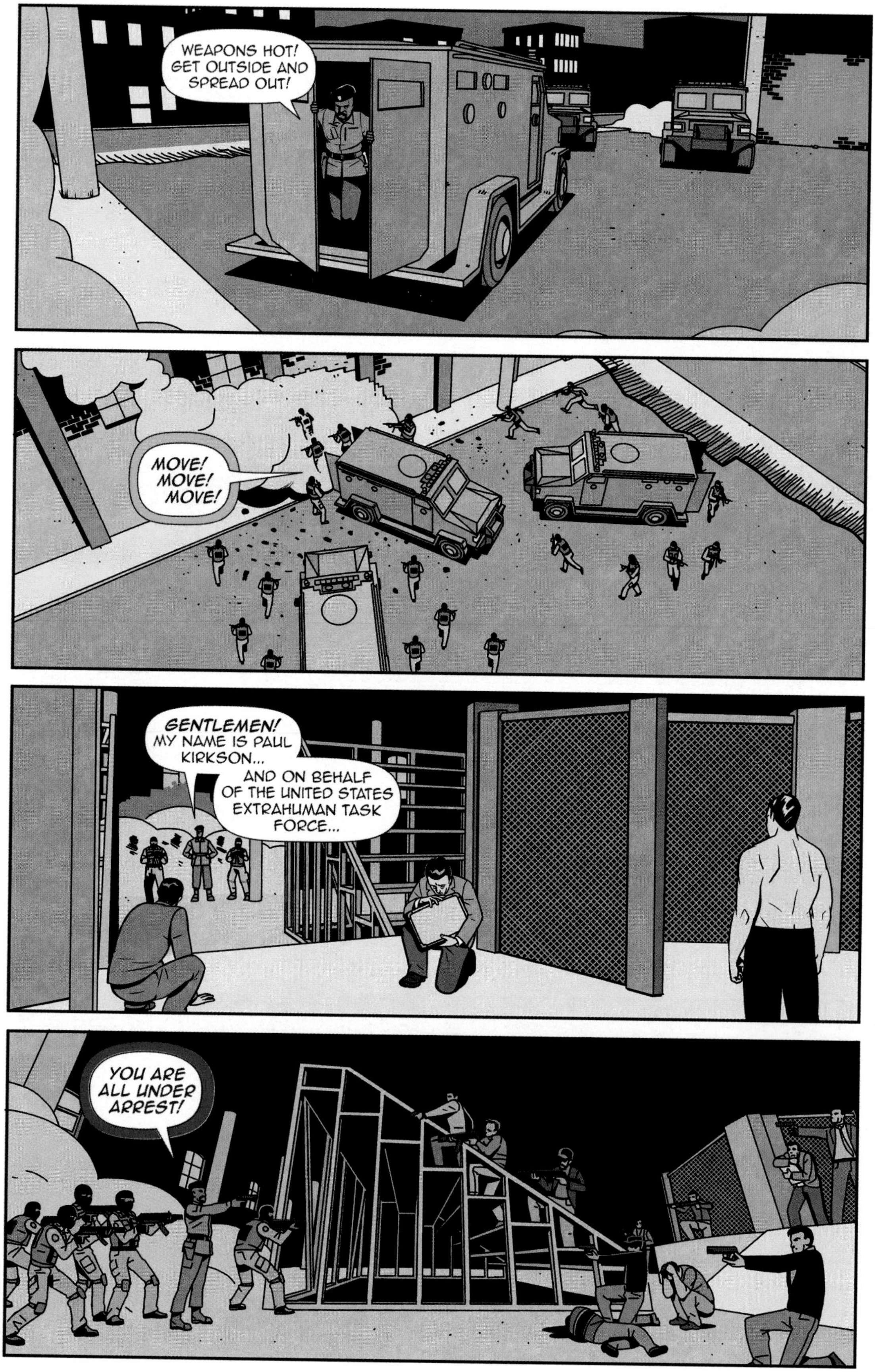
WEAPONS HOT! GET OUTSIDE AND SPREAD OUT!
MOVE! MOVE! MOVE!
GENTLEMEN! MY NAME IS PAUL KIRKSON...
AND ON BEHALF OF THE UNITED STATES EXTRAHUMAN TASK FORCE...
YOU ARE ALL UNDER ARREST!

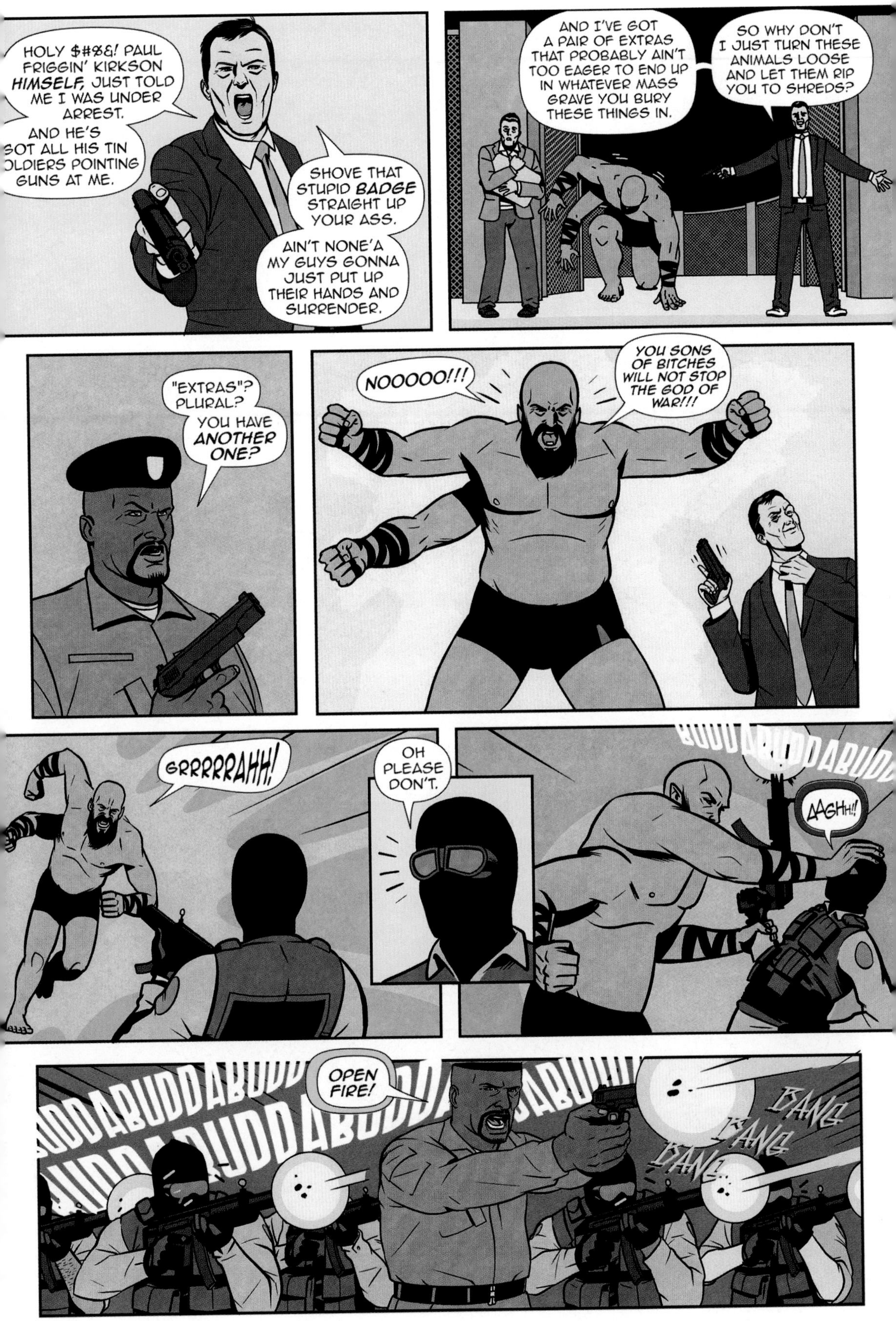
HOLY $#%&! PAUL FRIGGIN' KIRKSON HIMSELF, JUST TOLD ME I WAS UNDER ARREST.
AND HE'S GOT ALL HIS TIN SOLDIERS POINTING GUNS AT ME.
SHOVE THAT STUPID BADGE STRAIGHT UP YOUR ASS.
AIN'T NONE'A MY GUYS GONNA JUST PUT UP THEIR HANDS AND SURRENDER.
AND I'VE GOT A PAIR OF EXTRAS THAT PROBABLY AIN'T TOO EAGER TO END UP IN WHATEVER MASS GRAVE YOU BURY THESE THINGS IN.
SO WHY DON'T I JUST TURN THESE ANIMALS LOOSE AND LET THEM RIP YOU TO SHREDS?
"EXTRAS"? PLURAL?
YOU HAVE ANOTHER ONE?
NOOOOO!!!
YOU SONS OF BITCHES WILL NOT STOP THE GOD OF WAR!!!
GRRRRRAHH!
OH PLEASE DON'T.
BUDDABUDDABUDD
AAGHH!!
OPEN FIRE!
BUDDABUDDABUDDABUDD
BUDDABUDDABUDDABUDD
BANG
BANG
BANG

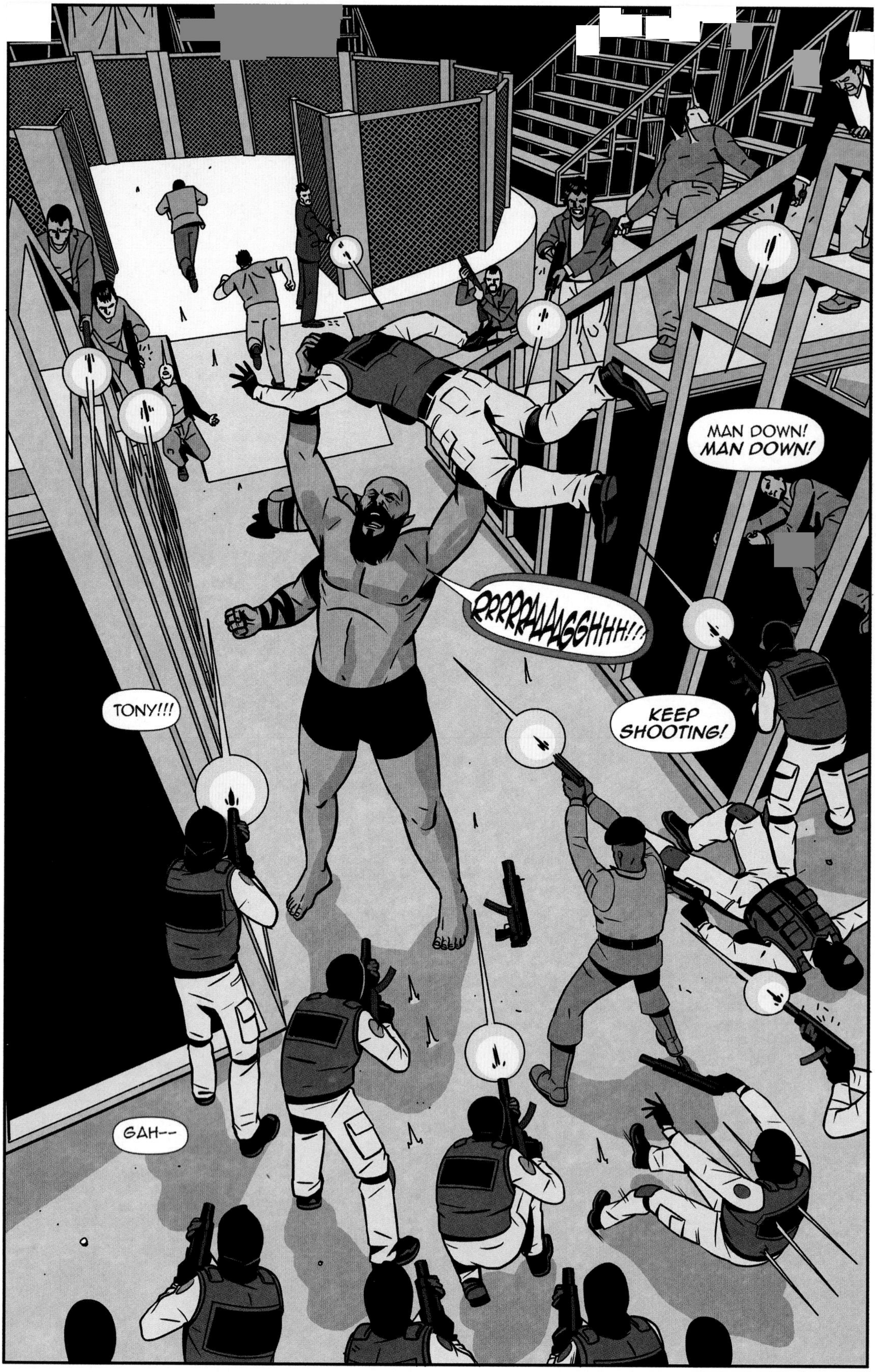
MAN DOWN! MAN DOWN!
RRRRRAAAAGGHHH!!!
TONY!!!
KEEP SHOOTING!
GAH--

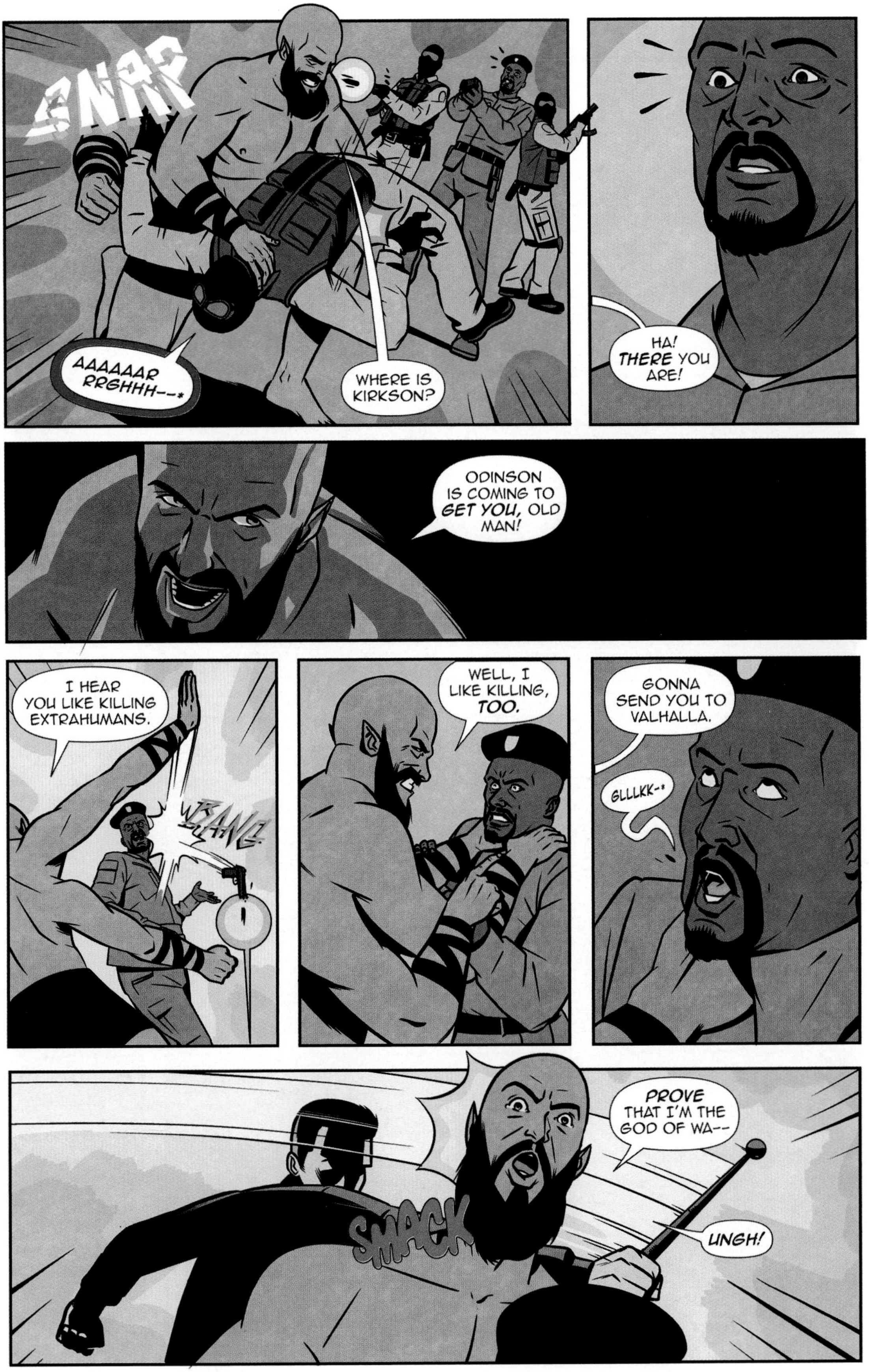
AAAAAAR RRGHHH--*
WHERE IS KIRKSON?
HA! THERE YOU ARE!
ODINSON IS COMING TO GET YOU, OLD MAN!
I HEAR YOU LIKE KILLING EXTRAHUMANS.
WELL, I LIKE KILLING, TOO.
GONNA SEND YOU TO VALHALLA.
GLLLKK-*
PROVE THAT I'M THE GOD OF WA--
SMACK
UNGH!

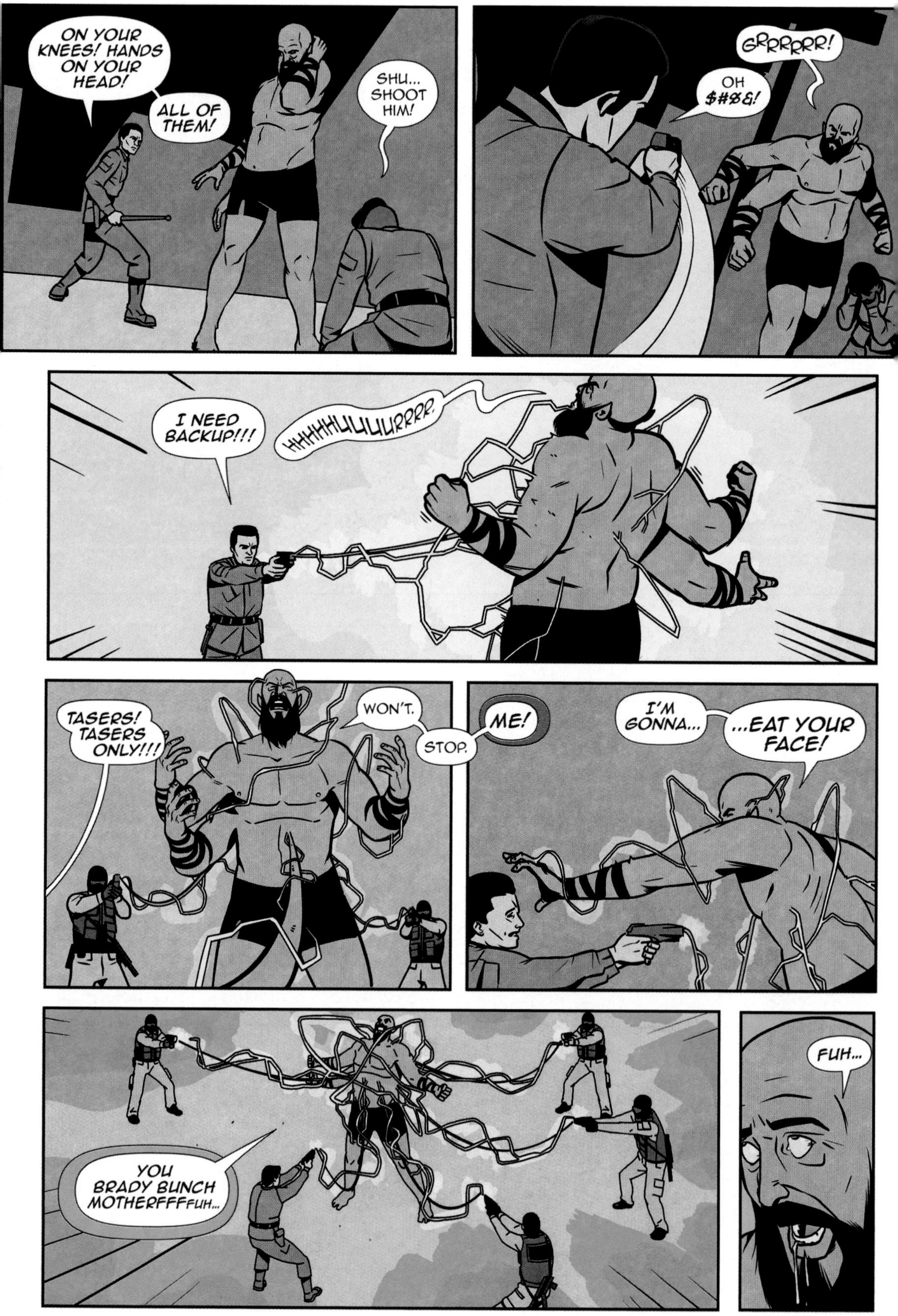

ON YOUR KNEES! HANDS ON YOUR HEAD!
ALL OF THEM!
SHU... SHOOT HIM!
GRRRRRR!
OH $#%&!
I NEED BACKUP!!!
HHHHHUUUURRRR.
TASERS! TASERS ONLY!!!
WON'T.
STOP.
ME!
I'M GONNA...
...EAT YOUR FACE!
YOU BRADY BUNCH MOTHERFFFFUH...
FUH...

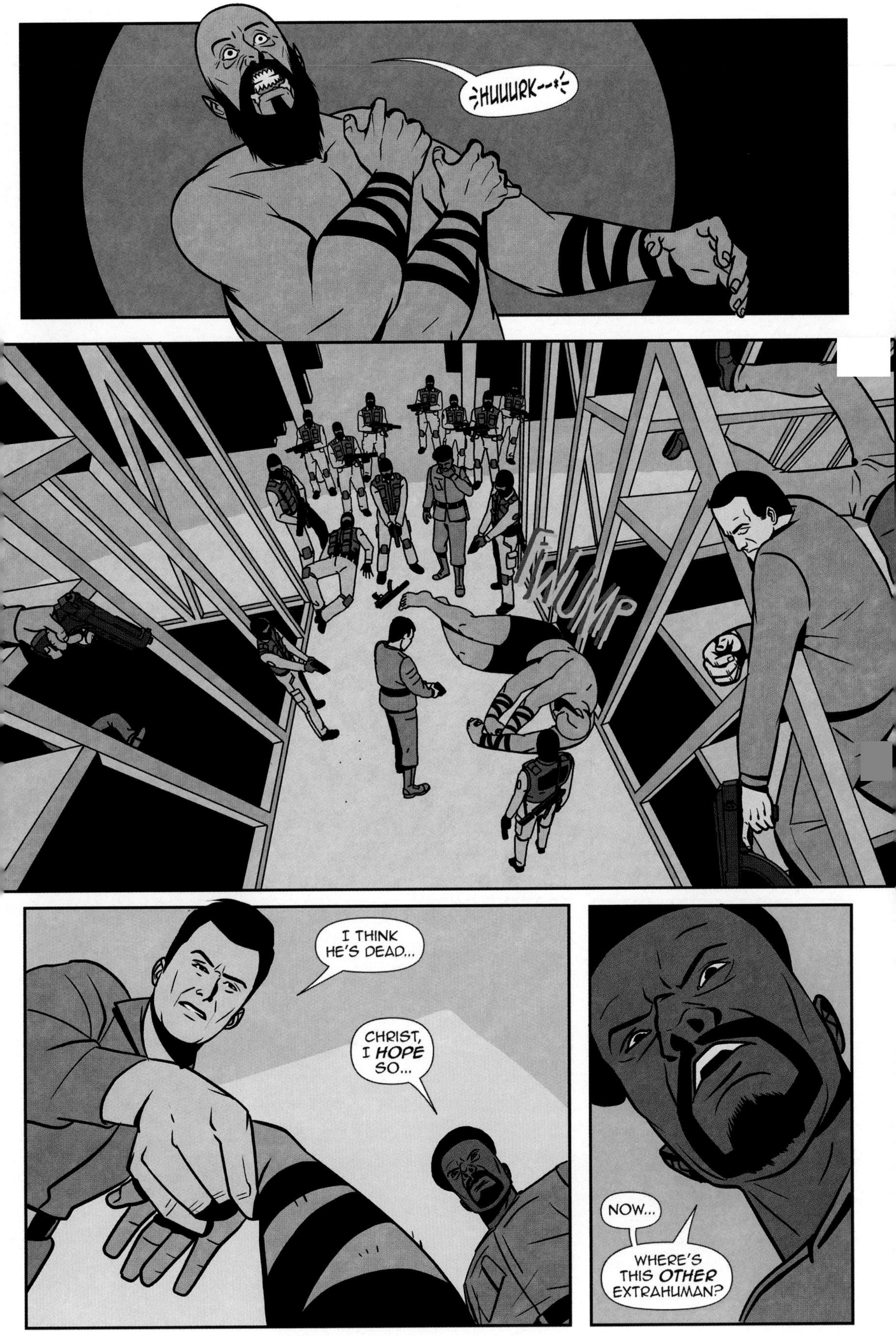
HUUURK--
THWUMP
I THINK HE'S DEAD...
CHRIST, I HOPE SO...
NOW...
WHERE'S THIS OTHER EXTRAHUMAN?

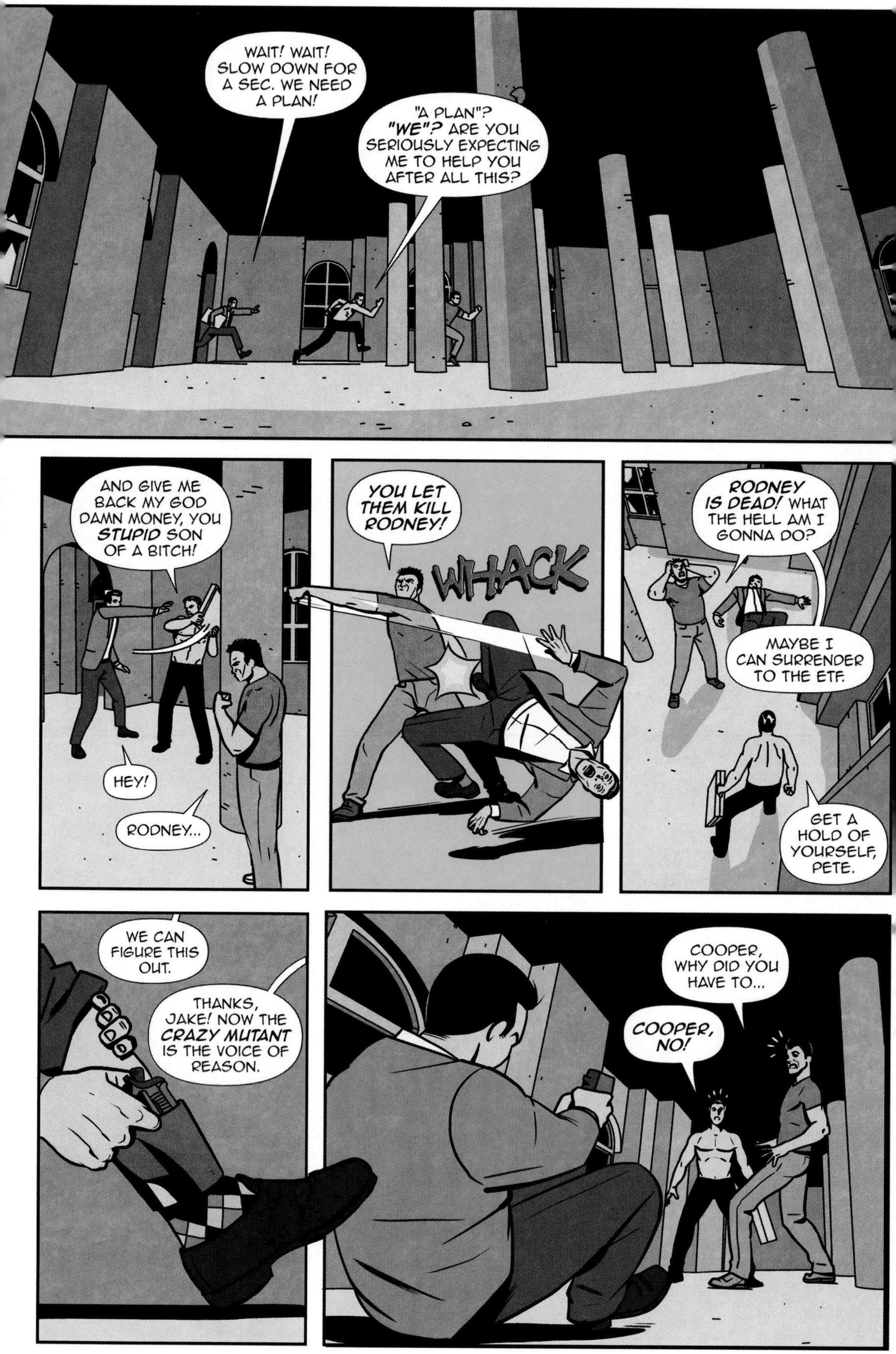
WAIT! WAIT! SLOW DOWN FOR A SEC. WE NEED A PLAN!
"A PLAN"? "WE"? ARE YOU SERIOUSLY EXPECTING ME TO HELP YOU AFTER ALL THIS?
AND GIVE ME BACK MY GOD DAMN MONEY, YOU STUPID SON OF A BITCH!
HEY!
RODNEY...
YOU LET THEM KILL RODNEY!
WHACK
RODNEY IS DEAD! WHAT THE HELL AM I GONNA DO?
MAYBE I CAN SURRENDER TO THE ETF.
GET A HOLD OF YOURSELF, PETE.
WE CAN FIGURE THIS OUT.
THANKS, JAKE! NOW THE CRAZY MUTANT IS THE VOICE OF REASON.
COOPER, WHY DID YOU HAVE TO...
COOPER, NO!

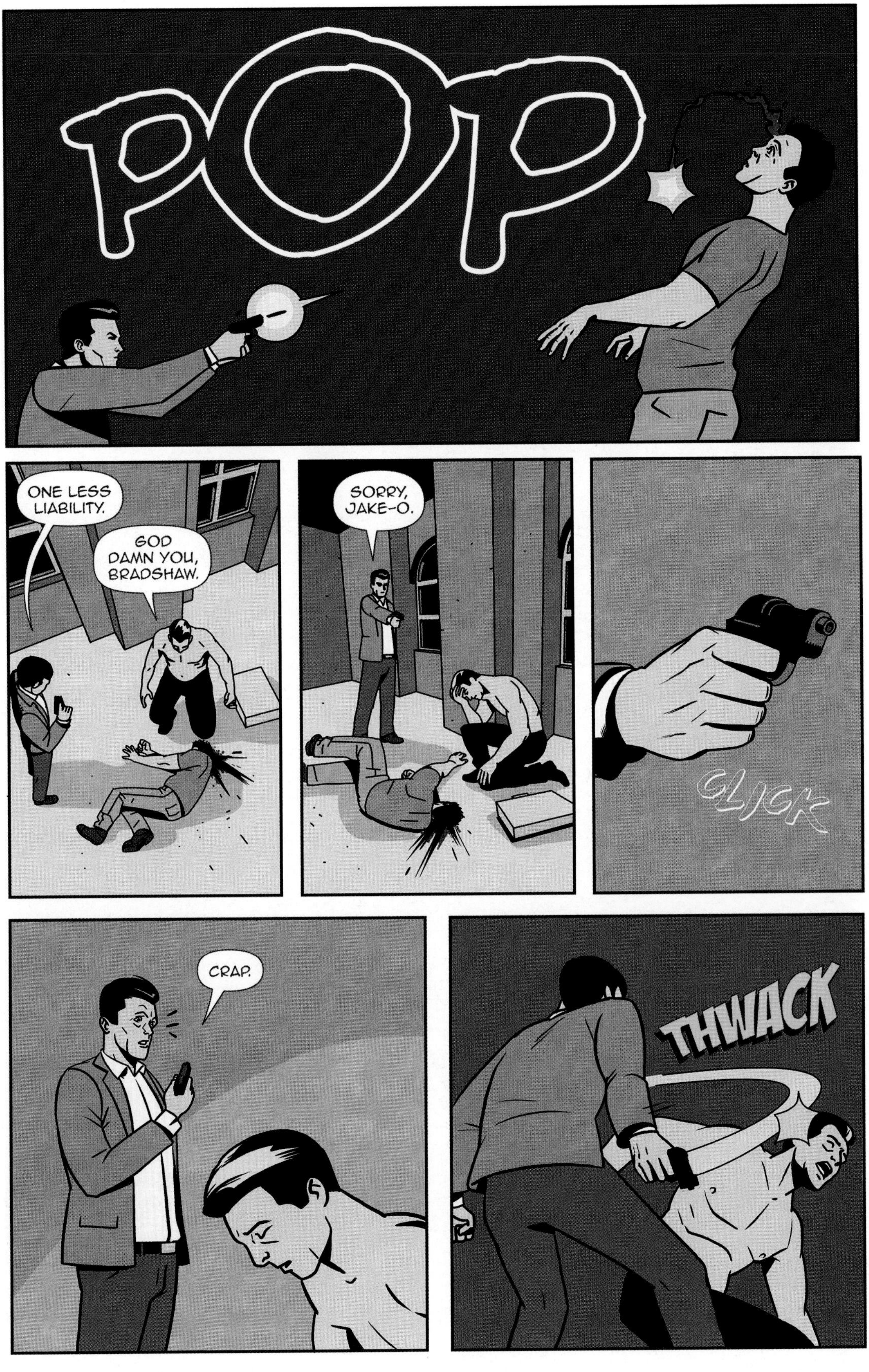
POP
ONE LESS LIABILITY.
GOD DAMN YOU, BRADSHAW.
SORRY, JAKE-O.
CLICK
CRAP.
THWACK

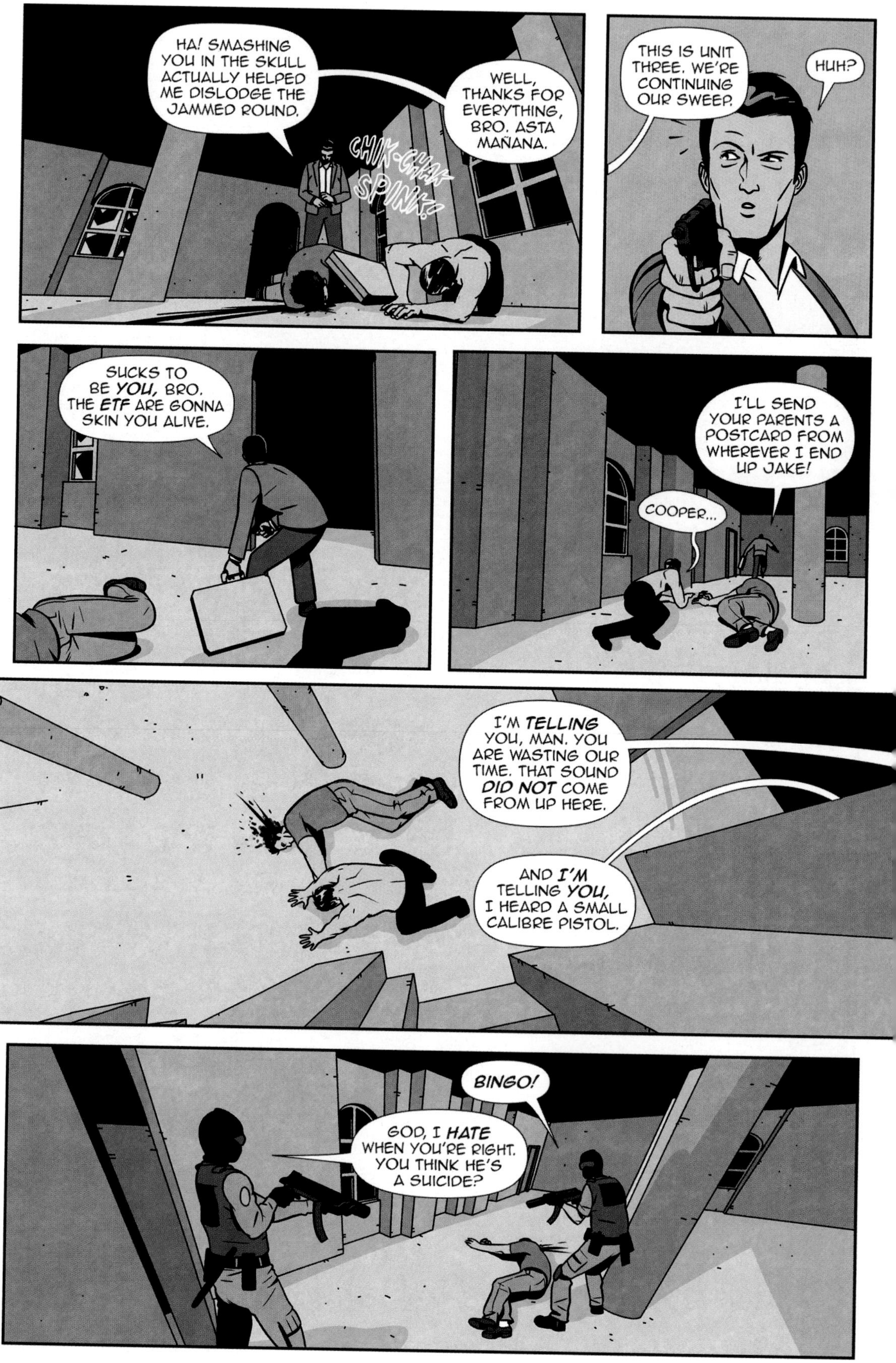
HA! SMASHING YOU IN THE SKULL ACTUALLY HELPED ME DISLODGE THE JAMMED ROUND.
WELL, THANKS FOR EVERYTHING, BRO. ASTA MAÑANA.
CHIK-CHAK SPINK!
THIS IS UNIT THREE. WE'RE CONTINUING OUR SWEEP.
HUH?
SUCKS TO BE *YOU,* BRO. THE *ETF* ARE GONNA SKIN YOU ALIVE.
I'LL SEND YOUR PARENTS A POSTCARD FROM WHEREVER I END UP JAKE!
COOPER...
I'M *TELLING* YOU, MAN. YOU ARE WASTING OUR TIME. THAT SOUND *DID NOT* COME FROM UP HERE.
AND *I'M* TELLING *YOU,* I HEARD A SMALL CALIBRE PISTOL.
BINGO!
GOD, I *HATE* WHEN YOU'RE RIGHT. YOU THINK HE'S A SUICIDE?

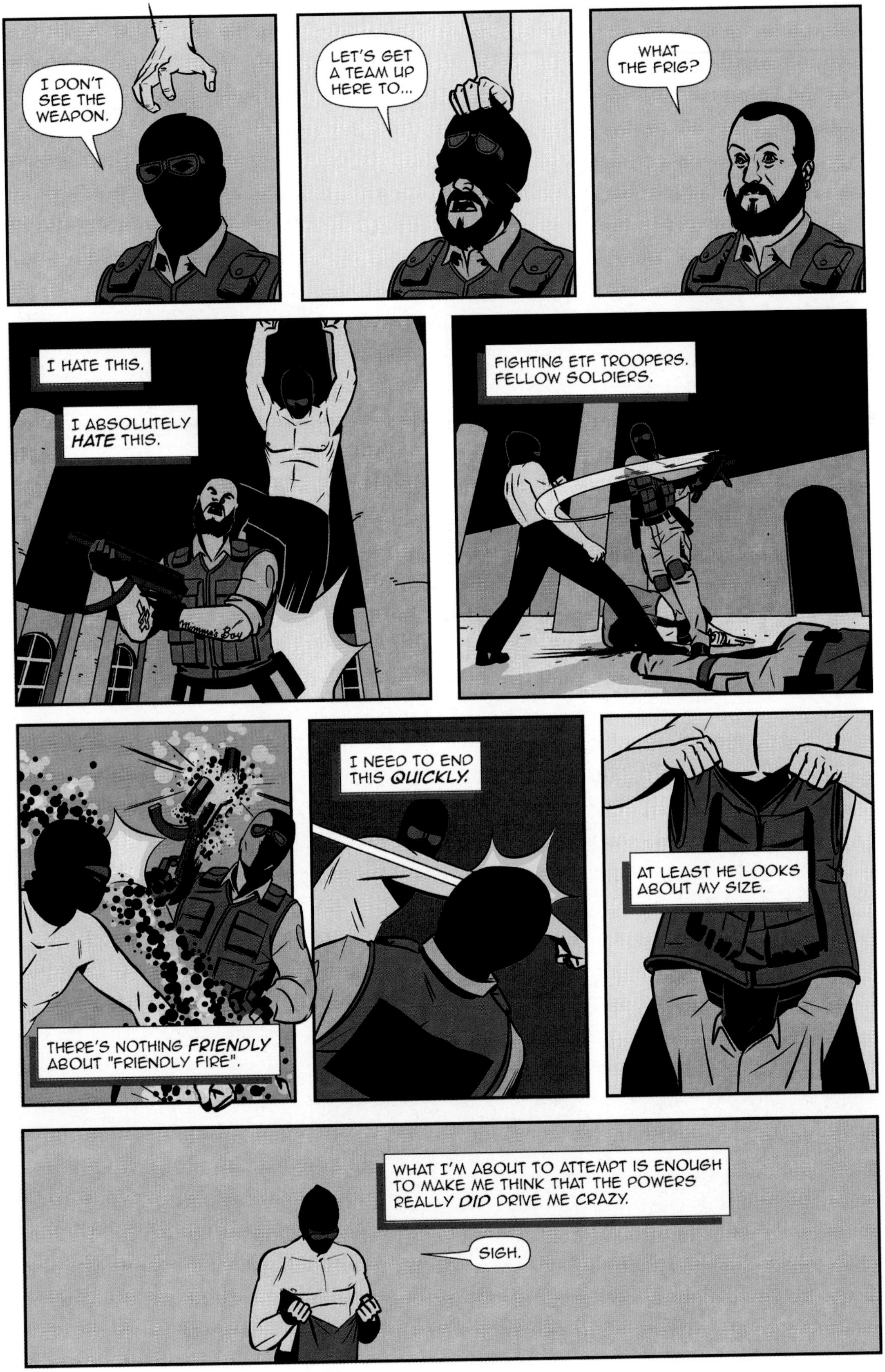
I DON'T SEE THE WEAPON.
LET'S GET A TEAM UP HERE TO...
WHAT THE FRIG?
I HATE THIS.
I ABSOLUTELY *HATE* THIS.
FIGHTING ETF TROOPERS. FELLOW SOLDIERS.
THERE'S NOTHING *FRIENDLY* ABOUT "FRIENDLY FIRE".
I NEED TO END THIS *QUICKLY.*
AT LEAST HE LOOKS ABOUT MY SIZE.
WHAT I'M ABOUT TO ATTEMPT IS ENOUGH TO MAKE ME THINK THAT THE POWERS REALLY *DID* DRIVE ME CRAZY.
SIGH.

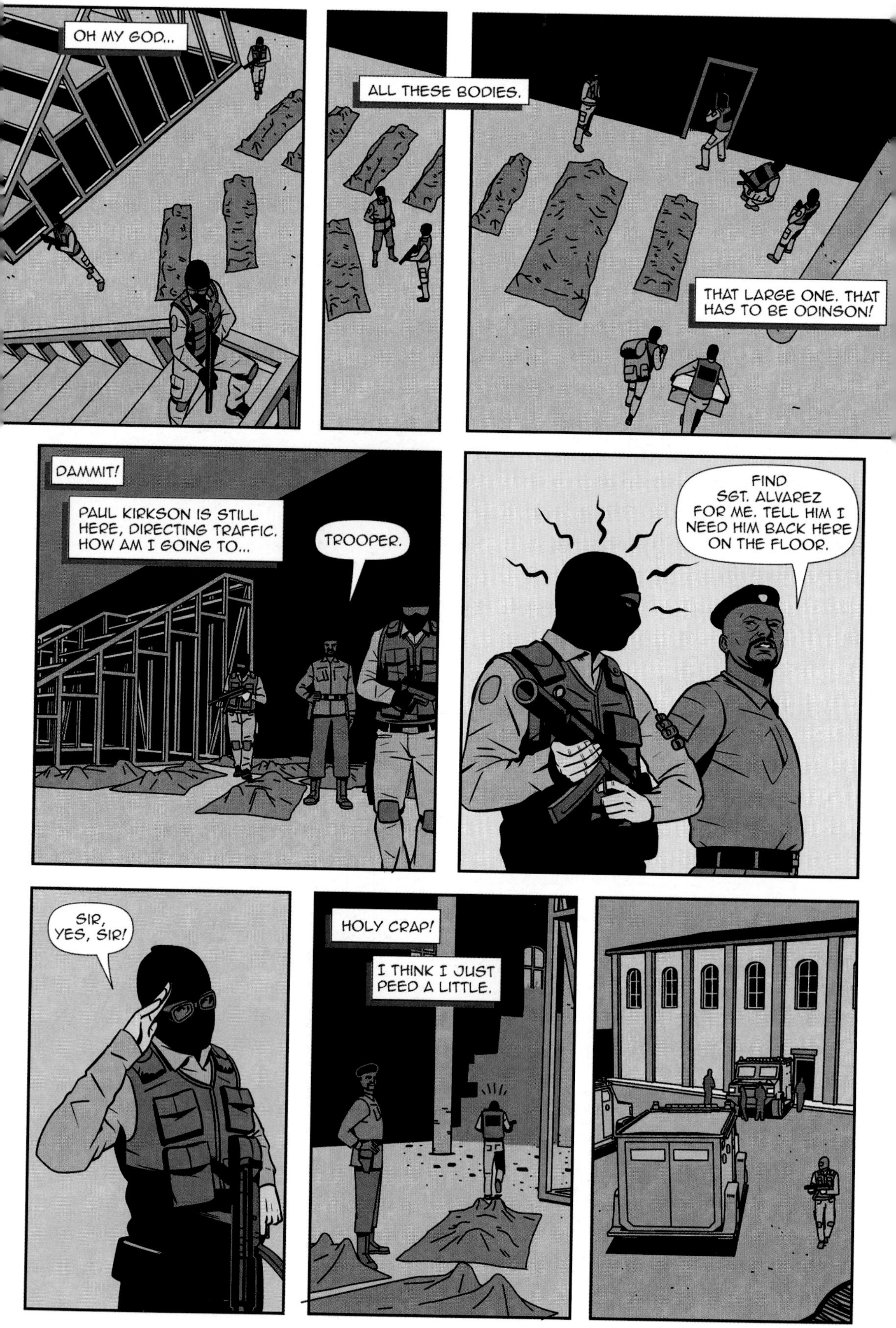
OH MY GOD...
ALL THESE BODIES.
THAT LARGE ONE. THAT HAS TO BE ODINSON!
DAMMIT!
PAUL KIRKSON IS STILL HERE, DIRECTING TRAFFIC. HOW AM I GOING TO...
TROOPER.
FIND SGT. ALVAREZ FOR ME. TELL HIM I NEED HIM BACK HERE ON THE FLOOR.
SIR, YES, SIR!
HOLY CRAP!
I THINK I JUST PEED A LITTLE.

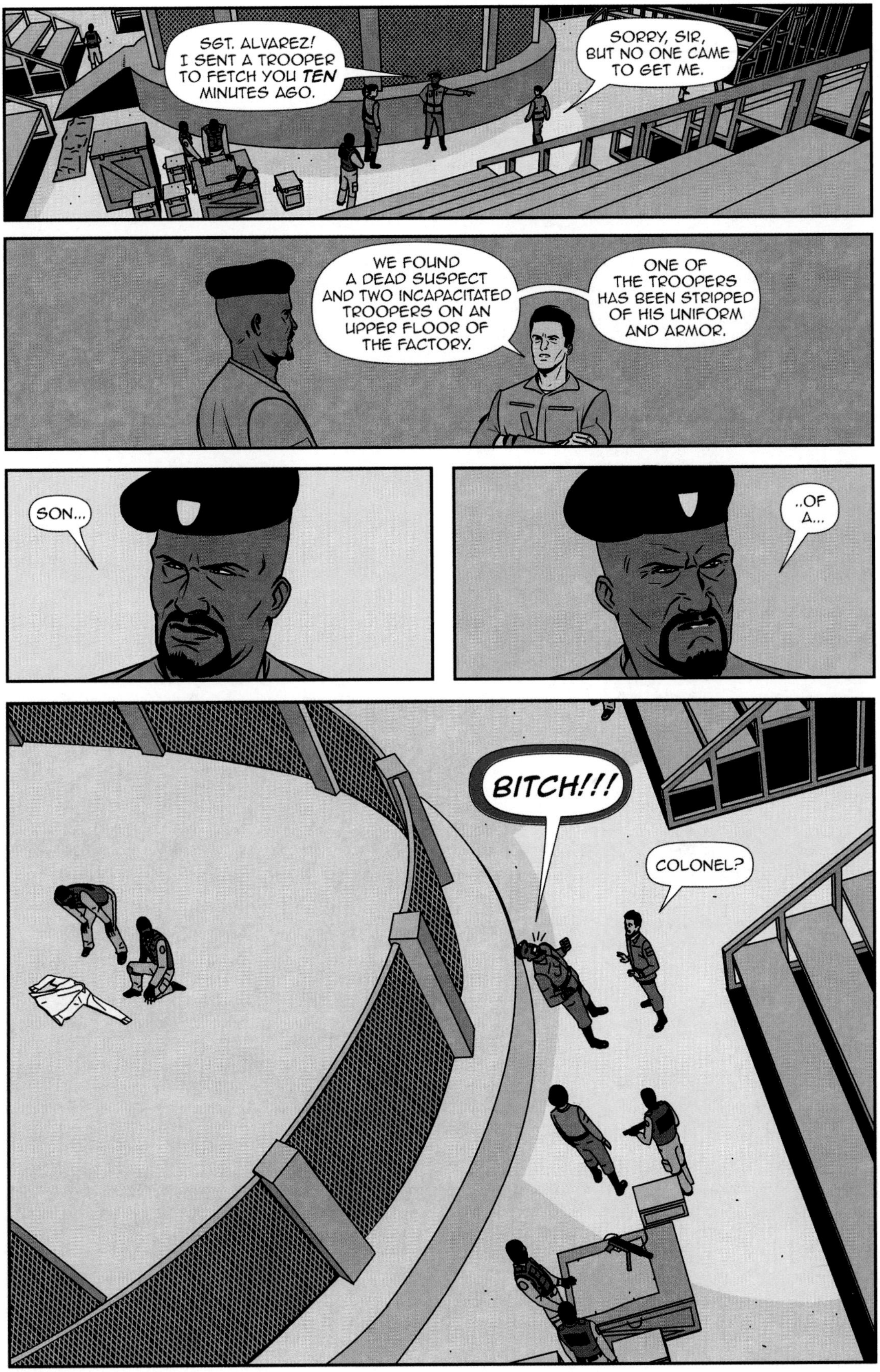
SGT. ALVAREZ! I SENT A TROOPER TO FETCH YOU TEN MINUTES AGO.
SORRY, SIR, BUT NO ONE CAME TO GET ME.
WE FOUND A DEAD SUSPECT AND TWO INCAPACITATED TROOPERS ON AN UPPER FLOOR OF THE FACTORY.
ONE OF THE TROOPERS HAS BEEN STRIPPED OF HIS UNIFORM AND ARMOR.
SON...
..OF A...
BITCH!!!
COLONEL?

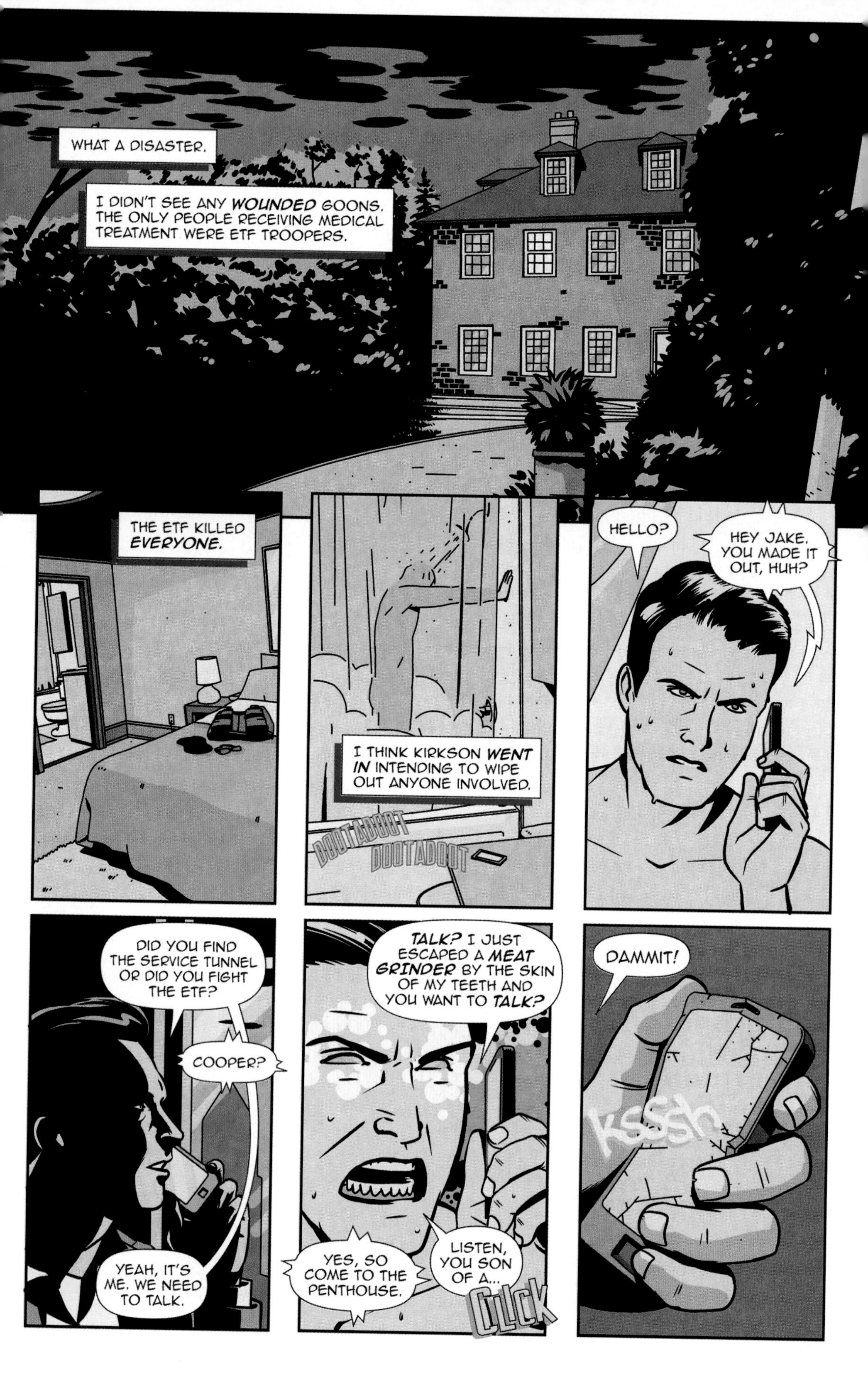
WHAT A DISASTER.
I DIDN'T SEE ANY WOUNDED GOONS. THE ONLY PEOPLE RECEIVING MEDICAL TREATMENT WERE ETF TROOPERS.
THE ETF KILLED EVERYONE.
I THINK KIRKSON WENT IN INTENDING TO WIPE OUT ANYONE INVOLVED.
DOOTADOOT
DOOTADOOT
HELLO?
HEY JAKE. YOU MADE IT OUT, HUH?
DID YOU FIND THE SERVICE TUNNEL OR DID YOU FIGHT THE ETF?
COOPER?
YEAH, IT'S ME. WE NEED TO TALK.
TALK? I JUST ESCAPED A MEAT GRINDER BY THE SKIN OF MY TEETH AND YOU WANT TO TALK?
YES, SO COME TO THE PENTHOUSE.
LISTEN, YOU SON OF A...
CLICK
DAMMIT!
KSSSH

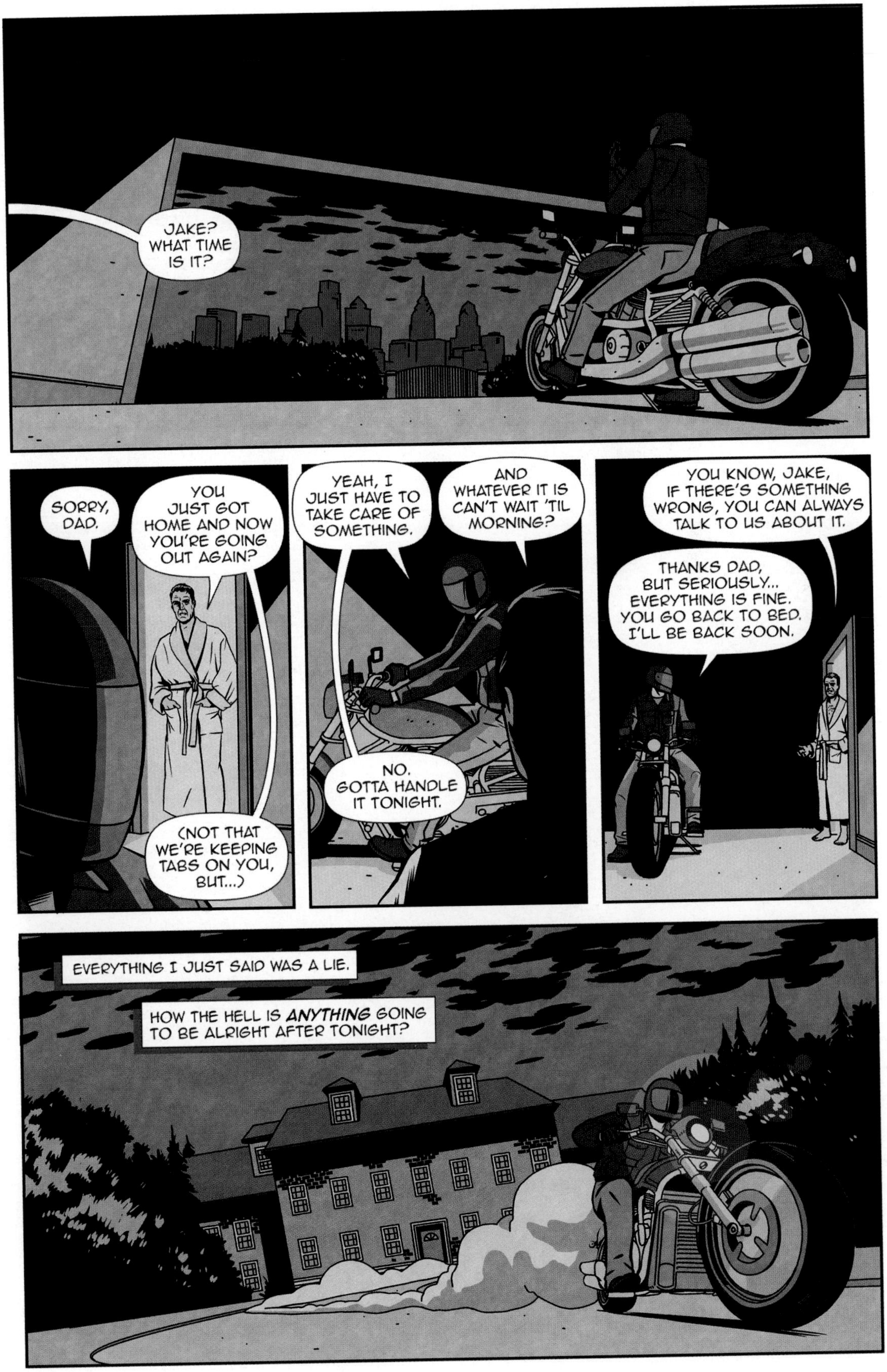
JAKE? WHAT TIME IS IT?
SORRY, DAD.
YOU JUST GOT HOME AND NOW YOU'RE GOING OUT AGAIN?
(NOT THAT WE'RE KEEPING TABS ON YOU, BUT...)
YEAH, I JUST HAVE TO TAKE CARE OF SOMETHING.
AND WHATEVER IT IS CAN'T WAIT 'TIL MORNING?
NO. GOTTA HANDLE IT TONIGHT.
YOU KNOW, JAKE, IF THERE'S SOMETHING WRONG, YOU CAN ALWAYS TALK TO US ABOUT IT.
THANKS DAD, BUT SERIOUSLY... EVERYTHING IS FINE. YOU GO BACK TO BED. I'LL BE BACK SOON.
EVERYTHING I JUST SAID WAS A LIE.
HOW THE HELL IS *ANYTHING* GOING TO BE ALRIGHT AFTER TONIGHT?

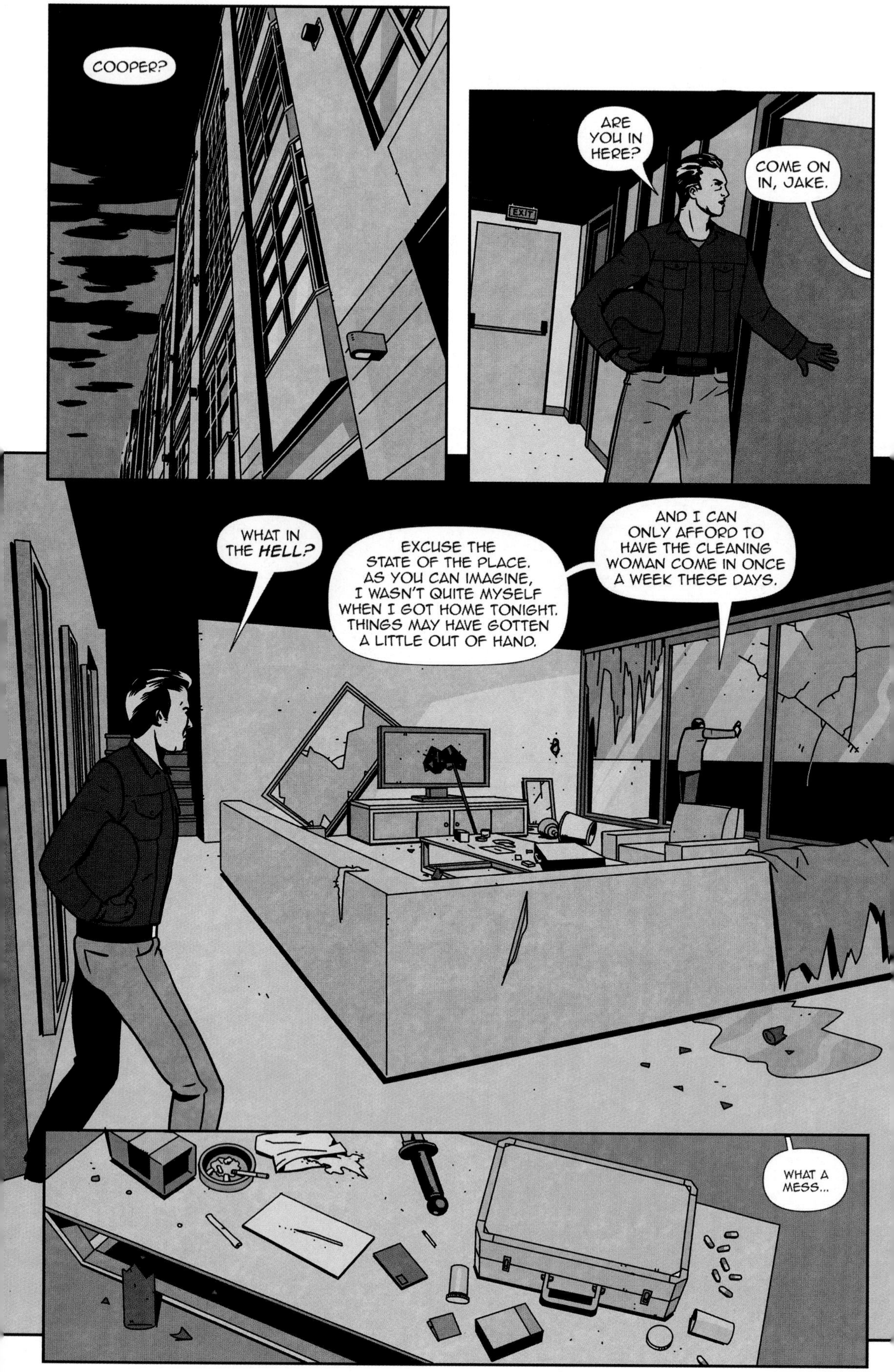
COOPER?
ARE YOU IN HERE?
COME ON IN, JAKE.
WHAT IN THE HELL?
EXCUSE THE STATE OF THE PLACE. AS YOU CAN IMAGINE, I WASN'T QUITE MYSELF WHEN I GOT HOME TONIGHT. THINGS MAY HAVE GOTTEN A LITTLE OUT OF HAND.
AND I CAN ONLY AFFORD TO HAVE THE CLEANING WOMAN COME IN ONCE A WEEK THESE DAYS.
WHAT A MESS...

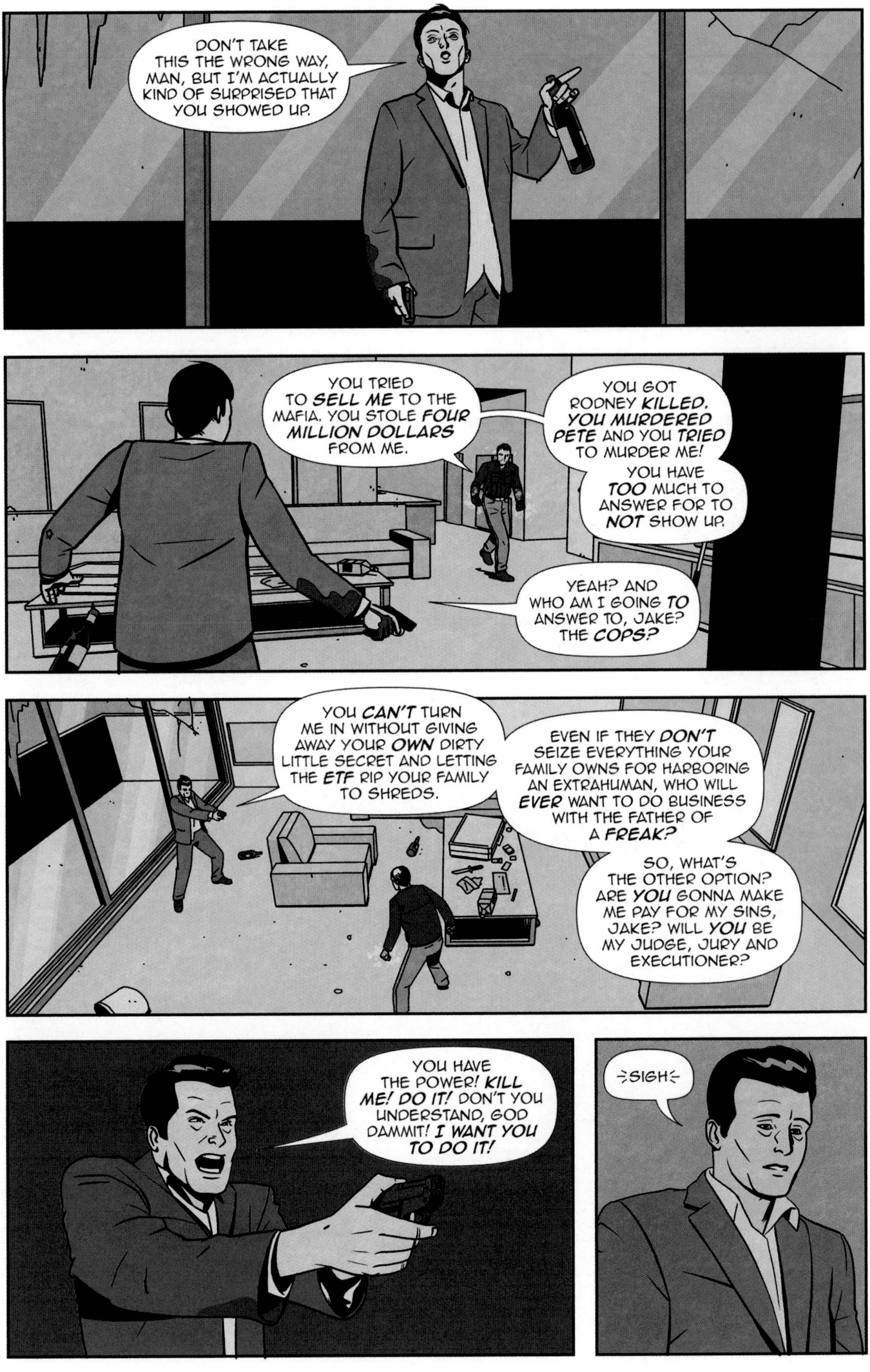
DON'T TAKE THIS THE WRONG WAY, MAN, BUT I'M ACTUALLY KIND OF SURPRISED THAT YOU SHOWED UP.
YOU TRIED TO SELL ME TO THE MAFIA. YOU STOLE FOUR MILLION DOLLARS FROM ME.
YOU GOT RODNEY KILLED. YOU MURDERED PETE AND YOU TRIED TO MURDER ME!
YOU HAVE TOO MUCH TO ANSWER FOR TO NOT SHOW UP.
YEAH? AND WHO AM I GOING TO ANSWER TO, JAKE? THE COPS?
YOU CAN'T TURN ME IN WITHOUT GIVING AWAY YOUR OWN DIRTY LITTLE SECRET AND LETTING THE ETF RIP YOUR FAMILY TO SHREDS.
EVEN IF THEY DON'T SEIZE EVERYTHING YOUR FAMILY OWNS FOR HARBORING AN EXTRAHUMAN, WHO WILL EVER WANT TO DO BUSINESS WITH THE FATHER OF A FREAK?
SO, WHAT'S THE OTHER OPTION? ARE YOU GONNA MAKE ME PAY FOR MY SINS, JAKE? WILL YOU BE MY JUDGE, JURY AND EXECUTIONER?
YOU HAVE THE POWER! KILL ME! DO IT! DON'T YOU UNDERSTAND, GOD DAMMIT! I WANT YOU TO DO IT!
SIGH

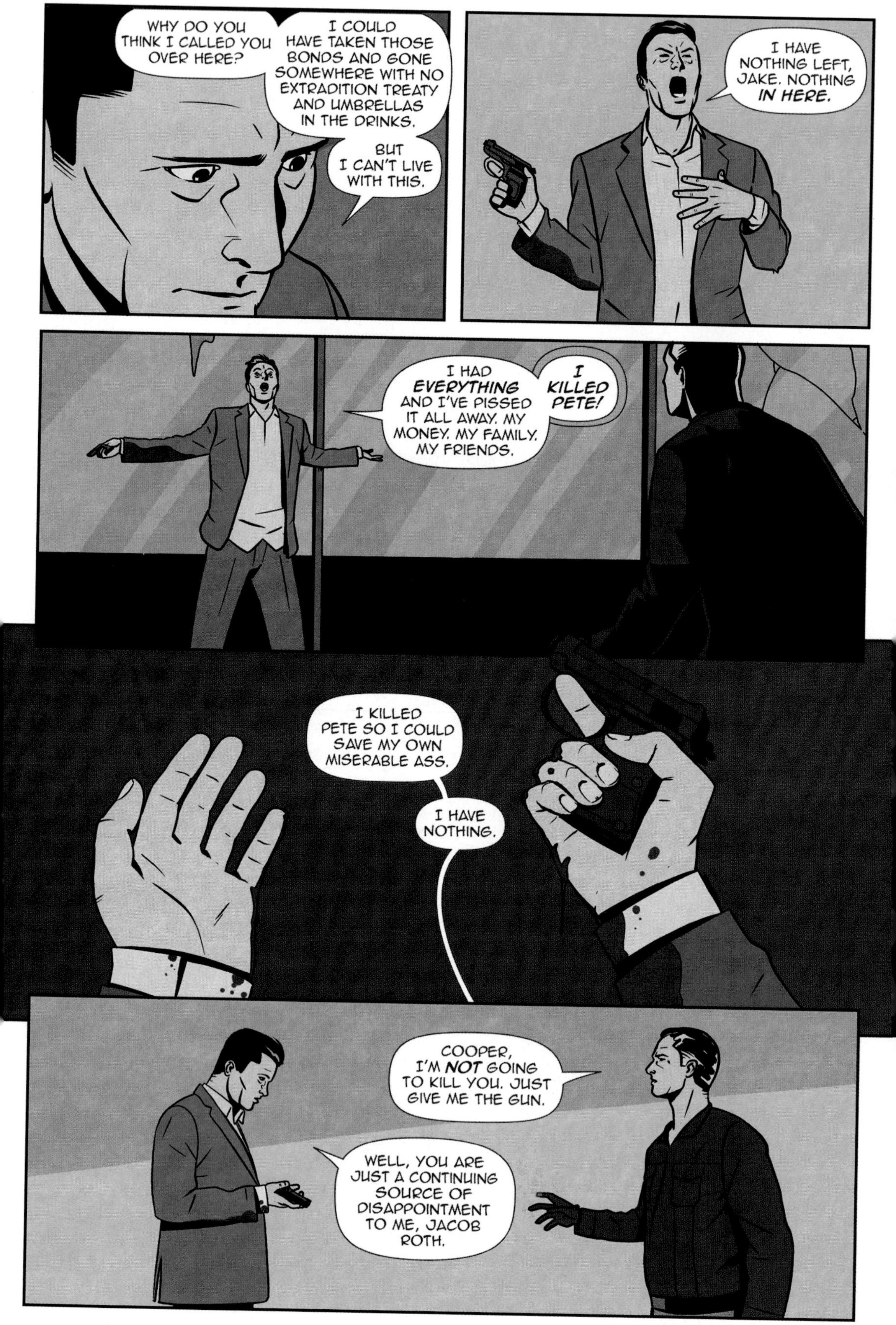
WHY DO YOU THINK I CALLED YOU OVER HERE?
I COULD HAVE TAKEN THOSE BONDS AND GONE SOMEWHERE WITH NO EXTRADITION TREATY AND UMBRELLAS IN THE DRINKS.
BUT I CAN'T LIVE WITH THIS.
I HAVE NOTHING LEFT, JAKE. NOTHING *IN HERE.*
I HAD *EVERYTHING* AND I'VE PISSED IT ALL AWAY. MY MONEY. MY FAMILY. MY FRIENDS.
I KILLED PETE!
I KILLED PETE SO I COULD SAVE MY OWN MISERABLE ASS.
I HAVE NOTHING.
COOPER, I'M *NOT* GOING TO KILL YOU. JUST GIVE ME THE GUN.
WELL, YOU ARE JUST A CONTINUING SOURCE OF DISAPPOINTMENT TO ME, JACOB ROTH.

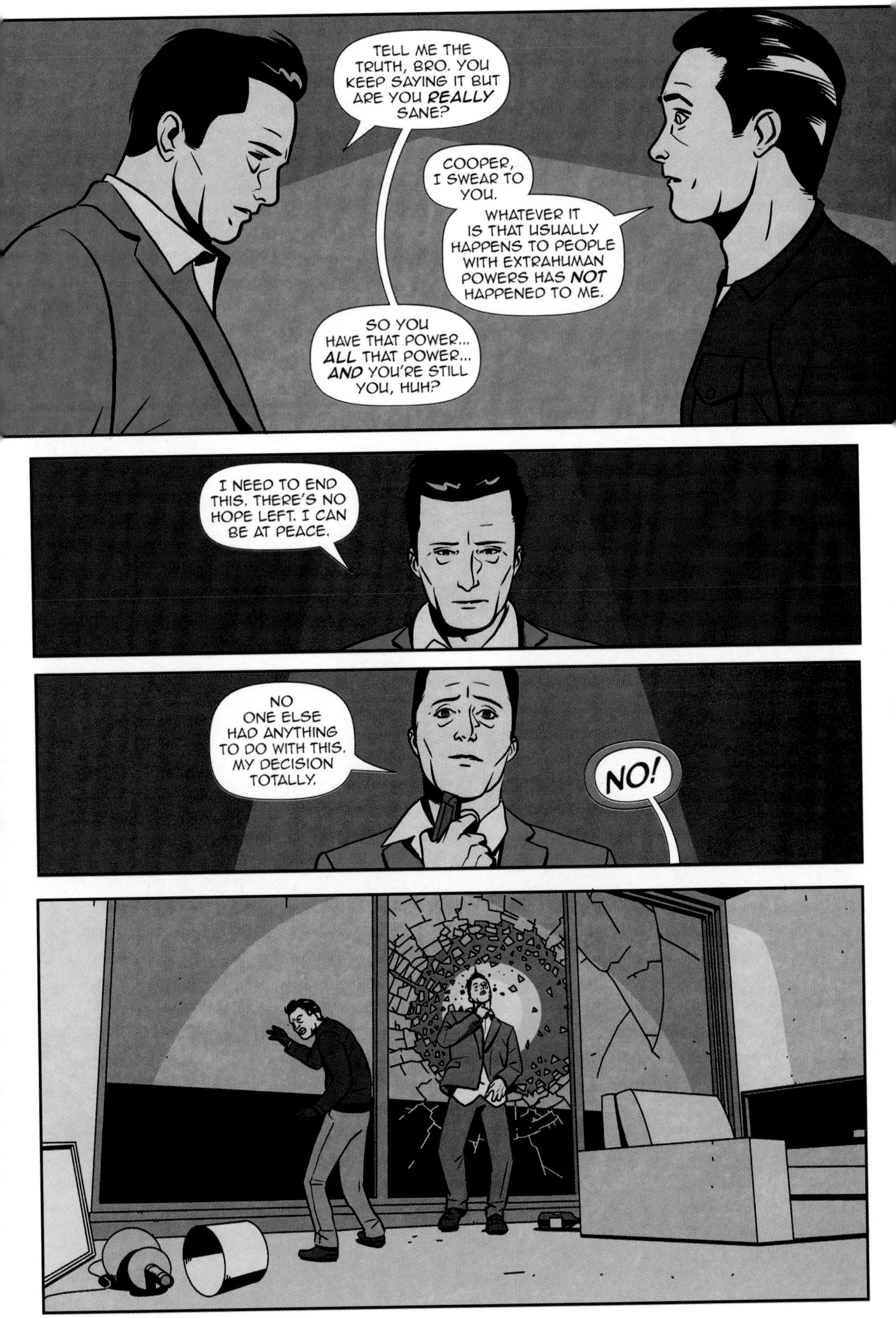
TELL ME THE TRUTH, BRO. YOU KEEP SAYING IT BUT ARE YOU *REALLY* SANE?
COOPER, I SWEAR TO YOU.
WHATEVER IT IS THAT USUALLY HAPPENS TO PEOPLE WITH EXTRAHUMAN POWERS HAS *NOT* HAPPENED TO ME.
SO YOU HAVE THAT POWER... *ALL* THAT POWER... *AND* YOU'RE STILL YOU, HUH?
I NEED TO END THIS. THERE'S NO HOPE LEFT. I CAN BE AT PEACE.
NO ONE ELSE HAD ANYTHING TO DO WITH THIS. MY DECISION TOTALLY.
NO!

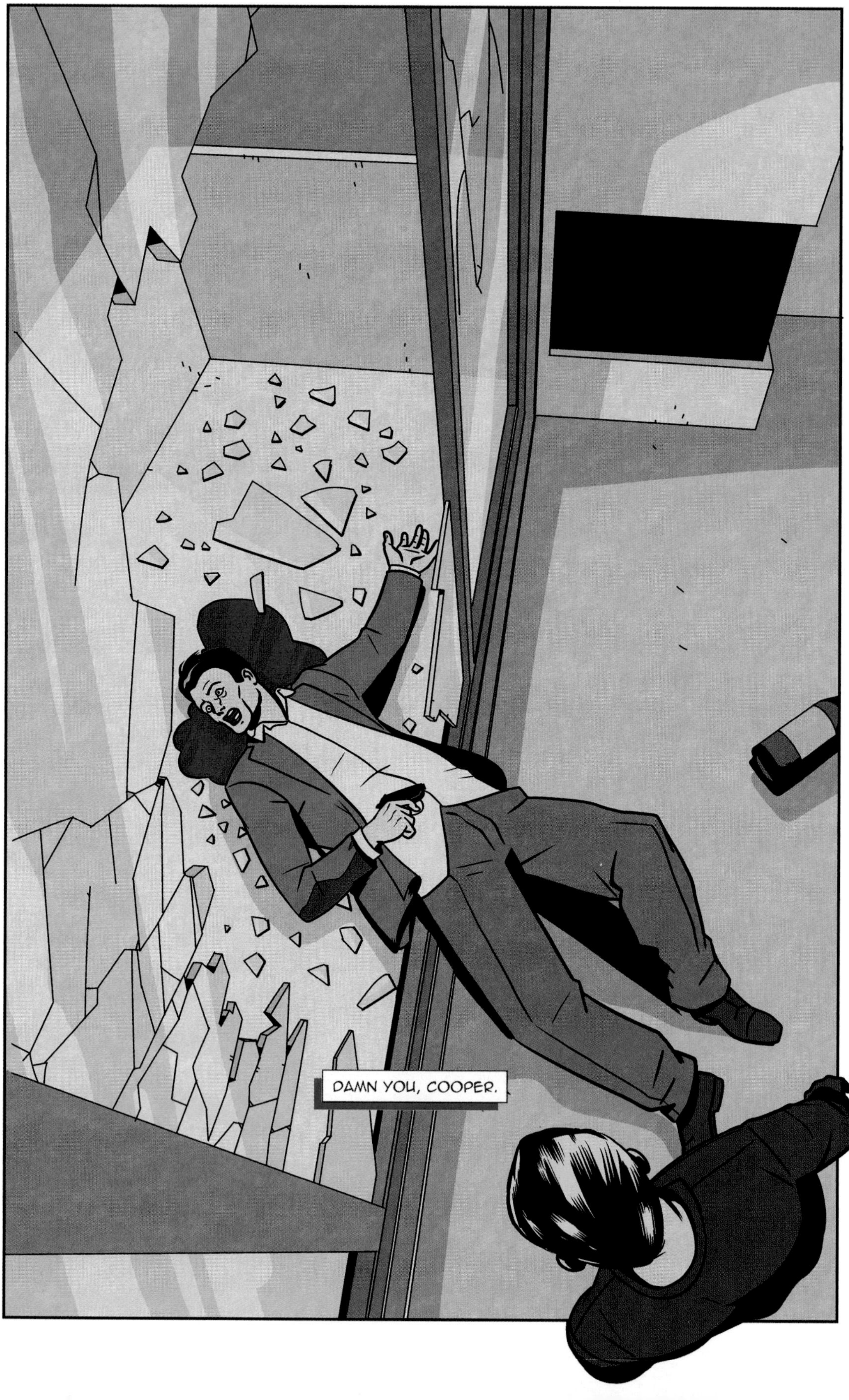
DAMN YOU, COOPER.

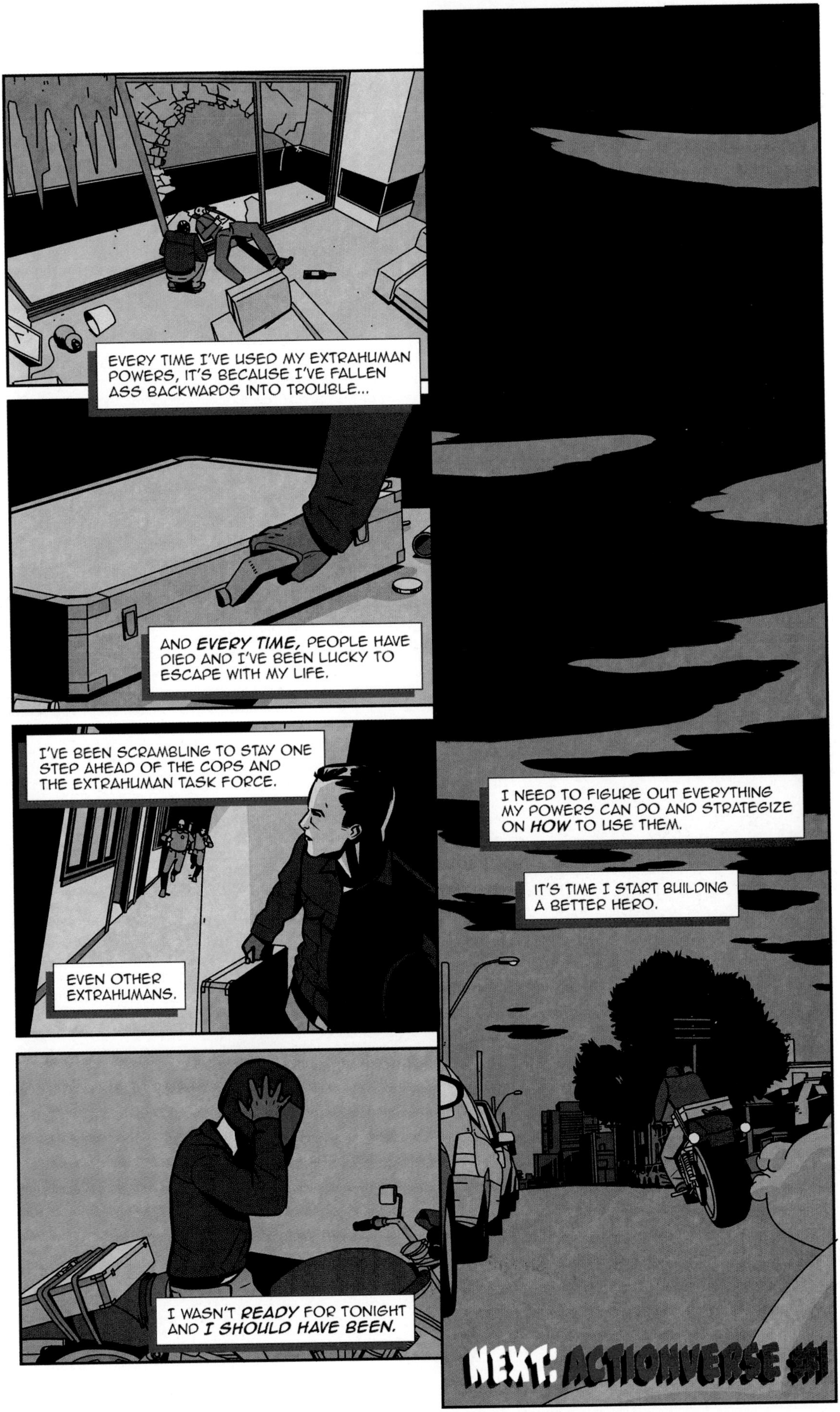
EVERY TIME I'VE USED MY EXTRAHUMAN POWERS, IT'S BECAUSE I'VE FALLEN ASS BACKWARDS INTO TROUBLE...
AND EVERY TIME, PEOPLE HAVE DIED AND I'VE BEEN LUCKY TO ESCAPE WITH MY LIFE.
I'VE BEEN SCRAMBLING TO STAY ONE STEP AHEAD OF THE COPS AND THE EXTRAHUMAN TASK FORCE.
EVEN OTHER EXTRAHUMANS.
I WASN'T READY FOR TONIGHT AND I SHOULD HAVE BEEN.
I NEED TO FIGURE OUT EVERYTHING MY POWERS CAN DO AND STRATEGIZE ON HOW TO USE THEM.
IT'S TIME I START BUILDING A BETTER HERO.
NEXT: ACTIONVERSE #1

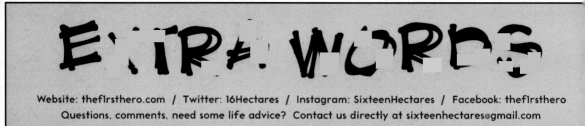

EXTRA WORDS

Website: thef1rsthero.com / Twitter: 16Hectares / Instagram: SixteenHectares / Facebook: thef1rsthero
Questions, comments, need some life advice? Contact us directly at sixteenhectares@gmail.com

And so ends Volume 2 of THE F1RST HERO.

And life isn't going to get any easier for Jake Roth as we move forward. The next time we see Jake will be in ACTIONVE FEATURING THE F1RST HERO #1, the first issue of a massive crossover series designed to create a new shared universe for Ac Lab's superhero comics. ACTIONVERSE will bring together Jake Roth, Molly Danger, Midnight Tiger, Stray and Virtue (along wit few special surprise guests) to fight an evil so powerful that it literally threatens untold billions of lives if it cannot be defeated.

The creative teams involved in the ACTIONVERSE mini-series started work on this project over a year ago and it's been non-stop e since. For all the nay-sayers out in the industry who shy away from doing superhero books because "Marvel and DC own market", we're going to force the door open and carve out some space of our own with well-told stories and exciting art. It can done. Hell, we're already doing it! We're just marshalling our forces to announce our presence in a new way and get more eyes our product.

Following that, we will be bring you our third big story arc entitled THE F1RST HERO: WEDNESDAY'S CHILD. Work on that serie continuing with artist Marco Renna turning in some incredible pages. I've said it before but it bears repeating: I've been so lu with the skill level of the artists who have joined my in bringing you Jake's journey. Phillip Sevy. Danny Zabbal. And now, Marco

But to close out THIS volume of the book, I need to take one final opportunity to say thank you to the aforementioned Danny Zak and the fantastic Fred C. Stresing for the work they put in to transform FIGHT FOR YOUR LIFE from words on the screen of iPad Mini into the truly amazing visual story you've just finished reading. Fred will be back for Volume 3. Danny will be moving to bring a project or two of his own to everyone. Don't sleep on this man's talent. When you see his name, buy his work. You never, ever be disappointed. And with any luck, Danny will return to THE F1RST HERO for either Volume 5 or 6. Fingers crossed..

* * *

I had the opportunity to visit with Raymond Rowe, the real-life Odinson, past weekend. Ray was wrestling on a Ring Of Honor event in Lockport, and a kayfabe-defying carload of us from Toronto drove down for the sh Ray has been very supportive through the creation process for FIGHT F YOUR LIFE (although, let's see how he reacts to watching Odinson DIE in issue!) and that support continued on Saturday.

Ray sat down and signed copies of the limited Kickstarter Edition of the #1 all the fans and friends who pledged to help make this series possible. once again, I need to thank Ray for being a true friend and letting me t him into a raving, three-armed, homicidal maniac.

Ray has a story of his own to share with you. A story of hard-earned succ sudden, terrible loss and triumphant recovery. It's the story of Ray's climbi through the ranks of the indy wrestling scene to reach Ring Of Honor, near-death experience of his horrific motorcycle accident in 2014 and incredible way he's comeback to the ring, stronger and better than ever.

And it's all available for you in the form of any hour-long documentary f called "THE PATH". Want to see it? Visit www.raymondxrowe.com to get y copy now! Do the right thing, kids.

* * *

Current Listening: Gonzo by Foxy Shazam, Professional Rapper by Lil Dicky, Transformation by FM, The King Is Gone by Big Toba and the Pickers and the Pittsburgh Underground podcast. Current Viewing: The League: Season 7, The Muppets and the fan-m "De-Specialized" versions of the original Star Wars trilogy. Current Doings: Shopping new series to publishers, preparing for N York Comic Con and getting ready for a "Loser Leaves Town" match against Brent Banks for Alpha-1 Wrestling in Hamilton, Canac

* * *

One last thank you to send out and that's to you, our loyal readers. It would be pretty cliche to say "without you, we're nothing" but that really is a true statement. I'm grateful to all of you who have come along with us for this ride. We are eight issues in w seventeen to go and I promise you that the craziest most exciting days in Jake Roth's extrahuman life are yet to come!

Thank y
Anthony Ruttga
Toronto, 28 September 2

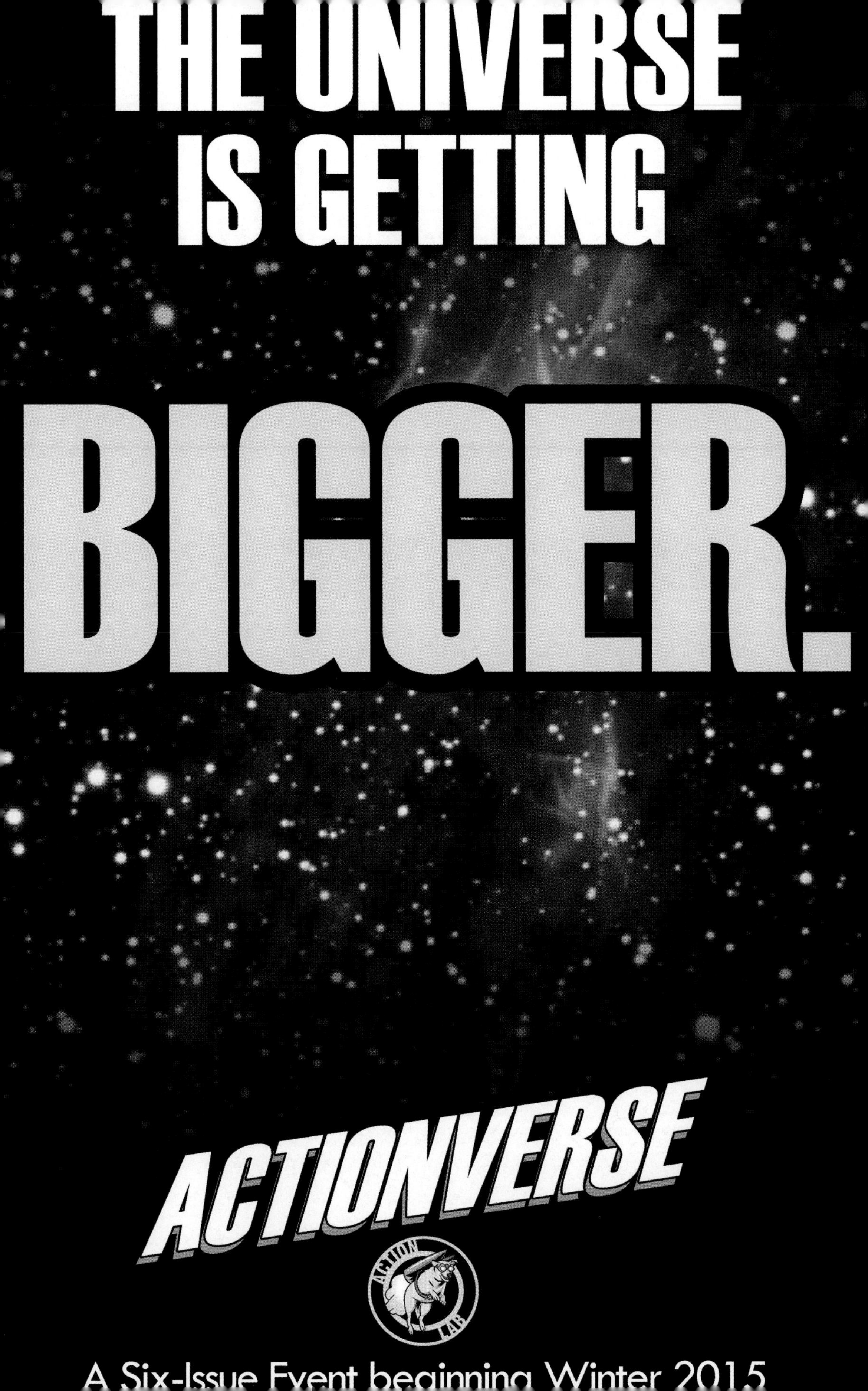
THE UNIVERSE
IS GETTING
BIGGER.
ACTIONVERSE
ACTION LAB
A Six-Issue Event beginning Winter 2015

After the tragic events of last issue, Cyrus Perkins has gone from aimless Taxi Cab Driver to amateur Detective. Teaming with Michael, the ghost boy trapped in his car, Cyrus speeds into mystery, danger, and a conspiracy too twisted for words!

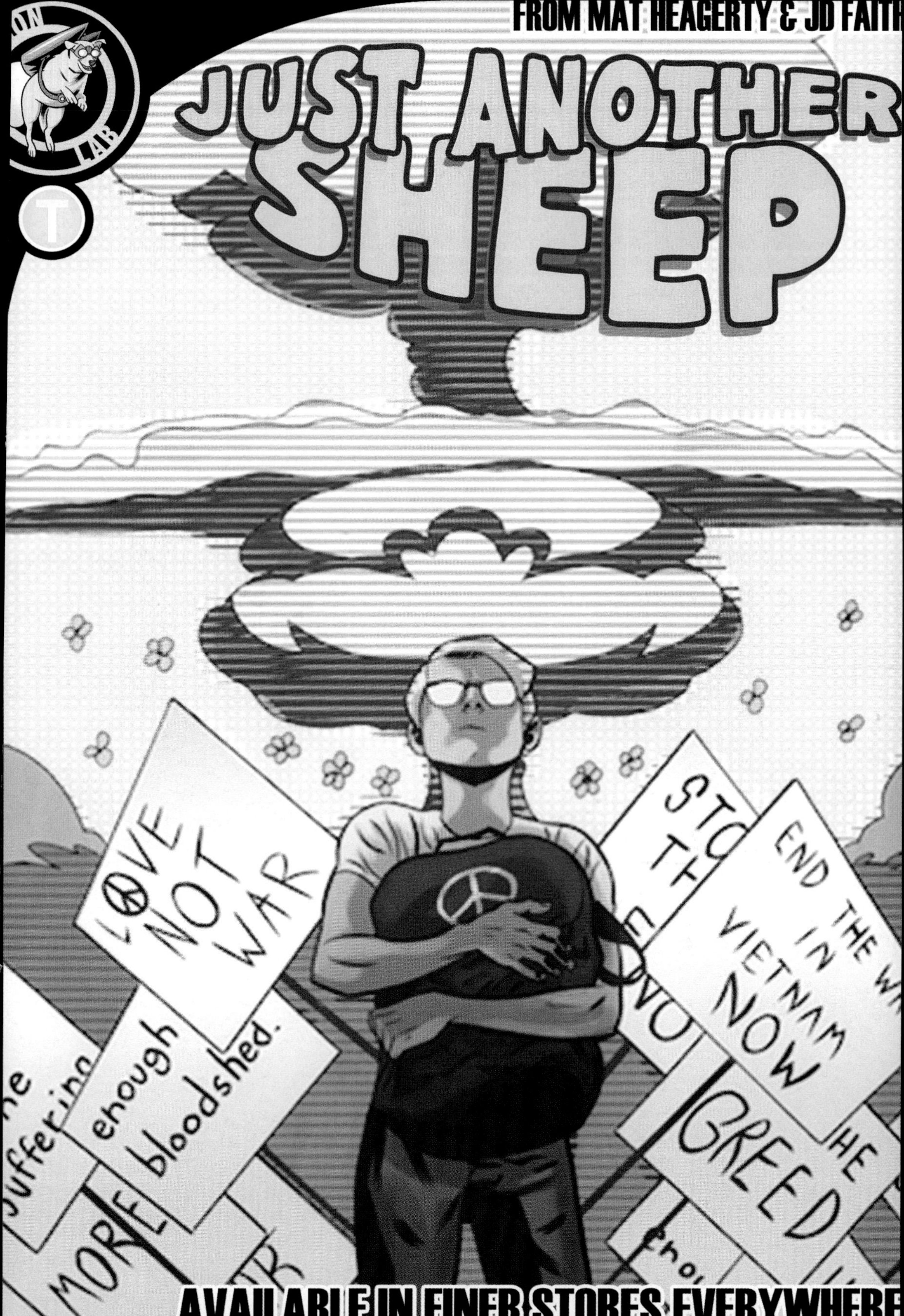
FROM MAT HEAGERTY & JD FAITH
JUST ANOTHER SHEEP
LOVE NOT WAR
enough bloodshed.
END THE W
IN VIETNAM NOW
GREED
MORE
AVAILABLE IN FINER STORES EVERYWHERE

In 1969 a timid teen sets out on a road trip. His goal? Find out the origins of his bizarre super human abilities. Always the follower, his trip is derailed when he befriends a group of extremist war protesters.

READ MORE NOW